RECOVERY

RECOVERY

*How to Survive Sexual Assault
for Women, Men, Teenagers,
Their Friends and Families*

Helen Benedict

DOUBLEDAY & COMPANY, INC.
GARDEN CITY, NEW YORK
1985

To all who need this book

The author gratefully acknowledges permission to reprint excerpts from:
Rape in Marriage, by Diana E. H. Russell. Copyright © 1982 by Diana E. H. Russell. Reprinted by permission.
Rape: The First Sourcebook for Women, edited by Noreen Connell and Cassandra Wilson. Copyright © 1974 by Noreen Connell and Cassandra Wilson. Reprinted by permission of Joan Daves.
Men Who Rape, by A. Nicholas Groth with H. Jean Birnbaum. Copyright © 1979 by Plenum Press. Reprinted by permission.
Your Children Should Know, by Flora Colao and Tamar Hosansky. Copyright © 1983 by Flora Colao and Tamar Hosansky. Reprinted by permission of the publisher, The Bobbs-Merrill Company.
Prison Sexual Violence, by Daniel Lockwood. Copyright © 1980 by Daniel Lockwood. Reprinted by permission of the publisher, Elsevier Science Publishing Company.
"Rape: A Personal Account," anonymous. Copyright © 1976 by National Association of Social Workers, Inc. Reprinted with permission from *Health and Social Work*.
Rape: Crisis and Recovery, by Ann W. Burgess and Lynda L. Holmstrom. Copyright © 1979 by Robert J. Brady. Reprinted by permission of the publishers.

Library of Congress Cataloging in Publication Data
Benedict, Helen.
    Recovery: how to survive sexual assault for women,
    men, teenagers, their friends and families.
    Bibliography: p.
    Includes
        1. Rape victims—United States.   2. Rape victims—
    United States—Psychology.   3. Rape victims—Services
    for—United States.   4. Rape victims—Medical care—
    United States.   I. Title.
    HV6250.3.U5B46   1985   362.8′83
    ISBN 0-385-19206-1
    Library of Congress Catalog Card Number 84–13821

Acknowledgments

I must first thank all the women and men who, by allowing me to interview them, put themselves through the pain of remembering. Thanks especially to those I have called Penny, Claire, Angela, Rachel, Kathy, Ann, and Mabel, who endured long, long interviews about their assaults; to Denise and Shelley, who told me, sometimes with tears, about their daughters; and to Larry, Clark, and Don, who went through so much unrecognized agony.

I want also to thank Anne Sparks and Doris Ullendorff at St. Vincent's Hospital's Rape Crisis Program for their knowledge and patient help. Thanks also to David MacEnulty, Tamar Hosansky, Flora Colao, Pam McDonnell, and Linda Fairstein for their expertise.

I am very grateful to Ann Jones and Roberta Israeloff for their meticulous readings of the manuscript, and to Gail Hochman for believing in it.

Above all, I want to thank my husband, Stephen O'Connor, for all his careful readings, for his tactful editing, for living with such a difficult subject, and for withstanding my occasional bursts of anger and despair.

Finally, I thank my son Simon, for being born between Chapters 4 and 5, thereby reminding me that there is innocence and joy.

Contents

Author's Note

When I was twenty-one, I spent nine days working in an English borstal—a prison for girls between fourteen and twenty-two years old. Those nine days broke through many of my sheltered, middle-class assumptions, but perhaps nothing shocked me as much as one piece of information the prison governor gave me. She told me that 70 percent of the girls in that prison had been raped by relatives. That opened my eyes to the injustices that can result from rape—a girl is raped by her father, she runs away, becomes delinquent, gets caught, ends up in jail. The wrong people, it seemed to me, were in prison.

After I moved to the United States, I pursued my interest in rape and its injustices first as a newspaper reporter, then as a magazine writer. For five years I interviewed survivors, their partners and families, rape crisis counselors, and researchers. I trained as a rape counselor at St. Vincent's Hospital in New York, and I read all that I could find.

This book is compiled with the help of all the survivors and counselors I have talked to. I asked the survivors what, ideally, they wish had happened to them after the assault, how they could have best been helped and what could have best been said. I asked the counselors what they have found survivors, their friends, and their families need the most. From all these people, whose names have been changed for their protection and privacy, I offer this advice.

Preface

In my work as manager of the Rape Crisis Program at St. Vincent's Hospital in New York, I have found that rape survivors and their loved ones have two major needs: comfort and information. In this book, Helen Benedict offers both: the warm, human voices of survivors, who talk about the horror of rape and yet provide encouragement and inspiration; and concrete, practical information about types of assaults, the range of reactions, ways to help, and issues that must be confronted.

Fifteen years ago, this book was not even conceivable. We had no idea at that time how many women and children were suffering in silence after a sexual assault. No one seemed to know or care about the ignorance, indifference, and cruelty experienced by the few victims who dared to speak out about the crime and their needs. The damaging attitudes toward women who were raped and the myths about rape that Benedict discusses were completely unquestioned at that time.

The reluctance to understand rape—and both men and women persist in this reluctance today—has two sources: rape is a shocking and depressing fact of life that we prefer not to face; and we cannot understand it without acknowledging the cruel and tragic way that misconceptions about rape have been used against women for centuries, something else we prefer not to face. It took the works of pioneer writers such as Susan Brownmiller, Susan Griffin, and Diana Russell, as well as all the consciousness-raising efforts of the feminist movement in the early 1970s, to force us to question the myths about rape and redefine rape according to the reality of survivors' experiences.

In this book, Benedict builds on these landmark works. Uniquely addressing the concerns of the rape survivor, she draws on the vast, largely unpublished knowledge that rape crisis workers and social scientists have gathered during the few recent years that rape has been taken seriously and survivors have been heard.

The original rape crisis workers were feminists who started their own programs and worked for free. They wanted to document the prevalence and manifestations of rape as well as diminish its traumatic effects on survivors by giving them understanding and assistance. Many women who had been raped volunteered as counselors so that other women would not have to experience the blame and isolation they had suffered. The same women who wrote letters and held demonstrations to bring rape to the public's attention and who agitated for changes in public attitudes, media portrayals of rape, the laws, and law-enforcement procedures also accompanied women who had been raped to police stations, hospitals, and the courts. They also held "speak-outs" so that survivors could hear each other's experiences and gain strength from each other, and so that other women could learn.

One of the most controversial innovations of this period was the development of the peer counseling model. Feminists challenged the professional counseling rule that said counselors should not share their personal experiences with clients and shouldn't work with clients whose experiences were similar to theirs. Instead, feminists suggested that professionals who couldn't identify with their clients and who couldn't acknowledge their own and their loved ones' vulnerability to rape would do survivors more harm than good.

Today, many programs blend the peer and professional counseling models. Some traditional psychotherapists have taken rape counselor training so that they will understand their sexually assaulted clients better. Some professional training programs offer courses on intervention with victims of sexual assault, but the training is often optional and not usually comprehensive. Physicians, nurses, social workers, school counselors, and pastoral counselors should *all* receive training in how to counsel in cases of rape, incest, and sexual abuse. And that training has to include time for people to sort out their feelings, fears, and questions. Although Benedict's book is aimed at survivors and their loved ones, it is also a valuable tool for such training, for it not only documents the reactions and needs of people who have been sexually assaulted—it tells friends, family, and counselors what *not* to do as well.

Before we accept volunteers for the training to become rape counselors for St. Vincent's Hospital Rape Crisis Program, we warn them that hearing about rape will be upsetting and that the training often makes women look at their lives and the world differently. They will become more aware of violence, they will feel more vulnerable as women and they may start to react angrily to remarks from men that they previously brushed off. They may recall a past incident, buried for years, when they were sexually threatened, abused, or attacked. They have to come to grips with their own reactions to rape before they are ready to help a survivor.

Eight years ago, I felt absolute dread coming to my first training session as a volunteer for St. Vincent's new Rape Crisis Program. I must have vaguely known that it would change my life. Before I could begin to feel the excitement and energy that comes from working with other women on a problem that affects the lives of all of us, I had to face this dread. Through my years as a volunteer, through years as a psychotherapist helping women recover from long-term effects of rape, and through recent years of trying to organize my own community to respond to rape, educating other professionals, and actually directing a rape crisis program, that dread, the fear of rape, has never completely left me. Now it is more like a familiar inconvenience that periodically catches me off guard: in the newspaper headline, on the deserted block, after seeing the survivor who was raped by the cab driver, watching a stranger approach a small child. . . . We all have to mourn the loss of innocence, the loss of the taken-for-granted feelings of safety that knowledge of rape brings.

There is no way to make the fear of rape go away absolutely, forever, until there is an end to rape. In the meantime we need comfort and information for everyone who, whether by choice or through being forced to confront the reality of rape, tries to find a way to live that can include, without being warped by, the knowledge of rape.

Helen Benedict is one who has by choice entered the territory of sexual assault as a writer. Her most difficult task has been to look at the raw, brutal facts and not lose sight of her mission, which is to heal. In the process of exploring women's issues and researching articles about rape, she became aware of a major gap in the literature. Among the excellent books for the general public on sexual assault and the growing number of works for professionals, where was the book to place directly in the hands of the survivor in the midst of crisis? In devoting herself to filling that gap with this book, Benedict had to listen to survivors as a woman struggling with her own reactions to the topic first. Thus she is able to speak not only knowledgeably but with compassion devoid of sensationalism or voyeurism. Not minimizing the violence or horror (there is much in the book that makes us wince; that is the nature of the crime), she tells us honestly, from her research and through the

voices of the survivors she quotes, that it is possible to look this horror
in the eye, survive, recover, and even grow.

Until we can change those aspects of our society that permit and
encourage sexual assault, we cannot "win" against rape. But by mobiliz-
ing our concern, as Helen Benedict does, we can conquer the silence,
the shame, and the isolation of suffering caused by rape.

Anne Sparks, C.S.W.
Program Manager, Rape Crisis Program,
St. Vincent's Hospital
Department of Community Medicine

RECOVERY

Introduction

There are many moments of despair after a rape. Whether you are a victim or someone close to a victim, your life has been violently interrupted. You wonder often if you will ever be the same. You wonder if recovery is even possible.

For a long time not much was known about recovery from rape. Until the mid-1960s, when the women's movement brought rape to the attention of the nation, no one had researched the long-term effects of rape on victims. Now this is being remedied. Several researchers are studying what rape does to people, how they recover from it, and how long it takes to recover, and some encouraging results have been found. One group of studies discovered that 20–30 percent of women who are raped recover within only one month.[1] A different study found that many women get over the severe depression that rape causes in six months.[2] The majority of women take longer than a year to recover, but they *do* recover. Rape does not have to destroy you.

A Definition of Rape

Rape in this book is defined as *any sexual act that is forced upon you.* The deepest horror of being raped lies in the fear of being killed. This fear is closely followed by devastating humiliation and the terror of having lost control over oneself. These feelings are present not only in vaginal rape but in forced oral and anal sodomy, in assault with other objects, and in sexual assaults that don't go "all the way." Therefore, this book concerns any woman or man, girl or boy who has been sexually assaulted, whether that assault be legally labeled rape, sodomy, aggravated assault, or attempted rape.

A Definition of Recovery

Once you have been raped, it is hard not to feel that you will never be the same person again, and to some extent you are right. You can't erase the memory of a horrible experience like rape, and so in that sense you can't ever be exactly the same person you were before it. But recovery doesn't mean erasing the assault. It means being able to enjoy life, sex, love, and work again. It means recovering your happiness.

This book will help you recover by showing you how to feel like a survivor instead of a victim. You do this initially by looking at what you did right instead of what you did wrong. Many victims of rape blame themselves for doing something stupid and risky that "invited" the rape and forget that the reason they came out alive was because they did something wise and safe. If you can be proud of yourself for that, you are on the way to feeling strong and powerful again. As one woman put it, "Now that I've survived that, I know I can survive anything. I feel tough." Being able to feel like a survivor means being able to fight for yourself. You can start by fighting against letting the rape destroy you. Recovering from rape is a way of fighting rape, even after it has happened.

How You Recover

Recent studies have shown that the speed with which you recover from rape depends primarily on two things: how you regard what happened to you and how supportive the people close to you are.[3] The circumstances of the rape—who did it, how brutal it was, where and when it happened—don't seem to affect how fast you get better.[4] Your recovery is therefore largely under your control. You can control how you look at your rape by understanding what rape really means, what exactly it has done to you, and what you need because of it. Other people in your life can learn how best to support you by understanding the same things.

Chapter 1 describes all the reactions that survivors typically have to sexual assault, so that you and those close to you can know what to expect and how seriously you have been affected. Chapter 2 tells you, the survivor, how to help yourself get through the various stages of recovery, and includes such practical matters as how to handle the hospital and the police. And Chapter 3 tells your spouse, lover, family, and friends how to help you and how *not* to make you feel worse. These three chapters lay the groundwork for the book and should be read by everyone. The rest of the book addresses people with special problems to overcome after a rape—victims of marital rape, male victims, older victims, teenagers, and lesbian and gay victims. At the end there is a list of resources that includes, for instance, rape crisis centers, victims' assistance programs, and national hotlines.

For Those Close to the Victim

As the spouse, lover, relative, or friend of a rape victim, you play an essential role in that victim's recovery, according to the findings of recent research.[5] If you can react sympathetically and supportively, you can stave off the victim's depression and help her recover faster. If you react with anger or blame, you can slow down her recovery dramatically or even *hinder* it. One current study is finding that the negative reactions of people close to the victim can be so harmful that even one such reaction outweighs several positive ones.[6] As one young woman said, "The way my family reacted was worse than the rape itself."

Most people don't mean to hurt someone who has been raped. They do it because they are feeling so many of the same horrors and fears as the victim that they find it hard to offer her strength and support. Also, without guidance, they have no idea what the right thing to do is. Coping with rape is not something that comes naturally. Rape is too strange and terrifying to rely on mere common sense for guidance. The right way to help a rape victim has to be learned, and that is why this book addresses you, someone who cares about a person who has been raped, in every chapter under the subtitle "How Others Can Help."

The Cycle of Injustice

Rape is an act of great injustice. Circumstances utterly out of your control hurl you into becoming a victim. Either you are chosen at random, picked out unfairly by fate to be degraded or tortured for having done nothing, or you are humiliated and punished out of all proportion for having made some small mistake, such as leaving a door open or trusting someone. As if this isn't enough, the sexual nature of rape adds to the injustice. The most intimate of physical interactions is forced upon you when you are raped, and your most tender, private parts, physical and mental, are invaded against your will; your most basic right as a human being—the right over your own body—is violated, again with no justification. These factors make rape a crime that is uniquely hard to bear. Yet the pain does not end there. Because so few people understand what rape really is and because almost no one has learned how to cope with it or how to help someone else recover from it, a rape victim is treated with continuing injustice by everyone else—and even herself; she is blamed for being a victim.

The blame habitually directed toward rape victims is reflected in jokes, movies, television, and the reactions of others to rape: those who say, "That's what women want"; those who don't believe a woman can be raped without her cooperation and say, "You can't thread a moving needle" or, "She didn't try hard enough to resist"; those who don't understand the horror and pain of rape and say, "But he didn't *hurt* you"; the fathers who say, "That's what comes of hanging out with the wrong crowd"; the therapists who say, "Let's look into your background and see what led to this"; the brothers who say, "You girls always say no when you mean yes"; the policemen who say, "You're just a prostitute who didn't get paid"; and the juries who say, "It happened because of your lifestyle." When the four men who raped a woman on a pool table in the celebrated New Bedford, Massachusetts, "barroom rape" were sentenced in 1984, demonstrators outside the courtroom shouted, "She should have been home in the first place!" and "They should hang *her*." [7]

There is also injustice in the way the legal system deals with rape. The police still notoriously mistreat people who report rape. If you are female and black, they may refuse to believe you or may even sexually accost you.[8] If you are female and white, they hint that you are a whore or a nut case. If you are male, you'll be lucky not to be laughed out of the police station, and if you are elderly you may be greeted with remarks such as "Who'd want to rape *you?*" There are exceptions to this, of course, but the police officer who is sensitive to rape is still a rare creature. And then in court, as has long been known, the system is more concerned with protecting men from false accusation than with convicting rapists or protecting victims from further humiliation.[9]

But the greatest injustice of all is that almost everyone sees a rape victim as less than human. The unsympathetic consider her contaminated and whorish, the sympathetic see her as neurotic, crippled, or at least pitiful.[10] Everyone, on some level, is ashamed for her. This is not true for the survivors of other tragedies. The survivor of a mugging is seen as someone who has merely had bad luck; his character is not permanently damaged and he may even be admired for handling the mugging coolly enough not to get hurt. The survivor of a war will probably be regarded as heroic, and the survivor of a car crash is considered lucky and strong to have pulled through. But the survivor of rape is thought of as a failure. "She did something stupid, so she got raped" is often people's first thought on hearing about her. Such a reaction comforts them with the thought that *they* won't get raped because *they* won't do anything that stupid. They ignore the fact that rape is caused by the rapist, not the victim and they forget that the victim did avoid getting killed—that she, too, could be admired.

The reason rape victims are seen as such failures lies in the myths about rape that abound in our society. Before you can recover from rape, or help someone else recover from it, you have to recognize those myths and understand how misleading they are. Once you are rid of the myths, you are rid of the many misunderstandings that can destroy the possibility of recovery and you are on the way to bringing the cycle of injustice to a stop.

Myth 1: Rape Is Sex

The most powerful myth about rape and the one that lies at the root of all the others is that rape is sex. This myth leads to the belief that rape doesn't hurt the victim any more than sex does, that women even enjoy rape and that therefore it is something to snicker at rather than worry about. But in fact, rape is much more akin to torture than to sex. A torturer puts his victim in a position of helplessness, makes clear to his victim that he is utterly at the torturer's mercy, breaks his will by humiliating and degrading him, and finally inflicts pain on him, usually to the most tender parts of the body. A rapist duplicates these acts. The horrifying testimony of a victim, cited by Ann Burgess and Lynda Holmstrom in their book *Rape: Crisis and Recovery*, serves to illustrate the point.

> He made me do such terrible things. He made me lick his whole body and he made me lick his rectal area. He knocked me around and knocked me out till I passed out. He ripped off all my clothes. When I woke up he picked me up by my breasts. That hurt so bad. . . .[11]

As long as rape is believed to be sex, not torture, women will be believed to have asked for it, but no one would ask to be treated like the woman quoted above. Yet even today one can turn on television and see this myth being perpetuated. The plot of the most popular soap opera, "General Hospital," had the heroine falling in love with and marrying a man who raped her. And in the British television comedy "Butterflies," an episode shown on Easter Sunday in 1984 had the heroine, a bored housewife, cry out in a paroxysm of defiant delight, "I want to be raped!"

Feminists, who understood rape long before most other people, have been saying "rape is violence, not sex" for years, but that statement is too oversimplified to be easily understood. What it means is that rape is motivated by a violent urge, not a sexual one. Rape is an act of violence in which sex is used as a weapon.

Myth 2: The Rapist Is Motivated by Lust

Because rape is seen as sex, the rapist is assumed to be a hot-blooded male, somewhat sexually frustrated, driven beyond self-control by lust. But studies have found that rapists are not sexually frustrated—most of them have normal sex lives at home and many of them are married.[12] Nor do they rape on uncontrollable impulse. In a well-known study of 1,292 offenders in Philadelphia done by Menachim Amir in 1971, it was found that 71 percent of the rapes were premeditated.[13] The specific victim wasn't necessarily picked out but the rapist had planned to rape. This was true for gang rape as well as individual rape.

Over the past few years much research has gone into the real motivation for rape. A. Nicholas Groth, director of the Sexual Offenders Program at the Connecticut Correctional Institute and coauthor of *Men Who Rape*, [14] is one of the leading researchers in this field. He has come to some interesting conclusions about why men rape that help to explain how little sex or lust has to do with it.

Groth divides the motives for rape into three main groups: anger, power, and sadism. Most rapists, he says, have a mixture of these motives but are dominated by one or another.

The Power Rapist. This type is the most common, a man who rapes primarily to feel a sense of control over someone else. Often he is without power in the rest of his life, or sees himself that way. He may have power but not recognize it—judges as well as messenger boys rape. His rapes are usually premeditated and ritualistic. He gets his kicks from the helplessness and submissiveness of the victim. As one man Groth quotes said about his rape of another man:

> I had the guy so frightened I could have made him do anything I wanted. I didn't have an erection. I wasn't really interested in sex. I felt powerful, and hurting him excited me. Making him suck me was more to degrade him than for my physical satisfaction. [15]

The Anger Rapist. This man rapes for revenge. He is furious at someone or something in his life—perhaps his whole life—and the victim, chosen at random, is a convenient object to take his fury out on. He wants to punish someone and, to justify himself, may blame that random victim for the rape. A convicted rapist, serving ninety-nine years for the crime in Texas, expressed this sort of victim blame when he tried to explain in a letter why men rape.*

> . . . most were traumatized by a woman earlier in life whether it be a mother, sister, aunt it doesn't matter. . . . Symbolically, he is getting back at them. A definition of rape is: R:esentment A:cceptance P:enetration E:go.

Another way to spell it would be R-E-V-E-N-G-E.

The anger rapist usually acts impulsively, his rape triggered by some frustration or insult. He is often brutal. He is likely to jump the victim suddenly and start the attack with violence.

* This letter was sent to me from prison in response to an article on rape I wrote for *Glamour* magazine.

The Sadistic Rapist. This man gets sexually excited by causing pain to others. He differs from other rapists in that he enjoys ritualistic torture and sometimes tortures a victim to death. His rapes also tend to be premeditated. Luckily, he is the rarest kind.

Dr. Gene Abel, professor of clinical psychiatry at Columbia University, has also studied rapists but does not agree wholly with Groth's theories. He believes that sex is part of a rapist's motivation but that the rapist has learned early in life to associate sex with violence. Perhaps, for example, he witnessed his father beating or raping his mother. Such a man cannot become sexually aroused unless violence is involved. Sometimes he becomes aroused by violence that doesn't even include sex. Sex for him therefore has to be violent—thus he rapes.[16]

The motivation of men or boys who rape in groups is generally agreed to be somewhat different from that of solitary rapists. Boys gang-rape for each other, in a kind of frenzied machismo, to prove themselves, to show off, to be part of the gang or, at best, out of fear of being ostracized if they don't. They do it as a dare or a joke, as an activity that goes along with robbery, as a sport—at least that is the explanation most analysts have given.[17] Group rape has traditionally been considered *less* perverted than solitary rape because of the assumption that gang-raping someone is some kind of proof of masculinity, a sort of rite of passage. However, a group of males overpowering one woman or girl isn't much of a challenge to manhood. Perhaps the real "proof" of masculinity is in being able to get an erection and maintain it long enough to perform some sort of intercourse in such a public situation. Indeed, not all men can get erections in gang rape. Burgess and Holmstrom cite a case when three men tried to rape a woman and all of them were sexually dysfunctional.[18] Despite the popularity of the one-of-the-gang explanations for group rape, gang rapists probably don't differ from solitary ones. The important factors that make men rape must still be there—being able to see the victim as an object of prey, not as a human being, and seeing sex as an act of power, not love.

A recent case in South Carolina illustrates the danger of believing the myth that men rape out of uncontrollable lust. Faced with a brutal case of gang rape by three men, who had tortured their victim so badly for six hours that she lost four pints of blood and had to be hospitalized for five days, Judge C. Victor Pyle suggested the rapists be locked up for thirty years or accept a suspended sentence on *agreeing to be cas-*

trated.[19] This suggestion is not only barbarous and primitive but it ignores the fact that a man doesn't need testicles to torture a woman. The acts these men performed that resulted in the loss of so much blood had nothing to do with sex. And, as castration is the removal of the testicles, not the penis, a castrated man can still have an erection and perform sex. Releasing a castrated rapist means releasing a man already full of hatred for women who now has even more reason to avenge himself.

Myth 3: The Rapist Is a Weird Loner

The popular image of a rapist is of an ugly, weird, seedy and crazy loner, creeping about alleyways waiting for his prey. This myth contradicts the one above of rapists being normal, hot-blooded males driven by uncontrollable lust, but that is the nature of myths: they aren't logical. In fact, the rapist can be just about anybody. A study by Diana Russell, professor of sociology at Mills College and author of *Rape in Marriage,* of 930 women selected in a random sample survey in San Francisco found that 44 percent of them had been victims of rape or attempted rape and that 60 percent of the assailants had been known to the victim.[20] Twenty-six percent of these assailants were acquaintances or dates of the victim. Eight percent were husbands or ex-husbands and 6 percent were lovers or ex-lovers. Six percent were friends and 6 percent were authority figures such as teachers and bosses. Three percent were relatives other than husbands and 3 percent were defined by the victims as boyfriends rather than lovers. Two percent were friends of the family. These rapists—uncles, doctors, lovers, therapists, policemen—hardly fit the stereotype.

Another popular image of the rapist is that he is black, criminal, and lower-class, but FBI statistics belie this, too. The 1980 FBI profile of a typical convicted rapist shows him slightly more likely to be white than black.[21] He is also very young—usually under twenty-five.[22] Another government study found that gang rapists tended to be only twelve to nineteen.[23] And the idea that the rapist is a loner is refuted by statistics as well. Amir's Philadelphia study found that *over half* of his sample raped in groups or pairs.[24]

Rapists, of course, differ from one another tremendously and, like any large group of people, defy accurate characterization. They are not all dumb or smart, they do not belong to any one class, race, or type, and most of them are never caught anyway and so can't be classified. But it is being found, among the convicted rapists who have been studied, that many of them were abused as children either sexually, physically, or emotionally.[25] And some recent studies indicate that although rapists tend not to be neurotic, they do have other personality disorders such as being antisocial.[26] Whether all the other men who rape—the fraternity boys and school kids who gang-rape, the dates, brothers, and husbands—fit into any of these classifications is not known. They may simply be men who do not see women as human beings with a right to say no.

Myth 4: Women Provoke Rape

Because rapists are believed to be motivated by lust, their victims are believed to have enticed them. This myth is terribly destructive for a victim, for it not only makes other people blame her for the rape but it makes her blame herself. She comes to hate herself for the way she looks, walks, dresses, and behaves—for being a woman. To get himself off the hook, the rapist is likely to reinforce the victim's self-blame by claiming that she provoked him. There are even ludicrous statements on record of rapists saying in court that they were tempted beyond endurance by "precocious" six-year-olds. (Precocious used to be a flattering adjective for a child, meaning she was ahead of her age in accomplishments. Nowadays it is used to suggest that she is inappropriately sexy.) Unfortunately, victims tend to believe these accusations. "He raped me because I gave him a come-on look," a woman might say, neatly taking the blame from the assailant onto herself. "It wasn't his fault for forcing me to do it, it was my fault for looking at him." But if, in order to find out how to avoid being attacked, you were to listen to all the justifications rapists have given for their rapes you would have to try not to be young or old, pretty or plain, male or female, thin or fat, short or tall, white or black, dressed in trousers or a skirt, made-up or not made-up, friendly or unfriendly, scared or confident, and so on. Of *course* the rapist is going to say "You asked for it," but that is no reason to believe him. Sadly, not only victims, but also lawyers, judges, and juries often do.

Blaming the victim in this way is so prevalent that it is even reflected in the way researchers gather rape statistics. In one major government study of rape, called *Rape Victimization in 26 American Cities*, the entire emphasis is on looking at who the victims were, something that was done to "examine the nature of rape and attempted rape victimizations by strangers."[27] This approach naturally led the researchers to draw such conclusions as, "Generally, women who had a high risk of being attacked were young. . . ." as if being young was the victim's fault and had caused the rape. But one shouldn't be looking at who the victims are, for the victims don't commit the crime. It's like compiling statistics about the people who get run over by cars, instead of those who drive the cars that run over people. To understand rape, one should be looking at who the *rapist* is.

Myth 5: Only Bad Women Are Raped

The myth that women provoke rape naturally leads to the belief that only sluttish women get raped. This idea is surprisingly common, even these days. Indeed, defense attorneys rely on this myth to discredit rape victims in court, as happened in the New Bedford, Massachusetts, "barroom rape." At the trial the defense attorney got the victim to admit that she had cheated the State Welfare Department by collecting payments for three years while she lived with her boyfriend, the father of her two children. The attorney, who incidentally was a woman, also revealed that the woman had told someone in the bar that she was seeing a psychiatrist and was having problems with her boyfriend.[28] This kind of evidence, completely irrelevant to the rape (after all, how many of us are "having problems" with a lover?) should never have been allowed in court. Clearly, the attorney was hoping to get the jury to see the victim as a "bad woman"—by implication, a woman who deserved to be raped.

But it is not only manipulative defense attorneys who tout this myth. When a writer suggested an article about rape to the editor of a prominent women's magazine two years ago, the editor said, "Our readers don't get raped." That's like saying they don't get colds.

Rape happens to everyone, the young and old, all races, all classes, and both sexes. The youngest victim seen at one New York hospital was only two months old. The oldest was ninety-seven.[29] It is true that the people who most often report rape are young, single women who live in poor, urban areas, but the middle-class suburbanite gets raped too.[30] The FBI now conservatively estimates that a woman is raped in this country every six minutes,[31] and it is being cautious to say that at least a million people are raped every year in the United States.† Recent research shows that one out of five of all these rape victims is under twelve and that 10 percent of those are children under five.[32] Also, contrary to popular belief, boys are sexually assaulted as often as girls[33] and men in the community are raped by other men; the estimate is that men make up 7–10 percent of all rape victims.[34] The reason this book is for men, teenagers, and the elderly as well as for women is summed up in these words of a director of the San Jose Rape Crisis Center in California, Jackie Read: "Rape can no longer be viewed as a crime against women, but a crime against people."[35]

---

† The one million figure is based on the 1980 FBI count of 82,088 forcible rapes of women over twelve and the New York *Times* report that 100,000 to 1 million children are assaulted each year *(Times*, May 13, 1982, pp. C1, C10). The number of male victims is unknown. No exact count of rapes exists because rape is the most unreported of all crimes (FBI, *Uniform Crime Reports, 1980*, p. 15).

PART ONE

RECOVERY
FOR WOMEN

The Survivors' Stories

This book looks at the stories of several women who have been raped and of some men who have been close to such women. Although every victim of sexual assault has a different experience, these stories illustrate that survivors have similar reactions and needs.

The women interviewed for Part One of this book will be called Claire, Penny, Angela, Rachel, and Joan. The men are Larry, Claire's brother; Clark, Angela's boyfriend; and Don, whose girlfriend Mary was raped.

The women quoted who are not named are eight survivors interviewed while participating in group therapy at St. Vincent's Hospital in New York and other women who have written accounts of their ordeals.

CLAIRE

Claire, a professional athlete in her mid-thirties, was attacked two years ago in the foyer of her apartment building at three in the afternoon. The assailant was a boy in his teens. He pulled a knife on her, forced her to lead him to her apartment and there, under the threat of killing her, raped her anally and terrorized her for three hours. Throughout the attack he kept a turtleneck pulled up to his nose. He asked her detailed questions about her life, examined her family photographs with fascination, and continually crossed himself. Claire said:

> It was very ritualistic and bizarre. Everything he did to me he could have learned from porn magazines or TV. I tried to answer all his questions and make myself as human as possible so he wouldn't kill me.

Afterward, he promised to come back.

LARRY

When I heard what happened to Claire, I wanted to murder someone. At the time, I thought it was just the rapist I wanted to kill, but
now I know I could have murdered anyone.

Larry, a successful sales manager in a large corporation, is a few years
older than his sister. He knows eight other women who have been
raped and the subject, to this day, makes him sad and furious.

PENNY

A writer in her thirties, Penny was raped seven years ago on a train
platform. New in town, she had taken the wrong train late at night and
ended up in a dangerous area with few people around. She was waiting
nervously for the train, writing "I don't want to be here" in her notebook, when three men approached. Two held her arms while the third
pulled the notebook from her and began reading it aloud. One of them
had a knife. Penny remembers:

> Everyone on the platform looked away when it started happening.
> The train came and the guys wouldn't let me go, but nobody
> helped. Everyone got on the train and it left. Then two of them
> held me down and the other one raped me. I can't remember how I
> got home afterward. It's a blank.

ANGELA

Angela, now a successful television producer of twenty-six, was raped
four years ago when she was a graduate student. Her boyfriend at the
time, Clark, was out of town for the night and she was alone in their
apartment for the first time. She went downstairs to the basement to
do some laundry and when she returned, the assailant jumped out at
her from behind the refrigerator and slashed her across the chest with a
knife. He was about nineteen and had been drinking. Angela said:

> I screamed and I think I slipped and fell to the floor. He didn't cut
> me deeply, but there was a lot of blood and I was terrified. He made
> me get up and take my clothes off, then he walked me into the
> bedroom with the knife at my back. All during the rape he was very
> jittery. When the phone rang (it was Clark), he panicked and I was

afraid he might do anything. I didn't fight because he had the knife in my back. Afterward, he said he'd come back and kill me if I told the police, then he left.

When I was sure he was gone, I got hysterical for a few moments. I wrapped myself in a blanket and ran upstairs to find help, but nobody was home. Then I called the police and after they came, I called Clark.

CLARK

I'd called Angela earlier and I wondered why there was no answer. It was because the rapist was there. Then I got a call from her. She sounded so calm. She just said, "Clark, I'm not hurt but I've been raped."

Clark, now in his late twenties, also works in television. He now lives in a different area than Angela. They are no longer lovers.

RACHEL

Now an editor, Rachel was raped six years ago when she was twenty-one and an undergraduate. She was walking home in the early evening when a well-dressed young man approached her and asked for help. He said he was looking for a place to stay and just needed her to sign a document for him to help him out. He told her he'd show her the place he was to stay. She believed him and followed him down the street. He pulled her into an alleyway and raped her. Rachel recalls:

It was strange, because although I knew I couldn't fight him, I didn't feel that scared. Once he tried to kiss me and I pushed his head away and he didn't even try again. I sort of felt in control. When it was over, I looked at my watch and I just said, "I have to go teach now," and I left. At the time, I thought being raped wasn't as bad as being hurt, but now I know that's not true. Now I'm pretty sure I'd fight back.

DON

Don's girlfriend, Mary, was raped when they were both students in their early twenties. Mary was visiting friends in another city and was

still asleep after they had left in the morning when she was awakened
by a man standing over her with a knife. He said he was looking for
money, and while he searched the apartment, she hid her wallet under
a pillow. He found it and said, "For that, bitch, I'm raping you." He
put the knife down and raped her, threatening to kill her if she made a
sound. Don said:

> She didn't tell me about it until she'd been back for a while. We'd
> just finished making love when suddenly she said, "I got raped." At
> first, I was more paranoid than she, I think, but six months later she
> started having a recurring nightmare. She kept dreaming that she
> was trying to scream but she couldn't and that she was trying to stab
> him with the knife but she couldn't reach it.

JOAN

Joan is a businesswoman in her mid-thirties who is the survivor of
incest and several robberies. She was entering her apartment building
at night when a man of about her own age came up behind her and
grabbed her arm. She offered him money, but he said, "That's not
what I want. You know what I want."

> I'd been burgled and robbed at gunpoint recently and because I'm a
> survivor of incest, my coping instincts are good. But I just gave up
> and said, "You guys have taken everything else, you might as well
> take this."

The man's answer to this was to say, "Can't you see my side of it?" and
to take her outside and sit her down on a step. They talked there for
almost two hours.

> He held my arm so hard I had a hand print on it for three weeks
> afterward. He told me his life story and said I was the first one who
> hadn't struggled or fought back. Then when I told him about how I
> was assaulted as a child, he was shocked! He didn't know about child
> sexual abuse.

The man not only let her go without raping her, but escorted her back
to her door to protect her from some men watching them from across
the street.

In a time when many people, men and women, still don't understand that rape is a violent crime, the victim of rape carries a special burden. She knows that she has just been through perhaps the most horrible experience of her life, yet no one else seems to know it. They seem to think the whole thing isn't that serious, that, somehow, it's kind of sexy.

When someone like Claire or Penny is met with leers from the police or doctors and hears jokes and impatient comments from friends, she feels utterly alone, as if the whole world has turned against her. One minute she was herself, minding her own business like anyone else, a private being with her own, small life. The next she is an object to be first brutalized and then sneered at.

The first thing everyone must understand in order to help a woman recover from rape, and in order for her to help herself, is that rape *hurts*. It is not titillating. It is not sexual. Rape is a life-threatening crime that no one asks for and no one wants. It is seriously near to murder.

1
Reactions to Rape

> It happened to me on a Friday night. Mainly, I felt relieved and
> grateful that I wasn't killed. It was disconcerting to feel grateful
> after what had happened. I needed to know that other women
> would react that way, that I wasn't crazy.

Like the woman quoted above, every survivor of rape interviewed for
this book said that her reactions to the rape made her seriously afraid
that she was going mad. She needed to know that what she was feeling
was what other victims feel. Examining reactions to rape is necessary
both for victims and the people close to them. Victims need to see how
similar their reactions are, and other people need to know exactly what
victims go through. Try to remember that nobody has *all* of these
symptoms. And if you have reactions that are not mentioned here,
don't assume you are abnormal. What follows is a composite—everyone is different and even a book devoted to the subject can't cover
everything.

When It Happens: The First Twenty-four Hours

Although most people will probably read this book some time after
rape has disrupted their lives, this section on how the victim reacts
immediately afterward is included for two reasons. First, it is important
for the rape victim and those close to her to know that she was not
alone in her seemingly abnormal behavior right after the rape. Second,
with luck some of you will be reading this even though you don't know
anyone who has been raped—yet. Rape is so prevalent now—the latest

estimates are that one in ten women will be assaulted at some time in her life—that the odds of everyone knowing someone who was raped are high.[1] This section will help you know what to expect.

He has this screwdriver in my stomach, and I think I'm dead—
that's all you think about is that you are dead.[2]

The single most terrifying reaction to being raped is the fear of being killed. Almost every rape victim is threatened with murder, for that is the rapist's main way of forcing his will upon her, and the threat is very convincing—two thirds of rape victims are threatened with weapons.[3] But the rapist doesn't even have to actually make his threat aloud for his victim to feel her danger. As one put it, "I figured if he's crazy enough to do this to me, he's crazy enough to kill me."

The terror of being murdered is the most traumatic part of the ordeal of rape and yet the one that is, oddly enough, the most ignored. People are so absorbed by the sexual aspect of rape that they forget the murderous side of it. It is essential that you, as a woman who has been assaulted, and your friends realize how much the threat of murder can affect you. As a victim said, "You come face to face with your own death and horrendous vulnerability. It takes a long time to recover from that."

The other great fear during a rape is that you will be badly hurt or mutilated. One woman remembers thinking, "They might beat me to a bloody pulp and leave me in a field someplace."[4] The fear of being hurt is also well founded. In a government study of rape, 91 percent of the victims received injuries other than those caused by the rape itself.[5] Most of them were not mutilations, but they did include bruises, broken bones, and stab wounds. So, those women who choose to submit to rape do not do so out of indifference or desire, they do it to save their lives. For the rest there is no question of choosing at all—they are simply forced.

How you feel during the rape itself depends a lot on the sort of person you are and on how the rape happens. If you are awakened from a deep sleep by the attack, for instance, or jumped suddenly out of nowhere, you may be so shocked that you freeze, unable to react or think. One young woman in Boston was grabbed by a drunken man on a street in broad daylight. He pinned her to a wall and tried to tear her clothes off, but she couldn't move or scream. The shock paralyzed her.

Luckily, someone came by and frightened the man off. Another woman found herself unable to leave her bed for two days after being raped there in the middle of the night. Some women, however, don't feel the shock until later and can only think about getting through the ordeal alive. A twenty-eight-year-old mother expressed this in a letter she wrote for other rape victims addressing the men who raped her.* "I could only think of two things. One was that I was praying my daughter would not wake up and walk in. The other was that if I didn't look at you, you might not kill me."

If the attack is not so sudden, you may be able to think extraordinarily clearly throughout the rape. You take in every detail of what the rapist looks like and what he says, think about what might happen next and try to calculate how to escape. You may even remember in photographic detail the advice you have read about how to resist rape.[6] Some people stay so calm that they are even able to set a trap for the rapist. A college student in suburban California reacted this way when she was jumped by a fifteen-year-old boy in a parking lot. After the rape, done at knifepoint, the boy asked to see her again, apparently under the common misapprehension that women like rape. The student agreed, gave him her address, and made the date. When he arrived at the appointed time with flowers and a box of chocolates, the police were there to greet him. This student's extraordinary presence of mind is, however, unusual.

A fairly common reaction during a sexual attack is to feel a complete separation of your mind and body, as if the rape were happening to someone else. Penny felt that way when she was raped.

> When the rape happened, it was as if time stood still. I wasn't even there. It was like a dream, not real. I can't even remember what the guys who did it looked like, if they were young or old or what color they were. I just remember seeing a little kid on the platform with his mother, watching me. He just stared like he knew this shouldn't be happening and he couldn't believe no one was doing anything. I know my mind was racing during it, but I can't remember the men, just that kid.

Right after the rape, you probably feel stunned. You find it hard to believe all this even happened and that you haven't walked into some

---

* This letter, "A Letter to the Men Who Raped Me," is used by the rape crisis center at St. Vincent's Hospital in New York City to train rape counselors.

cruel nightmare. One woman bit herself on the arm to make sure she was there and alive. Others wander about in a daze, literally in a state of shock.

When you talk to friends or officials after the rape, you may cry or you may find yourself acting supremely self-controlled. You might be calm, sensible, and even indifferent, as if you are explaining a math problem rather than describing a brutal attack. You might even smile in a tense way and crack jokes. This control is a way of protecting yourself from the shock, but it can be most confusing to friends, who expect to see you shaken and sobbing when they arrive at the emergency room. Some women become upset immediately, laughing senselessly or sobbing so hard they cannot speak. Others become hostile, defensive, and edgy. You might go into a trancelike state, removing yourself from all that is going on around you. All these reactions are normal, the reactions of anybody to shock and terror. They have been seen in countless women across the country by counselors at crisis centers and nurses at hospitals.[7] They are signs of the awful ordeal you have just been through, and are remarkably similar to the reactions of people who go through any other terrible crisis, such as war, a flood, or a hurricane.[8]

During the first twenty-four hours after the rape, and probably long after that, too, you are likely to be afraid of being alone. You especially fear that the rapist will seek you out again, for many rapists do threaten to come back. You are jumpy and nervous and shaken up. None of this is surprising. When you have been raped, you have had the deepest part of yourself violated: your body and your control over your own will. As Claire's brother Larry put it, "We are normally propelled by the idea that we are masters of our destiny. That's one of the ways we can get out of bed in the morning. He robbed Claire of that." The world as you knew it before has been shattered. It is no wonder that you feel suspicious and terrified of everyone.

Physically, you may be experiencing trauma, too. Not everyone goes through this, but nausea and pain are common aftermaths of rape. If you were raped orally, you may develop a sore throat, a common physiological reaction of disgust. The ordeal might also have left you exhausted and racked with headaches, stomachaches, and genital pain. Some of these symptoms will be physically caused and some psychologically, but they are genuine, need to be recognized and, if possible, treated.

A Day to a Month Later

Every woman who has been raped recovers in her own time and her own way. Some women show almost no reactions until a couple of weeks after the rape. Others get all their reactions over with immediately and then feel back to normal. Most, however, take years to feel completely recovered. If you don't feel better in a month, you should realize that you are the rule, not the exception. As one victim said, "People say, 'Oh, she's okay now,' because the hurt isn't visible anymore. The bruises may be gone, but we still hurt."

The first few weeks after a rape are not easy for anyone. On the one hand, you may want to collapse, give in to the horror of what has happened and weep, stay in bed and succumb to your depression. On the other hand, you may want to conquer your fears, and prove to the world and yourself that the rape has not destroyed you. One woman expressed this contradictory impulse when she said:

> I went back to work two days after the rape. I had to do it. A girl I
> knew wrote me a letter saying I was so strong, but I wanted to be
> looked after, not seen as Superwoman. I had to act strong out of
> self-respect, but I wanted someone to see I wasn't.

You may go through a period, after the initial shock is over, of acting as if nothing has happened, a kind of suspended time before you can deal directly with it that may last days, weeks, or only hours. You need that time and should not be pushed to hurry through it. It's a time when your survival instinct is in full force. Meanwhile, however, there will be frightening things going on underneath.

THE SYMPTOMS

You may have only one, several, or none of these symptoms. They are all symptoms experienced, in one form or another, by most rape victims and they all eventually go away.

- Fluctuating Emotions. Your feelings seesaw dramatically. One minute you are feeling calm, the next your heart is beating wildly, your legs are shaking, and you are in tears. Such mood swings will seem to come on with no warning and no control, as if something inside you has gone haywire. Your body is coping with shock.
- Physical Ills. Loss of appetite and nausea after a rape are common,

especially after an oral rape. You may have difficulty sleeping. You might also develop vaginal irritations such as itching, burning, or soreness, and have stiff limbs, stomachaches, and headaches. You may also get sick in other, seemingly unrelated ways: perpetual colds, the flu, and other, more serious illnesses. Claire got sick after her rape.

> After the rape I got a bad result on my Pap smear for the first time in my life. I went to a holistic healer who said it was to do with my internalized rage about the rape. She did a laying-on-of-hands type of thing. I don't really believe in all that stuff, but after letting my rage out more, the gynecological problems did actually go away.

Whether illnesses unrelated to the rape occur because the stress caused by rape has lowered your resistance to infection or whether they are psychologically induced is not known—probably both factors play a part. Several women who had been raped said they thought getting sick was partly to do with feeling neglected. "We were signaling people that we weren't better yet, that we still needed attention."

• Flashbacks. Images and memories of the rape are likely to plague you for some time, either coming out of the blue or triggered by some reminder, such as the sight of a man who looks like the rapist, the place where it happened, or the time when it happened. Some women who were attacked in their sleep wake up at the exact time of the attack every night for a while. If the rape happened during your regular routine, flashbacks are especially likely to be a problem, because you can't avoid repeating that routine—going to work or passing a particular alleyway, for example.[9] You might be able to overcome this by deliberately going to the place the rape happened until it is neutralized, but you might also find that flashbacks can only be cured by time.

• Depression. Not only will the rape depress you, but having to cope with all these other reactions to it will too. One study found that depression is the most common reaction of all, the kind of depression that makes you feel anxious, down, and restless.[10] The depression was acute during the first month, but most of the women in the study had recovered from it by six months.

• Loss of Self-esteem. In a way, loss of self-esteem is an offshoot of the depression, because feeling down usually makes you dislike yourself. You may feel angry at yourself for getting raped, for instance, and as a result feel unable to stand up for yourself or even to care about what happens to you. Something like this happened to Claire.

I was so intimidated by the rape that for a time I became immobile whenever any other danger presented itself. I had to ride the trains a lot to commute to work, and some freak or drunk was always sitting next to me. It was as if they could sense my fear and so would pick me out. I'd sit there, unable to move, unable to change seats. I'd be frozen.

Low self-esteem also disrupts your work. Without realizing it, you begin to feel incapable, confused, or even a failure. These feelings might be so subtle that you don't even connect them to the rape. Try to remember that no one can go back to work and perform excellently after a crisis like rape.

Another form this loss of self-respect can take is disgust with your own body. You may feel so sullied by the rape that you despise your femaleness and believe others despise it, too, especially lovers. One woman actually bathed herself in Clorox because she felt so befouled by the rape.[11] Another, who had been gang-raped at age seventeen by fraternity boys who had ejaculated all over her, felt for two years afterward that she couldn't wash the smell of semen out of her hair.[12] Older women sometimes feel contaminated by the rapist and worry that they will pass a venereal disease on to their children or grandchildren.

Some women come to hate their bodies for a different reason—they believe that being female is what caused the rape and so blame their femaleness for it. Burgess and Holmstrom quote a woman about this. "My womanhood turned suddenly from the center of my source of identity to the cause of my woe."[13] Some also hate their bodies for being attractive to men. Gaining a lot of weight after rape is not uncommon because it is a way of hiding your sexuality. The writer of the "Letter to the Men Who Raped Me" reacted against her body.

> For a long time after what you did, I felt shame to be a woman. I would look at my body in the mirror and I did not like what I saw. I could not wear makeup or jewelry. I wanted to be with a man in a normal way again, but I couldn't. You did all of that to me.

Other women react in an opposite way; they need to emphasize their femininity as a kind of self-reassurance. Rachel found this:

> I went to class two days after the rape wearing a dress, which I hardly ever did in those days. It was subconscious then, but now I realize I was saying, "I'm still a lady, even if a violated lady."

• Nightmares. Nightmares about the rape can be a real curse, forcing you to relive your terror over and over again, but they can also be a relief. In an early study of ninety-two rape victims by Burgess and Holmstrom, twenty-nine of them described rape dreams that divided into two types: dreams where the woman tried to fight off the attack but woke up frustrated and crying because she could not, and dreams where she fought off the attack successfully. This second kind usually came later on, as the woman was progressing in recovery.

> I had a knife and I was with the guy and I went to stab him and the knife bent. I did it again and he started bleeding and he died. Then I walked away laughing with the knife in my hand.[14]

• Phobias. Developing phobias after a rape is extremely common and extremely disturbing, for it is one of the things that makes you certain that you are going crazy. Some of the phobias are obvious: you fear men who look like the attacker(s), for instance. Claire found that whenever she saw someone who resembled the teenager who raped her, she would be filled with such terror that she had to go directly home and stay there. Don and Mary found themselves both reacting to large black men with fear because Mary's rapist was large and black. Phobias of people who are the same physical type or race as the rapist are very common, which can be upsetting for people who've struggled against racism all their lives. But you might develop phobias that are less obviously related to the rape. Don said this happened to Mary. "She would sit in a theater and insist on being near an exit in case of fire. She was never like that before." You might develop a fear of indoors or outdoors, of being alone or in a crowd. You might get paranoid about certain people you know and even feel plotted against. Although you are convinced that these phobias are sure signs of madness, they are in fact quite natural after a rape. Eventually, phobias will fade to a manageable level if not go away altogether.[15] If they don't, therapy can help.

• Nervous or Compulsive Habits.

> After the rape, I developed a nervous twitch in my face. It would come on at work or anytime when I was not dealing directly with the rape by crying or talking about it.

Like Angela, you might find yourself getting into odd, compulsive habits, such as washing many times a day, or developing a nervous twitch. The stress you've been through has to come out in some way.

• Disbelief. You will probably find it hard to really believe that such a horrible thing has happened to you, not only immediately after the rape but for some weeks later. Angela said, "I kept thinking, it couldn't really have happened, it just couldn't. Then the details would come flooding back and I knew it had."

• Taking Crazy Risks. Because rape shakes up your sense of security so much, leaving you with a fear of men, of solitude, and of nightfall, you might go overboard in an attempt to prove to yourself that you won't let the rape intimidate you. You then start taking risks, such as walking dark streets alone or sitting in deserted parks. Some people might see this as an attempt to invite another rape, or as a sign of self-destructive mental instability. It isn't. It's a gesture of defiance.

YOUR SEXUALITY

"Will I ever like sex again?"

This question is one of the biggest and most upsetting for any victim of rape. The answer seems to be that you will, but it might take time. Unless you are lucky enough to have a sensitive, gentle partner *and* an ability to immediately disassociate sex from the rape, you probably won't want to engage in any sexual activity for the first month after the rape. This is perfectly normal. See "Resuming Sex" below and "Your Relationship with Your Partner" in Chapter 2 for a discussion of the problems you might have then.

There are two circumstances that may make you worry particularly about your sexuality. The first is if you had an orgasm during the rape and the second is if you were a virgin.

A few women do have orgasms when they are raped, something they usually don't want to admit to anyone. If this happened to you, you are probably devastated. You might think it means you must have secretly enjoyed the rape, that the myths about women being masochistic and wanting rape are right. And you know that if people found out, they wouldn't sympathize much with you as a victim. You are also deeply ashamed and likely to despise yourself. To some extent, your worries are justified—most people will take your orgasm as evidence that you enjoyed the rape and so won't sympathize with you. But those people are wrong.

Doctors and psychologists give this explanation of how a woman might climax during rape: When the body is in a state of acute fear, the physiological system becomes highly excited. Adrenaline washes through the body, the heart races, and the senses are keyed up. Sometimes the body gets in such a state of excitement that its different responses become confused. As some people urinate involuntarily when excited or afraid, others can climax.[16]

People who are familiar with rape should understand this, but, in order to protect yourself, you might want to refrain from telling anybody else about this detail of your rape. Wait until you find somebody you can trust.

If you were a virgin before the rape, or have almost no sexual experience, you may be very confused by it, especially if you were brought up to see sex as something shameful. You may fear that you will never be able to develop a normal sexuality, that you'll always be afraid of sex or that no man will want you because you've been sullied by the rape. If you value your virginity for cultural or religious reasons, having it "stolen" from you can be devastating, particularly if your family or fiancé regard you as spoiled as a result. In some cultures an unmarried woman's virginity is her primary value. Hindu and Moslem women have told rape counselors that they cannot tell their families about their rape for fear of being murdered; a nonvirgin is a disgrace to the family, unmarriageable and a financial burden.† Otherwise, simply being initiated into sex in such a violent, degrading way can leave a psychological scar. But this can be overcome by a gentle partner, by sex education, and by understanding that what happened to you was an act of violence, not sex. (See Chapter 2 for more on your sexuality and Chapter 8 for more on virgins.)

FACTORS THAT EXACERBATE YOUR REACTIONS

How exactly any one woman reacts to rape depends on what else is going on in her life. For some women rape simply is not as horrible as for others. If there has been a death in your family or some other crisis,

† If you are in danger like this, be assured that a rape crisis center won't inform your family of your rape. You may want to ask them for a referral to a battered women's shelter, where you can be temporarily hidden.

for instance, your rape might not seem so terrible in comparison. One study found that people who have had a family crisis before a rape actually recover faster than others, because the rape doesn't seem so important and because they've learned how to cope with trauma.[17] On the other hand, some women just see something like this as the final straw, just a further example of their bad lot in life. Then they feel more defeated than ever, and even more depressed. There are certain other factors that seem to make your reactions more acute, too. Here are a few examples:

• When you've been raped or assaulted before, a second rape can be doubly traumatic.

> I was just getting over the first time—not sitting up every time I heard a strange noise or getting jittery being alone. What makes me mad is my life is disrupted [again]; every part of it upset.[18]

Not only will you feel picked out for double misfortune, but you'll worry about how other people will regard you. "They might say, 'Well, once I can believe, but twice, well you must have been asking for it.' "[19] You will feel ashamed and persecuted. It is true that having two or more incidents of terrible bad luck is extraordinarily unfair but, still, it *is* only bad luck. Since the statistics on rape now officially predict that one woman in ten will be raped in her lifetime, the chances of its happening more than once to someone are not so unlikely.[20]

For some women the chances of being raped more than once are higher because of the environment they live in. If you are poor and have to live in a dangerous neighborhood, for example, violence may be a part of your everyday life. That might mean that you cope with rape better on the surface—"That's just part of my life"—but it doesn't mean you aren't affected by it. Many women in such circumstances have such low self-esteem that their entire image of themselves is that of victim. This might mean that you take less care to protect yourself or feel so beaten down that you accept rape as merely one of many abuses. Counselors say that the women they see who are already on drugs or drinking too much can be the hardest ones to treat for rape, for they don't have the will anymore to fight to get over it.[21] This makes recovery much harder.

• When you come from a strictly traditional family that has a disapproving attitude toward sex, you might find it particularly hard to tell them about the rape or get their support. You fear their anger and disgust and you fear causing them trauma and shame. Angela said she didn't tell her parents about her rape for two years for reasons such as this.

> As far as I knew, they thought I was still a virgin. They didn't even know about Clark. I was embarrassed to tell them about the rape and afraid they would blame me and say I asked for it. When I did tell my father about it, though, he didn't react like that after all. He was very supportive.

Burgess and Holmstrom cite a case where the woman did get a bad reaction from her family. She told her counselor:

> No one wants to have anything to do with me. My grandmother doesn't want to tell my brother and I want him to know. She says it is a shame on the family. No one is talking to me. They won't even say hello to me. I never would have told anyone if I thought this is what would happen. I didn't have to tell anyone; that is what makes me so mad. I told people because I thought they would understand. Even my husband is ashamed of me; doesn't want me around his family. It is as though it were my fault.[22]

In cases like this the intervention of a counselor can be invaluable. She can explain rape to your family and help them sympathize with you instead of blame you. Getting your family to read this book could help as well.

• When you've had a strongly religious upbringing, you might find your religion can be a great comfort after an ordeal like rape, but you might also find it making recovery more difficult—it may shake your faith or lead you to find religious reasons for blaming yourself. This book is not the place to tackle the spectrum of religious beliefs, but do be cautious about jumping to conclusions. If you are strongly religious, you may be tempted to look for godly or cosmic explanations for the rape that are really just a way of blaming yourself—you decide that the rape is a punishment for something you have done wrong, for example. You can then get so carried away with guilt and self-hatred for being bad that you forget the badness of the rapist, you forget your own innocence. How your rape affects your religion may be a problem you can only discuss with your priest, minister, or rabbi, but beware of being self-destructive. Consider the attitude of the woman who wrote the letter to her rapists.

For a moment I thought about asking God for His help. But then I
thought that this was ridiculous. If God had been watching over me,
He would never have let you in my window. *I am not an evil person.*
If God were watching over me, He would not have let you be doing
this. I knew that God had nothing to do with it. The only person I
could count on was myself.

• When you were raped in the presence of someone else, such as a
boyfriend or husband, your sense of safety might be especially hard to
regain. When someone you thought of as your protector was violated
along with you—tied up, made to watch the rape, sexually attacked as
well—it makes you feel as if your very last barrier of safety has been
destroyed. That is terrifying. It also means that, with both of you being
primary victims, you may find it harder to give each other support.

• When you know the man or men who raped you, you may take
the rape particularly hard. The fear that your assailant will return and
attack you again, for instance, will be frighteningly realistic, for he may
know where you live, who you are, or have other powers over you.
Perhaps he lives with you. You may also be afraid to report him because
he has threatened you or people close to you and because you know
that people are going to be less likely to believe you anyway, especially
if you went on a date with him or had a previous sexual relationship
with him. And if you both live in a small town, he might spread rumors
that you offered yourself to him, thus making you look promiscuous and
him look like an innocent man who's been seduced, a trick that often
works because society has such double standards about the sexuality of
men and women: a man who sleeps around is a virile stud, a woman
who sleeps around is "loose." You might also find it harder to get
sympathy from friends than you would if the rapist had been a stranger.

Rape by a friend also shatters your self-confidence, because it calls
into question your judgment of people. You may feel very foolish.

If you know the rapist well, you are going to have to make some
tough decisions. Are you going to face the hate and ridicule of his
friends and family by accusing him? Are you going to risk his revenge
by exposing what he did? Are you going to ignore his threats to do it
again or kill you and try to get him arrested? And what will you do
about loyalty? "He's my sister's husband. How can I put him in jail?"
"He's my brother's son. How can I bring disgrace on them like this?"
Black women may feel the question of loyalty is a problem when they
are raped by black men. By reporting the rape, will you be betraying

your own kind by putting the man in the hands of white police, the white court, and the white-run prison? A black woman who was raped by a white Puerto Rican expressed her version of this dilemma like this: "I felt I would be guilty in turning in another Third World person who had raped me. I felt . . . it was wrong. . . ."[23]

The more you fight the man or men who raped you and the more you fight the thoughts that make you blame yourself, the less of a victim you will be. By raping you, your attacker was not worrying about loyalty to family or race. By raping you he was not responding to some mysterious come-on you unwittingly gave him. He raped you to fulfill his own sick fantasy. The more you keep quiet and let him get away with it, the more you are allowing him to victimize again. You owe him nothing. (See Chapter 5, "Rape by Husbands," for more on this subject.)

Long-term Reactions

A few months after the rape, Clark was planning a trip to Europe for the summer. I told him I needed him to stay. I didn't want to be left alone. We were living in a bad neighborhood and I didn't feel safe there. I was terrified, and I said I felt I'd kill myself or something horrible would happen. But he went anyway. I could understand a stranger hurting me and not caring about ruining my life, but I couldn't understand why someone who loved me would abandon me.

That summer I was in the lowest state I've ever been. I kept thinking, "How could he do this to me? Does he understand what he's doing?" He didn't see how the rape had changed everything totally.

I went into therapy because I'd lost weight and was feeling lousy. I was locking myself in my room at night and drinking and not sleeping. I was really unhealthy and getting worse. I'd spent twenty-two years living a safe, secure life that I'd built up brick by brick and in half an hour some stupid, illiterate, evil person had knocked it all over. I had to start over again with a cracked foundation, and I felt I'd never get back to where I'd been before, so why even try?

Not everyone goes through as bad a time as Angela after a rape, but everyone is likely to feel at least a few moments of despair during the weeks and months that follow it. People recover at different rates and continue to have reactions anytime from six weeks to ten years or more; one study of 146 rape victims found that 74 percent of them took four to six years to recover.[24] Other studies have shown that about a quarter of the women who never seek help consider themselves recovered within three months to a year.[25] It is important to realize that there is no norm for the time it takes to get over rape; it is a highly subjective phenomenon—what one woman considers recovered another might not—and most studies on the subject can never be wholly reliable because they only look at women who come to rape crisis centers to volunteer information, a very select population. Basically, it can safely be said that *the majority of women take longer than a year to feel completely recovered from a rape.* If you don't realize how long it usually takes to recover from rape, you might worry that you will *never* recover. It *is* a long road to recovery, but most people do get there eventually.[26] You will be able to be happy, successful, and back to your old self again. As one of the women interviewed for this book said, "I've lived through this and I've survived it. Now it's time to get back to my life."

For some women the worst reactions to rape are over within three to six months. The acute symptoms described above—phobias, eating and sleeping disorders, nightmares, physical ills—have gone, the woman has returned to her usual life, and things look, at least outwardly, back to normal. For others these symptoms don't even begin until after a month or more has passed. It's as if the psyche gives you a respite until you are ready to think about the rape. But even if you do feel recovered after a month or so, you will probably still have a higher level of anxiety and fear than you did before the rape. As one victim found, "I was not a fearful person before the rape, but afterward I found that I became frightened when alone and was less likely to stay out as late as I had before."[27]

It is only natural that the rape is going to leave you more wary of being alone. Angela said:

> I still don't like being alone at night. I live with a male roommate
> 'cause it feels safer, and when he's away I lock myself in my room.
> I'm also very careful on the street and cross repeatedly to get away
> from people who scare me. But I do go out at night now, which I
> was afraid to do for two years.

This sort of fear is probably going to restrict your everyday life for some time, something that is unpleasant to bear. As a result, you may have bouts of depression. Claire recalled:

> I went through a time of about four months after the rape when I couldn't talk about it without getting depressed. Talking about it would get me so upset that it'd take two weeks to get back to normal.

One of the hardest parts of your long-term reactions to rape is impatience with still having reactions at all. You don't want to feel afraid and depressed anymore, you've had enough and you despair of ever getting better. There will be many moments when you feel that you want to just give up. As one victim put it, "I felt a lot of impatience with myself. I saw other people thinking, 'Why aren't you better yet?' and I felt that about myself, too." Luckily, these feelings come and go. On some days you'll be able to see that you are improving and it won't all look so bleak.

A few months after the rape is often the time when you can finally get angry about the whole thing. At first, you may have been too scared or intimidated or simply glad to be alive to let yourself react that way, but as you mend, your fury at the rapist can come out. Counselors consider it a sign of recovery when you can release your anger. You might, however, not be able to let yourself get angry. Like a good little girl, you turn your anger inward, blaming or hating yourself for what happened instead. Claire still has trouble with her anger. "Learning to get angry about the right things is very difficult. I tend to blow up about little things instead."

When you do finally feel rage, you'll show it in various ways. Sometimes you might burst out at someone you love, which is difficult for everyone. Other times you will indulge in endless fantasies of revenge, as the woman did in her letter to her rapists.

> More than anything in the world, I want to be strong enough and brave enough to kill you. I know that I did the right thing by not resisting. I probably saved my own life, and perhaps the life of my daughter. But still, as I lie awake in bed and think about you, I want it to happen over again. Because the only thing in life that would satisfy me now is the chance to kill both of you.

Fantasies of revenge like this often come out in nightmares as well as in daydreams, and the nightmares may not begin until several months after the rape. When reactions like bad dreams and renewed fears don't start until more than a month after the rape, they can be extremely upsetting. You thought you were over that stuff, and here it is again. Or you thought you wouldn't go through it at all, and then it begins just as you should be better. The nagging persistence of symptoms is part of recovering. It's as if a lot of ugly demons were imprisoned inside you, and gradually they are getting out and leaving you free.

Another long-term reaction to rape is that you may be more sensitive in many ways. You are more easily hurt by people because your self-esteem is low, more likely to be angered by street harassment, jokes and stupid remarks about rape, and more vulnerable to reminders of it. Often, if another type of trauma happens, it will temporarily bring back some of the reactions you had immediately after the rape. The trauma might be another sexual assault, a burglary, or a mugging, but it might be quite unrelated, too, such as the car breaking down, a fight with a lover, a crisis in the family or at work, or even a movie. Don remembered, "One of the last times we went out together, we saw *Looking for Mr. Goodbar*. It was Mary's idea, but afterward she sat in the theater for twenty-five minutes and cried." Don said that Mary had also been retraumatized when two of her friends were raped.

> They were raped more horribly than she was, and this awakened the whole thing for her and the rage. It was especially bad when a friend was raped at Mary's best friend's house. The guy held her for six hours, terrorized her with her three-year-old child in the room all the time. He even pointed a gun at her and pulled the trigger, but it didn't go off. Mary and I were breaking up then, and she had been staying there a lot. She felt her second home had been violated.

On the practical side, money and work can also be sources of trouble for some time after a rape. Claire still has financial problems as a result of her rape. She said:

> People need to know that they may not be as good at their work as before for a long, long time. And the money thing is hard, too. You take cabs because you're afraid of public transport, you pay more for a secure place to live, moving costs you. The rape was a huge setback for me financially, and I still can't save anything because I

need to live some place safe, and that costs all I earn in rent. It's specially hard for a single woman trying to be independent, not letting her parents help her.

It is also especially hard for poor women, single mothers, women in low-paying jobs. A middle-class woman like Claire could choose to move out of the area if she really wanted, but many a victim of rape can't afford to leave even if she is terrified of where she lives. She is simply stuck, and this may exacerbate her reactions to the rape.

If the rape occurred at work or while you were traveling to or from work, you may find yourself unable to go back. The work place or the route there is simply too terrifying. Circumstances like this are particularly unbearable, for the rape seems to have invaded every corner of your life. You will not only have to pull the private part of yourself together, but find a new job as well. Be sure to contact a victims' assistance program to help you win worker's compensation. If you were raped at work, you may be able to sue the company for negligent security. If you were raped by a colleague, you will have similar problems as those women who are raped by friends or acquaintances (see pages 33 and 34).

RESUMING SEX

After a month or so has passed, you may be feeling ready to try having sex again, especially if you are in a steady relationship. Or you might feel pressured into having sex again even though you aren't ready; see "Your Relationship with Your Partner" in Chapter 2 for a discussion of how to cope with this. But when you do resume sex, you may find yourself having problems.

In a long-term study of how rape affects women's sexuality, Judith Becker, associate professor at the Columbia College of Physicians and Surgeons, found that the most disturbing factor was continual flashbacks of the rape.[28] Sometimes these flashbacks would appear out of nowhere, but usually they were triggered by a particular touch or position that reminded the woman of the rape. One woman, for instance, could not stand to have her breasts caressed because her rapist had caressed them. Angela still finds, four and a half years after she was raped, that she reacts badly to certain movements. "The guy clutched my stomach during the rape, which no one had ever done before, and even now when that happens I struggle to get out of it."

Many women who have been raped resume having sex as frequently as before but feel less desire and find it more difficult to get aroused.[29] Becker found that by three years after a rape, the majority of women felt their sexuality was back to normal, but 39 percent of them said they still had sexual problems because of it.[30] The problems were an inability to have orgasm, low levels of desire, and repulsion toward certain positions and actions that reminded them of the rape.

Measuring how rape affects sexuality is tricky because sexuality is so elusive. It is not always easy to tell how much the problems are caused by the rape and how much by other things. Tensions between couples after a rape can affect their sex lives. Trauma or anxiety of any kind is likely to interfere with sex. Penny expressed her confusion about the effect of her rape on her sexuality when she said:

> I don't know if it affected me much. My sexuality is erratic anyway, but I don't know if it's the rape, getting older, or being in one relationship for a long time. I did become absolutely asexual for about a year though, some time after the rape.

Angela, too, was uncertain about this.

> I wouldn't say I'm unchanged sexually. I used to love sex and I used to dress in a sexy way. I don't anymore. On occasion, I enjoy it but not like before. But this is also a product of things that have happened since the rape. I had an abortion last year, and that caused trauma with the person I was with. I don't feel like a sexual person anymore. That started with the rape but then other things added to it.

Close, solid relationships are usually the best cure for sexual problems after a rape. If the problems persist, it's often because they were there to begin with, and it is worth trying to work them out by yourself or with the help of therapy. But you might find that you don't regain your normal sexuality until you are in a new relationship with someone you met after the rape, someone who is not associated with it in your mind.

If you are single, enjoying sex again may be particularly difficult because the rape has made you afraid of new men. Learning to trust men again is one of the hardest aspects of recovery. Claire said she still distrusts men.

> I don't believe they can really understand what I went through, so I can't get too close to them. It's a problem. I was in between relationships when the rape happened, then my two subsequent boyfriends were good about nodding and saying "I understand" when they didn't. I could feel they couldn't. I don't think any man can, really. And I couldn't and wouldn't do a lot of sexual things I used to—it became a power thing. I wouldn't let them make me do anything anymore. The man I'm with now said, "I can't pretend to understand, but it seems like the grossest violence that can happen to you." That's the best I can expect.
>
> At certain times I still can't deal with certain sexual things and at other times I can; I feel as if I have to keep on explaining myself to my boyfriend. I don't think he really understands.
>
> You see, in my heart of hearts, I still feel that I'm used goods. Part of me wonders if I can ever have a marriage or a good relationship.

Worries such as Claire expresses, although sad, are typical. You feel ruined emotionally and sexually by the rape, and you worry that you'll never be stable enough to sustain a good relationship with a man. Yet studies are finding that the majority of women are able to resume satisfactory sexual relations by about six months after being raped,[31] and the women interviewed for this book have all pulled their lives back together well. Seven years after her rape, Penny is now happily married to Pete, the man she was living with at the time of the rape, and is an outgoing, energetic, and anything but fearful woman. Claire, two and a half years after her rape, is now in the best relationship that she's ever had and is continuing her career as an athlete. And Angela, although still somewhat troubled four and a half years later, is newly married, successful in her work, and full of fun and life.

Recovery takes time. Meanwhile, you are suffering because it is hard to be alone, to go out, to concentrate on work, or to settle back into previous relationships. This in turn upsets you, and a spiral of anxiety ensues. "What is the matter with me?" you wonder, and you often despair. The matter is that you are in trauma. But you needn't be a helpless victim of all these reactions. There are ways you can help yourself through it.

2

How to Help Yourself

For a long time it was thought that a woman's recovery from rape had a lot to do with the circumstances of it. If you were a virgin, if the rape was particularly brutal, if you had numerous attackers, or if you knew the rapist, it was supposed to be harder for you to get over it. But recent studies are finding that this isn't so; these circumstances may make your initial reactions more severe, but they don't necessarily make it harder to recover.[1] What really counts is how you perceive yourself and how you perceive what happened to you. In other words, the key to recovery is within you.

It's important for you, as a survivor, to have faith in your own strength. It's important to know how normal all your seemingly bizarre reactions are. And it's essential to remember that the rape is no reflection on your worth as a person.

Women who are proud of themselves for surviving not only recover well from the rape but also learn something positive from their recovery. Several studies have reported women saying they feel more serious about life and more self-reliant since the rape.[2] This is not to say that they are even remotely glad it happened, but that it made them reexamine their lives in a new way. Surviving a tragedy can teach you a lot about yourself, and although all your life you will wish the tragedy had never happened, you nevertheless may come out the wiser for it. Claire said the rape made her rethink her life.

> It's a self-revealing exercise to be a victim of violence and humiliation. It's not pleasant to learn about, but it made me look deeply into my family and the way I'd been raised. I began to think a lot

> about how part of a woman's sexuality is to be submissive, and I
> began to want to change that.

Claire's brother said she did change.

> She began to see how she'd allowed herself to be victimized by all
> her relationships with men and that her whole relationship pattern
> was a form of emotional rape. She didn't want that type of thing
> anymore. Now she's with a guy who's much better than the ones
> before.

Here are some ways you can help yourself recover.

When It Happens: The First Twenty-four Hours

By the time you read this book, you may already have lived through
the first day after your attack, but this section will still be useful. It will
allow you to see what options you have left and what you have done
right so far. Also, much of the advice here applies for longer than the
first twenty-four hours. If you manage to read this section before you
have sought any help, it will give you guidance. It will help everyone
know how to help other victims, too.

Immediately after a rape, you have three main concerns: you want to
get somewhere safe, you want to wash off the filth of the rape, and you
want to find someone to turn to for help, whether that be a friend, a
rape crisis counselor, someone at a hospital, or a police officer.

SOMEWHERE SAFE TO GO

Once the rapist has left you, your immediate concern is to get somewhere safe. You may just want to go home, but if he took your money
and your keys, you have no form of transport, or you are afraid he will
follow you, you might have to go to a hospital or to the police first. Or
you might want to go to a friend's house. If, however, you were raped
in your home, you will probably want to leave immediately. Some
women put themselves in more danger by fleeing their homes without
anywhere else to go and wandering the streets, maybe late at night.
Whatever the circumstances of your rape, try to think of a friend or
family member you can contact right away. A friend can keep you
company, go to the police or hospital with you, provide you with shel-

ter, and just make you feel safer. If no one sympathetic comes to mind, think of a less obvious person such as a cousin, aunt, or friend you haven't seen lately. How about someone from work? If you don't want to tell the person about the rape yet, you can still turn to them for shelter. Say that you can't stay home for the time being because you were just robbed, if you like, and leave the explanations for later. If you still can't think of anyone suitable to turn to, call a rape hotline number and ask for advice. Hotlines are listed under "Rape Crisis Programs" at the back of this book.

WASHING

Rape victims are always warned not to wash after a rape, a command that is highly uncomfortable to follow. If you decide to go to a hospital right away, it is wiser to refrain from washing so that medical evidence of the rape can be gathered, especially if the rapist ejaculated. But if you aren't going within a day, go ahead and wash. If there is any of the rapist's semen in you—and one study found that fewer than half of rape victims showed any evidence of sperm[3]—it will only last about twenty-four hours anyway. But even if you are going right to the hospital, you can at least change your clothes first. Just put the clothes you were wearing when attacked, especially the underpants, in paper bags and take them with you.

FINDING HELP

You may be afraid to ask for help after the rape. You might think you don't deserve it because you believe you invited the rape in some way and so are ashamed to tell anyone about it. Or you may tell yourself that nothing really serious happened, since you are alive and relatively unhurt, and so shouldn't make a fuss. Perhaps you are afraid that no one will believe you anyway and that if you tell, you'll only be laughed at, further humiliated, or even attacked again. But you always deserve help and you need it. Visibly wounded or not, you have been through a serious trauma. As someone who has survived a rape or attempted rape, you have the right to make all the fuss you want.

Choosing who to tell about the rape is not always simple. You need to be listened to, sympathized with, and believed, and not everyone you know will be able to do this for you. You might not be able to tell your

parents, for instance, because they are too old-fashioned, religious, sheltered, or vulnerable to handle the news. Or you may be afraid to tell
the man in your life for fear that he will get angry at you. Sadly, these
worries often have foundation. One study found that 40 percent of the
men close to rape victims reacted negatively when they were told about
the rape.[4] (The remaining 60 percent, luckily, were kind and concerned with the victim's welfare.) Another study found that women
who aren't visibly brutalized by the rape tend to get much less support
from friends and family than those who are.[5] If you are met with anger,
blame, or lack of sympathy, it will make you feel worse. You'll be less
willing to seek help or talk about the rape and more likely to blame
yourself. Therefore, in choosing who of your friends or family to turn
to, either immediately after the rape or sometime later, protect yourself
by choosing carefully. Ask yourself who is the most understanding and
kind and who is the least ridden with myths about rape. You may want
to choose someone like a woman friend over a more obvious person
such as your mother or husband. Penny said: "I never found any man
who had a good response. Women seem to just know, to just understand in some way. The first thing that helped me was talking to
another woman."

If you do get tactless reactions from people close to you, you will
probably feel hurt and unloved. Try to remember that such reactions
may come from their own fear, mixed with relief that you are all right
and anger at you for frightening them. They are reacting like a mother
who loses her child in a supermarket, searches for him frantically, then
hits instead of kisses him when she finds him. Also, they are probably
traumatized themselves by the realization that they live in a world
where such things happen, something no one likes to face. The husband who comes tearing into the emergency room shouting, "I told
you not to open the door to strangers!" may not mean to hurt you, even
though to you it sounds like blame.

Because the people close to you might need to protect themselves
from facing the horror of what happened (and their own vulnerability
to similar violence), they might try to minimize the importance of the
rape. One woman described her husband's attempt to depreciate her
assault.

> My husband inadvertently made me feel worse. He said, "Try not to
> be so upset. The guy just stuck his fingers in you and put his penis in

your mouth—that's not really so terrible." It created a conflict in me. If it was not so terrible, I thought, why was I so upset? Was there something wrong with me?

A common reaction of others is to try to force you to calm down, another way of protecting themselves. Your shouting, crying, and railing with fury shakes them up and scares them, even though it may be just exactly what you need to do. Penny found this happened with her husband Pete after she got home after the rape.

> When I finally got home that night, Pete had locked me out because he was pissed at me for being so late. I stood outside and screamed and yelled until he finally let me in. It was late at night and I was scared! I screamed at him for hours—I don't remember what I said—and cried, and I remember I didn't want him to touch me. Pete kept telling me, "Calm down, calm down," but I didn't want to calm down. I needed to scream and cry. He just wanted me to calm down for his sake, not mine.

Penny still feels angry at Pete for this, seven years later.

All these unhelpful reactions of other people may not only hurt you but may make you feel guilty. "I shouldn't be throwing a scene, I shouldn't be scaring them so much," you tell yourself. At a time when you should be able to think only of yourself, you may already be trying to curb your reactions for the sake of others. As this young victim said: "I told my mother and she cried and cried. That was so hard to take. She didn't know how to deal with it. I had to take over and figure out what to do on my own."

If you have been raped, you should not be silenced, blamed, forced to calm down, yelled at, bossed about, or scolded. If the person you turn to does these things, you need not put up with it. Tell him or her to leave you alone, and if you don't have the strength for that, call someone else for help instead. Now, at this point of crisis, is not the time to work out problems with someone you love. You can do that later.

RAPE CRISIS CENTERS

If there is no one you can possibly turn to for help, then you will need to consider the help that organizations such as rape crisis centers offer. To find such a place near you, try the following:

• See Part Three "Resources" at the back of this book for listings of rape crisis programs in your area.

• Call a rape hotline listed at the front of your telephone directory or a national number listed in "Resources."

• Call Women Against Rape (WAR). If there is one in your area, it should be listed in your telephone book under "Women."

• Call your local YWCA and ask for a rape crisis center number.

• Call a local women's center and ask for a reference to a rape crisis center.

Rape crisis centers, which are usually affiliated with hospitals or women's centers, are primarily set up to help you through the first hard weeks after the rape. A counselor will either talk to you by telephone, if that's all you want, or arrange for you to visit her. She will accompany you to the police and hospital, although she won't force you to go if you don't want to, and will provide "crisis intervention counseling" designed to get you over the immediate horrors and fears caused by the rape. She will even help you break the news to your family, boyfriend, or husband if you wish, and refer you to any further therapy or counseling you may need.

Rape crisis counselors, or advocates, are volunteers who have been trained to understand rape and sympathize with rape victims. Many of them have been raped and chose to help other victims as a way of helping themselves. The counselor's duty is to stick by you and make sure you aren't bullied into doing things you don't want to. She will help with practical matters, too, such as filling out hospital forms about who you are, what insurance you have, what injuries you've sustained, and how the rape happened. You may find yourself being asked to describe the rape in detail over and over again by the police and hospital personnel, which is no fun, and a counselor can be a comfort when the questioners are officious males in uniform. She will also explain the procedures of the police and hospital to you and, in many places, will be able to arrange transport for you to and from the hospital. (See "Therapy" below for more about counseling.)

Sometimes, unfortunately, rape hotlines don't work. Either there isn't one in your area, you can't find it, the number is disconnected, or there is only a tape recording on the line instead of the instant attention you need. If this happens, you have two more sources of immediate help: you can go to the police or to the emergency room of a hospital near you.

THE POLICE

Reporting your rape is important for the obvious reason that if a rapist isn't reported, his chances of getting caught or convicted are zero. He's free to rape again and again and he is highly likely to do so.[6] However, you should never be made to report if you don't want to. Most rape crisis programs have a policy of not pressuring rape victims to report—the decision is completely up to them. If you do choose to report, remember that this does not commit you to pressing charges or to prosecuting. You can report a rape and specify that you don't want to press charges. If you do choose to press charges, though, you should be willing to follow this up by appearing at trial if the rapist is caught.

Some women find reporting emotionally satisfying. They see it as a step toward revenge and toward protecting other people from the rapist. And more women nowadays are treated well by police who have been trained to be sensitive about rape. Several cities now have special sexual assault divisions in their police departments. These are not guaranteed to provide you with sympathetic treatment, but if you do get a good one, you will be assigned a female police officer or at least someone who knows not to give you the stereotypical brutish responses. The police are gradually learning not to treat rape victims as criminals. Claire's rapist was never caught, and she was not treated well by the police even though they had a special sexual assault program, but even so, she said:

> I believe strongly that it's very important to report to the police. If you report, your rape becomes known, it becomes a statistic. You can't let people know how serious and prevalent the crime is or fight society's tendency to sweep it under the carpet if you don't let anyone know about it.

When you go to the police, try to get a friend to accompany you. As Claire said:

> My advice to any woman is to take an understanding man with her when she reports. I hate to say that, but the police treat you so badly if you're a woman alone. If you can't find a man, then bring a girlfriend. It's hard to do alone.

If no family member or friend is available, a counselor from a rape crisis center will accompany you as will members of Women Against Rape.

Having someone there who is familiar with the police procedure and who is on your side can be a great comfort.

If you go to the police right after the rape, before getting any medical attention, their job is to get you to a hospital before asking any but a few basic questions, such as "What happened?" "Where did the crime occur?" "What can you describe about the assailant?"[7] At some point, however, you will have to answer questions for a fully detailed report, and this can be harrowing. Sometimes this report will be taken by an officer who comes to you, especially if you were raped at home and called the police from there. Otherwise, it will happen at the station or hospital.

During the questioning, the police will note any visible injuries and how you look and behave. All of this may be used as evidence that the rape actually happened, which is why it is important to report the rape immediately, if you can bear to. They will also ask you what seem like hundreds of questions. They'll want a full description of everything the rapist did to you, no matter how embarrassed or upset you feel about telling it, because they want evidence of the force he used and any violent and "unnatural" aspects of the rape—all useful for proving it was rape in court. They may well ask you the same question over and over again in different forms. Repeated questions often make you feel as if the police are trying to trick you or are doubting your word, but in fact they are usually just trying to make sure your memory is clear and that they have the facts right. One victim said:

> The police kept asking me if the guy had a weapon. It was a real preoccupation with them. But I was thinking, "What's the difference?" Are they suggesting I could have got away if he hadn't?

Often, because of the state you are in right after a rape, the police seem to be more suspicious and threatening than they really are. A few weeks later quite a few women have second thoughts and realize the police weren't so bad after all.[8]

The police will also want to know of any other evidence of the rape —witnesses, bruises, your memory of what the rapist looked like, the car he was driving, his clothes and so on. Because many rapists have rituals that they repeat with all their victims,[9] your detailed description of what happened might match someone else's and give the police a clue about who they are looking for.

In spite of all the positive reasons for going to the police after a rape, most women don't. The current estimate is that nine out of ten rapes are never reported.[10] Women don't report because they don't trust the police, they are scared of being disbelieved or jeered at, they are afraid of getting into trouble, or, simply, they are afraid of being treated rudely. These fears have foundation. Claire remarked, "The police said, 'What are you complaining about? You're alive, aren't you?' "

Joan also had a bad experience with the police.

> For two days after the rapist jumped me, I was hysterical. I couldn't leave my apartment because I was afraid to come through the foyer. But finally, when I went to the police, they didn't believe me. One of them looked at me and said, "Oh, just an attempted rape," and he slammed his notebook shut with this fed-up expression, like I was just wasting his time.

Penny didn't want to go to the police at all after her rape.

> Pete wanted me to report it, but no way was I going to tell the police in my precinct. I know what they're like, I've met them. They're sexist, filthy-minded pigs. Nothing in the world could have made me go to them.

Minority women especially distrust the police. If they were raped by a white man, they fear they may be laughed out of the station, if not threatened. And if they were raped by a minority man, they're afraid of getting some remark like, "So, that's what you people are like. What do you want me to do about it?" As one black woman said to explain why she didn't report her rape, "I was sure that if I went to the police that (1) they weren't going to do anything and (2) they weren't going to protect me. . . . And (3) black women are supposed to be whores anyway."[11]

Police racism can work in reverse, too. Claire, who is white, discovered this when she reported her rape to a black detective.

> I assumed that having my brother Larry with me when I went to report would stop any funny business with the police, but I was wrong. The detective had a real hate toward whites. I told him the guy was black and had pulled up a turtleneck to his nose during the rape but that I'd recognize him anyway, and the detective was just scornful. "That would never hold up in court," he said. I told him I'm an athlete and I'm very aware of how people move and I'd recognize him anywhere, plus I was so close to his face for hours, but the detective kept scoffing at me. Then he flung down a picture

of a black man's profile next to a monkey's! We were shocked at the racism of this. The detective seemed to be saying that whites think all blacks look alike and so I'd never be able to identify the rapist.

Then when I told him the guy had an unusually enormous penis, he said, "How do you know?" He was full of innuendos about my life, my knowledge, and about my being racist. It was awful.

This detective's dismissal of Claire's assertion that she would recognize the rapist was a serious mistake. There are few crimes in which a victim is exposed to the assailant as long as during a rape, so a rape victim is uniquely likely to know what he looks like. Lawyers are well aware of this and know that it can, contrary to the detective's assertion, be very useful in court.[12]

Teenagers are often afraid to go to the police because they think they'll get into trouble, especially if they've been buying drugs or drinking when the rape happened. It's true that you might find yourself treated unpleasantly by the police in these circumstances, but you won't get arrested. If you are a minor, however, the police will probably call your parents whether you want them to or not, unless a rape crisis counselor is there to intervene.

Another major reason many women don't report rape is that they don't believe the police will do anything anyway, particularly if they live in a crime-ridden city. This ought not to have any foundation, but, alas, it does. A woman, call her Ann, who was raped when she was sixty-one by a man who forced his way into her home (Ann will appear again in Chapter 7, "The Older Victim"), had this story to tell:

> The man was high on drugs, very talkative, very jittery. So I told him I'd give him something to calm him down. I had some strong drugs for my husband, who had been very sick. The man took a pill and it knocked him out. Then I called the police.
>
> The police came and got him—he didn't even deny that he'd done it. Then they wanted me to come down to night court right away. I just couldn't. I was shaken and exhausted—I'd just been raped! I said I'd come the next day instead.
>
> The following morning, the man was standing outside my house screaming and yelling. The police had let him go.

The mother of a young girl who was raped by a gang of schoolboys, cited by Burgess and Holmstrom, was so fed up with the police not doing anything that she took over the detective work herself.

I don't know why the police haven't been able to find those boys. I
went to the area where it happened and asked two little boys playing
if they knew who attacked my little girl. They said they did and gave
me [one] name. I called the police and they were able to arrest three
of the boys.[13]

People are also discouraged from reporting rape because even if the
police do try, rapists are so seldom caught. (The FBI declared that 49
percent of reported rapes were "cleared" by arrest in the 1980 *Uniform
Crime Reports*, but this high figure is regarded skeptically by experts in
the field of rape.) And they often won't report because they are afraid
of being put through a trial if the rapist is prosecuted. This last fear is
quite unfounded, because reporting does not commit you to partake in
a prosecution. You can decide whether to do that later, and if you don't
want to be a witness, the prosecution will rarely try to force you because a reluctant witness is no help.

Because of these fears about the police, you may not be able to face
reporting your assault right away. This is understandable, and it doesn't
mean that your chance to report is over. You can do it later. If you do,
however, be prepared for a hard time from the police. When Claire
reported her rape two weeks after it happened, the police said, "The
only people who wait this long are prostitutes trying to get back at their
pimps." Reporting later also means that your evidence will lose much
power in court, should there be a prosecution, for there will be no
record of your immediate state after the rape. Late reporting might
even be used against you by a defense attorney. However, reporting late
is still better than not reporting at all—the rape gets on record, and
since the most important evidence against the assailant is your word, he
still can be convicted for what he did to you.

If there is going to be a delay in your reporting, you could try writing
down everything you remember about the assault to aid your memory
and help you keep your story consistent. Evidence of your reactions to
the rape can be used against the rapist. If you do write down anything,
however, in a diary, letters, or anywhere, *it can be subpoenaed by the
defense* and used against you. Supposing, for example, that you wrote
to a friend that, oddly enough, right after the rape you felt clearheaded
and calm. You were able to walk home, make some phone calls, and fix
some coffee before you fell apart. Although such calmness is a common
reaction, the defense could try to use it to show that you were not

scared, not traumatized, and therefore could not have been raped. Bear this in mind as you write.

Reporting rape is no fun, and you should never be forced to do it. You have been through enough force already. But if you can bring yourself to do it, you might find it surprisingly satisfying—for you are fighting back.

THE HOSPITAL

Going to the hospital after you've been raped is advisable even if you don't think you've been hurt. You may be in more shock than you realize. Getting a prescription for a sleeping pill or tranquilizer to see you through that first night after the rape can be a blessing. Also, you can be checked for any internal damage, which is quite possible if you were raped anally, if the rapist used instruments on you, if you are a virgin, if you are elderly, if you are frail, or if the rapist was violent.

Going to the hospital also enables you to get preventative injections for venereal disease and an antipregnancy pill, if you want. If you would rather not go to a hospital right after the rape, however, these last two precautions can wait, but do at least see a doctor or gynecologist a week or so later to check for any infections or other medical aftereffects of the rape. For the same reason be sure to keep any follow-up appointments a doctor suggests.

The "morning-after pill," which is so popular as a preventative of pregnancy for rape victims, has fallen into strong disfavor lately. It is made of diethylstilbestrol, or DES, which has been found to cause terrible nausea in many women who take it. The pill has a 10 percent failure rate in terminating pregnancy, and if you do remain pregnant, a female child will be in danger of getting vaginal cancer later in life and a male child may get testicle cancer. The pill can also cause existing breast, cervical, or vaginal cancers to grow. If your family has a history of these cancers or of diabetes, high blood pressure, or blood clotting, you should not take DES.[14]

Some hospitals give you DES automatically when you come in as a rape victim. Others may offer you newer variations of the "morning-after pill." Ask the prescribing doctor what pill you are being given and demand to be informed of its dangers before you swallow it.

Only 3 to 5 percent of women get pregnant from a rape.[15] The chances of pregnancy from one act of unprotected intercourse are always slim, and 50 to 70 percent of rapists don't even ejaculate.[16] Pregnancy is slightly more likely from a gang rape or a repeated rape, such as happens to a long-term victim of rape by a relative. But the likelihood of your needing an antipregnancy treatment is small.

Nevertheless, many women understandably worry a great deal about becoming pregnant from a rape. If you think there might be a chance, discuss it with a counselor or doctor. You can also check your fertility cycle to see how likely pregnancy is. Women are only fertile about two days a month, so if you were in any other part of your menstrual cycle, the chances of your being pregnant are tiny. (The most fertile time is about two weeks after the end of your last period, if you have a regular cycle. It is possible to conceive earlier than that and even during a period, but this is rare.[17]) Often you can be reassured that you aren't pregnant without needing any medical procedure. Otherwise, if your next period does not come you can have a pregnancy test done. Your period may be delayed by the trauma of the rape. If you can't bear to wait, you can have a blood test that will give you pregnancy results within six to fourteen days of the rape; the length of time depends on where you are in your menstrual cycle. If the result is positive and you don't know what to do about it, you may want to talk to your religious representative or a counselor at a rape crisis center or hospital. That's what counselors are there for. The counselor can help arrange an abortion or adoption or help you deal with keeping the child if you wish. If you have no objection to abortion, you can set up an appointment for yourself as soon as possible. Planned Parenthood (their number will be in the phone book) is a good agency to help you with this.

If you are pregnant when you are raped, it is essential that you see a doctor. The trauma will present a danger to your baby, but you won't necessarily miscarry. Burgess and Holmstrom describe the case of a woman who was six months pregnant when she was raped.[18] Even though she went through terrible trauma, even at one point wanting to die, she eventually recovered and gave birth to a healthy six-pound boy.

Another great medical worry is whether you have caught a venereal or sexually transmissible disease from the rapist, something that often happens to victims of rape. Some of these diseases will have obvious symptoms such as itching, soreness, irritation, or a discharge. Others don't manifest themselves in symptoms at all. Sexual diseases can be maddeningly persistent, going on for months and months, and they can also be dangerous if they go untreated, affecting your fertility and your health. Getting medical tests and treatment is thus essential. If you have caught a disease from a rapist, whether it be gonorrhea, syphilis, a chlamydia infection, herpes, or something simple like pubic lice, be sure to follow all the medical instructions and take all the medication, even after the symptoms seem to have gone away. The treatment for these diseases may be a nuisance, but it is not painful—most of the diseases can be treated with penicillin or antibiotics. If your doctor is not giving you adequate information about the disease, contact a Planned Parenthood office near you. They have pamphlets that explain sexually transmissible diseases.

In some emergency rooms, a dose of antibiotics is given to rape victims automatically in order to prevent the development of a venereal disease. Automatic dosage is not a good idea because some strains of VD are resistent to the usual medication, so it is best to be tested first and wait for the results. The problem with this approach, however, is that you may have to wait several weeks and you will have to keep going back to the hospital or clinic, which can be distressing after a rape. Tests for gonorrhea, for instance, must be done a week after exposure to it and tests for syphilis must be done four to six weeks afterward.[19] If you don't think you can bear to wait that long, or you won't be able to go to the follow-up appointments, have the preventative treatments—they are better than nothing.

The examination for evidence is not a pleasant thing to go through at any time, but especially not after a rape. You have to have a pelvic exam for signs of abrasion and the collection of any semen left by the rapist, and you also have to be checked for any sign of his hair, blood, skin, semen or some soil on the rest of your body. Fingernail parings will be taken, in case you scratched the rapist and got some of his skin under your nails; the clothes you were wearing when attacked will be taken away to a laboratory for examination; and you'll be looked over for bruises, scratches, cuts, and other injuries. All this will be noted down for use in court. If the rapist tried to strangle or choke you, remind the doctor to look at the back of your neck as well as the front for bruises. These marks, which doctors often forget, are good evidence of the violence done to you. None of these examinations should hurt much (although the pelvic exam can hurt after rape), but having your body touched by strangers yet again can be upsetting. It will be worth it, however, because the hospital's report that you came in stating you were raped can help the prosecution's case, even if no medical evidence of the rape is found. And if there is evidence, it can reveal much that can help to catch and convict a rapist. In a rape case that took place in the Bronx, New York, for example, the rapist tried to claim that he hadn't had sex with the victim at all. Medical evidence of his sperm showed clearly that he had, so his defense failed. Sometimes medical evidence can reveal patterns in the rapist's violence that the police have seen in other cases, thus helping the police identify the rapist.

Rape victims have mixed experiences in hospitals. Some find it a relief to be in a safe, sterile environment, surrounded by doctors and nurses and well-protected from the rapist. They feel it is therapeutic to go because it is one of the few things they can do to help get the rapist. Others find indifferent, hurried hospital staff and the pelvic examination humiliating and distressing after the ordeal of rape. Claire said:

> After it happened, I didn't want to go to the hospital because I wasn't hurt in any visible way, but my friends insisted I go. We went to the emergency room and they kept us waiting for *two hours.* I told a nurse that I had to catch a plane in half an hour and if they didn't see me, I'd leave, so finally a doctor examined me. He was very brusque. He asked me if I'd ever had anal intercourse before, and I didn't understand why he had to ask me that or why it mattered. I still don't understand that. Then they told me I had to wait for the police, but I didn't because I had to catch that plane.

Several things went wrong for Claire here, but none of them are unusual. It is miserable to be kept waiting in the gloomy and disturbing atmosphere of an emergency room for hours right after a rape, yet it happens frequently. Emergency-room staff understandably don't consider rape a priority over cardiac arrests, wounds, or accidents. Then, doctors and nurses are often hurried and under pressure, which can make you feel further ashamed, as if you have no right to be there. They may ask you tactless, leading questions out of carelessness or for sound medical reasons that they just don't bother to explain. And it is possible to get a nurse or doctor who has a "sexy" idea of rape. Ask for a rape counselor, or take a friend or advocate with you to the hospital, for he or she can provide you with comfort and company during the long wait, stand up for you if you are being bullied and don't feel capable of fighting for yourself, and escort you to and from the hospital, especially at night when the streets are unsafe.

Many hospitals around the country use controversial kits for the collection of evidence from rape victims.[20] One of the reasons the kits are controversial is that they give hospitals an excuse to turn you away if they have run out of kits. But every hospital has the basic equipment for gathering evidence and that excuse is not valid. No hospital should ever turn you away. In order to avoid that trouble, either go to a hospital you know and like, or call Women Against Rape or a rape hotline and ask which hospital to go to. Some cities have special hospitals designated to treat rape victims.

A major fear for many rape victims is that going to the hospital is automatically going to bring their case to the attention of the police. This is true in some areas, but not all. The hospital staff in an area where this isn't true may not know it, however. If they have an evidence collection kit, they are especially likely to inform the police—another reason these kits are controversial. Just remember that ultimately it is up to you and you alone to report the crime. Even if your assault is reported to the police by someone else, you don't have to talk to the police, press charges, or carry through with prosecuting if you don't want.

You should also feel free to object to the manner of a doctor or nurse or to insinuations they make. Everybody, man and woman alike, is too easily intimidated by those people in white uniforms. If you don't like the tone of the questions you are asked, refuse to answer. Or, better still, ask why those things are being asked of you. Remind the questioner that his job isn't to prove whether you were raped, his job is simply to take the evidence and to treat you. This posture takes nerve, of course—something you may feel decidedly short of after being assaulted—but if you do have the strength, use it. It can be most satisfying not to let yourself be pushed around by hospital officials, especially after you've just been pushed around by a rapist.

On an optimistic note, there has been an increased effort over the past decade to make hospitals more welcoming to rape victims. Many places now have connections with a rape crisis program and will call a counselor at any time of the day or night to see you through the hospital procedure and to make sure you aren't left alone unless you want to be. If you can, call the hospital before you go to it and ask if they are linked to such a program, and if they aren't, ask which hospital in your area is.

It is brave to allow yourself to be put through a hospital examination after rape and you should be proud of yourself if you do it. If you simply can't bear the idea of doing it, though, don't feel guilty. You've been through enough.

A Day to a Month Later

During the first month after you were attacked, you are still in crisis, so don't expect too much from yourself. The days will get easier. Meanwhile, you will have some specific problems to face: How will you deal with the physical reactions listed in Chapter 1? How will you get back to normal functioning, socially and at work? How will you cope with the overwhelming emotional reactions? And, how will the rape affect your relationship with your partner?

There are no simple answers to these questions, but the rape victims and counselors interviewed for this book have made the following suggestions. Not every one of them is going to be relevant to you, but if you even find one or two that help, that's a start.

DEALING WITH THE PHYSICAL REACTIONS

If irritation of the genitals, itchiness, or soreness persist after the first twenty-four hours, see a doctor. Venereal disease and vaginal infections take some days to incubate before you feel the symptoms. If other symptoms such as sleeplessness, nausea, or lack of appetite persist, you should seek some medical advice, too. You might need tranquilizers or sleeping pills for longer than that first night, and you deserve all the help you can get. If your sickness seems to be psychologically caused, consider therapy (see "Therapy" below). You may find that being encouraged to let out some of your feelings about the rape will cure your physical ills.

GETTING BACK TO WORK AND FRIENDS

Going back to work right away is difficult at best, but may have some benefits. It keeps you busy and distracts you from brooding about the rape. It can, however, put pressure on you,—to keep up a happy face, to not tell anyone what happened, to not let yourself succumb to tears or rage. Also, it can lead to more anxiety if you find that you can't work as well as before because you are tired and distracted. If this happens, consider taking some sick leave and going away to stay with a relative or friend. Perhaps you need to collapse for a bit, to be pampered.

As for seeing friends, that too can either be a help or a hindrance. Angela found that the rape eventually changed her from a loner to a socialite because she felt safer around people. She still makes sure that she surrounds herself with friends on the anniversary of her rape and that she is not left alone too often at night. At first, however, the strain of keeping up social behavior might be too much. Rather than shutting yourself up in a room, spend time with just one or two people you are close to, people who won't expect you to be charming.

DEALING WITH THE EMOTIONAL REACTIONS

Studies have found that women who report themselves completely recovered from rape used these ways of coping with their emotional reactions to it: they talked about it to friends; they found ways of explaining why it happened without unreasonably blaming themselves; and they took positive actions on their own impetus to make themselves feel better, such as traveling, moving, or reading about rape.[21]

Talking about the rape is important because it helps you get it into perspective, helps you feel less alone, and helps you share the burden. Yet a natural reaction is to withdraw and not mention it, either out of shame or simple bewilderment and hurt. Without realizing it, you may be isolating yourself even more. Angela advised:

> It's so important to reach out to people. A lot of friends didn't contact me after it because they didn't know if I wanted to be comforted or left alone. It was up to me to bring it up, but I didn't. It's crucial to give people the opportunity to help you, but they won't if you don't ask.

Once you seek out people to talk to, you'll be surprised at how many women you know have been through assaults, if not actual rape, themselves. Rachel discovered this when she began to talk about her rape.

> My first impulse was not to say anything about the rape. Then I thought, "I'd tell if I got robbed or mugged, why not raped?" The more I talked to people the better it was. I found out a lot of other people had been through the same thing and that I wasn't a freak. And other people helped me quit thinking it was my fault for get-

ting suckered in by a smooth-talking guy. They helped me realize
that rape is not a punishment for being stupid.

After a few weeks have passed, talking may well become easier. You
are more prepared to handle the occasional bad reaction from other
people yet you can still benefit from sympathy and support. After some
time of not wanting to talk about the rape to anyone but her brother,
Claire found herself bringing it up all the time. Sometimes people
didn't want to hear about it, but mostly talking about the rape was, she
said, a relief.

There are always going to be elements of the rape that are not so
easy to talk about, however, especially the sexual ones. As one victim
said:

> There were certain aspects of the rape that I felt embarrassed about,
> certain aspects I felt were too "brutal" for others to hear about.
> . . . Also, there are some things, such as certain feelings of messi-
> ness and dirtiness that, for various reasons, I have been able to share
> only with another victim.[22]

Sometimes a family member is the only person you can discuss these
things with, but often only a professional who doesn't know you as a
friend will do.

You might find that men friends are a great help after rape, both to
talk to and to just be around. Rachel found this to be true:

> I immediately wanted to hang around men for a while after the
> rape. I wanted assurance that men aren't all bad. The women I
> knew all had this attitude, "Well, what do you expect from men?" I
> needed to know that all the men in my life were not like that.

Don said this was the case for Mary, too.

> One of Mary's best friends was a tall black man who was gay. That
> had a therapeutic effect concerning blacks for both of us, because
> after she was raped by a black man, we found ourselves getting a lot
> more racist. Also, most of her friends were men and that was good.
> It helped her not generalize and hate all men. But she still retained
> a horror of big men for a while, black or white.

If there are times when you just can't talk to anyone, or if there is no
one in your life you can tell, try writing down your feelings instead.

Even if you do have people to tell, writing can be a release. One woman said:

> I kept a diary while I was going through the worst part. Now every-time I do something good, I write down how I feel. I have such extreme ups and downs. When I'm down, I read over the good times and it shows I'm making progress. I was thinking suicide at one point, and now I can't believe I ever thought that.

Another woman, "Adrienne McAllister," expressed how much writing helps her deal with her rape in a poem.

> There is so much I need
> and want to say
> that words and analogies can
> not capture.
>
> blotting my pain in poetry
> letting it ooze out
> filling the page
> and spilling.
>
> And maybe just by writing it down
> it will make me feel better
> or at least clearer
> on how I feel
> and why.

There are other therapeutic actions you can take to help yourself get through those awful first weeks after the rape, too. Here are some suggestions:[23]

· Remind yourself that recovery takes time. There are many dark moments after a rape when you will feel as if your life and your sanity have been ruined forever. They haven't, but recovery takes patience and it takes courage. Sometimes, you're bound to feel worn out.

· Remember that you are safe now, even if you don't feel it. The rape is over. This is hard to remember, because the rape seems to have destroyed your safety in the world. But you haven't been marked as a special target for misfortune. You were unlucky, but so are millions of other people. Perhaps the world isn't as safe as you thought, but that doesn't mean you are in danger every minute. If you want to do something active about protecting yourself and making yourself feel safer, take some safety precautions, as Claire did.

> I made sure I felt secure in my apartment, and that's helped me feel better. I carry my keys in my hand all the time now, and I don't unlock my mailbox if anyone is near me. I always look around when I go into a building.

Consider also taking a self-defense or martial arts course (see "Self-defense" below). This is a way of *actively* protecting yourself and boosting your confidence.

 • Don't blame yourself irrationally. A common reaction to rape is to go into paroxysms of self-hatred for causing the rape. Some such typical twists of self-blame heard from rape victims are:

> It wouldn't have happened if I hadn't left my husband.
>
> I'm a loser and a bad person.
>
> I must have done something to get raped. My father always said whatever a man did to a woman, she provoked it.

Some women go to even more extraordinary lengths to blame themselves. One told a rape counselor that she was a rapist in her former life and was "paying for it now." "It's in my karma," another said. None of this self-blame is going to help you feel better.

There is another way of explaining the rape, however, that can be constructive. As long as it does not make you hate yourself, seeking an explanation for why the rape happened has been found in studies to help victims recover faster.[24] You might be able to acknowledge, for instance, that the rape happened partly because you took a knowing risk, such as hitchhiking, leaving an apartment door open, letting a stranger into your house, or going home with a man you didn't know. If you think, "Well, I made a mistake. It's too bad and I'll know not to do it again," you can turn the rape from something out of your control to something you can have some power over, because you know that you can avoid making that mistake again. You also know that there is a difference between making a mistake and inviting rape; you didn't provoke the rape, because the rapist would have raped regardless of what you did. You just accidentally increased your chances of becoming his random victim. You didn't leave the door open or hitchhike because you wanted to be raped, you just took a gamble and, this time, you lost.

If you met the man under sexual circumstances before he attacked you, your self-blame may be especially bitter. If you flirted with him in a bar, for instance, or accepted a ride home from him, you might feel that you did indeed provoke the rape. Perhaps you agreed to have sex with him, but then he turned violent or insisted on bringing another man into it against your will. Many rapes take place in circumstances like these. A counselor told a story of one woman who met a man at a business conference. They flirted, had a few drinks, and decided to go to bed together. In bed the man demanded anal intercourse. When the woman refused, he picked up her stiletto-heeled shoe and threatened to beat her in the head with it unless she complied. "Was that rape?" she asked the counselor afterward, considerably upset. His answer was a firm "Yes." "Anytime you say no and that no is not honored," he told her, "you have been raped." Flirting or agreeing to have sex does not mean that you are asking for violence or coercion, or that you deserve it. Everyone has the right to court sexual partners without being punished or tortured for it. The person you should be furious at is the rapist, not yourself.

Sometimes you can find no reason to blame yourself at all, even when you want to. The rape happened in such wildly random circumstances that you could have done nothing to prevent or avoid it. You made no mistakes, you took no gambles, you just had terribly bad luck. This sort of circumstance can be a comfort or even more frightening, depending partly on how you regard it. You could feel glad that you were in no way even remotely responsible for having fallen victim, or you could feel terrified that fate played you such a cruel trick. Penny chose to view her rape as an example of the random bad luck that can happen in the world, and she found this a comfort.

> I wouldn't recognize the guys who did it, and I think I'm lucky. Instead of thinking about them, I think of it as an impersonal crime, as random violence. I reacted against the whole world after it happened—that such things can happen, that such violence goes on and it happened to me—instead of those particular guys.

• Keep your days structured so that you don't fall into a slump of brooding depression. Make a list of things you have to get done and try to accomplish them one by one. Regard each successful accomplishment as a triumph. It's like building a wall—you are slowly stacking your old life back together.

• Keep a weekly schedule listing all those activities that give you a sense of mastery and pleasure. When you feel down, do one of those things.

• Give yourself special treats.

> I pampered myself after the rape. I had my hair done; I had a facial and a pedicure. I did whatever I could to make myself feel better.

• Travel, if you can. A change of scene can do wonders for your spirits and sense of security. Go on vacation or visit a friend.

• Move, if you can. If you were raped at home, you probably won't want to ever live there again. You no longer feel safe there and the place is associated with the rape now. These days, however, leaving a home isn't so easy. Apartments and houses are hard to find and many people can't afford to move. Claire faced this dilemma after her rape.

> I had just moved into my apartment when I was raped there. It was a beautiful place, and I was hoping I'd have the courage to stay there after the rape so I wouldn't have to go through all the trouble and expense of finding someplace else.

You need not make the decision about whether to move during this first month after the rape. Stay somewhere else for the time being, with friends or family, and think about whether you could cope with living there again eventually. Or consider alternatives to moving out: getting a roommate, changing and reinforcing the locks, changing your phone number and taking your name off the bell if you live in an apartment building. (See "Victims' Services" at the end of this chapter for information on getting your locks changed for free.) If you are certain that the rapist knows where you are—and many don't actually remember their victims' faces or addresses—and he is still on the loose, or if the place fills you with fear, moving out may well be your only option. It may also be surprisingly therapeutic.

• Ask people to stay with you. If you were raped outside your home, you still might be afraid to be alone there for a time. Don't be shy about asking people to stay with you and don't feel that you have to tell them the real reason why if you think they won't sympathize. Needing company for several weeks after a rape is not a weakness, it is natural. If you have to lie to get that company, do so.

• Rearrange your home. One woman who could not afford to move found that rearranging the furniture in her apartment helped her get over her fear of the place, even though she had been raped there. By making her bedroom look different, she was able to stop associating it with the rape.

• If you really think you are going crazy or breaking down, seek professional care. See "Therapy" below for more information on this.

YOUR RELATIONSHIP WITH YOUR PARTNER

Life with your husband or lover is not going to feel normal for quite a while. You will need him desperately at the beginning, more than ever before and in a different way, but you won't be able to give him back much support or love. Angela had this problem with Clark.

> I'd always been the supporting one with Clark before the rape. I ran the household, bought the food, typed his papers even when I was tired, cooked, got up early to get the film we were making together done—I was the mother. Then all of a sudden, I was the baby and I couldn't take care of myself at all. He had a hard time switching gears that quickly, anyone would. I can't remember ever being supportive of him after the rape. I was trying to conserve my energy for myself.

Even if he doesn't complain about this imbalance, you will probably feel guilty. Don't. This first month is a time to be selfish. You can worry about giving to him later.

Sex may cause problems between you, too. For this first month, you probably won't want to resume sex yet, and standing up for yourself about this is essential. If your partner is pressuring you to have sex and you don't feel ready, *refuse*. The worst thing you can do for your recovery is to submit unwillingly—it is only being raped again.[25] You don't have to refuse unkindly. Explain that you aren't rejecting him but that you simply cannot stand the thought of sex yet. You are still healing.

At the same time, if you would like to be held and just cuddled at night, tell him. If he is avoiding cuddles or sexual contact with you, don't assume that it's because he finds you "soiled"—he may be so sensitive to your state of mind that he's afraid of seeming to pressure you at all. Indeed, your touchiness and his wariness of hurting you can easily lead to a tangle of misunderstandings: He won't touch you for fear of scaring you. You think he's avoiding you because he finds you disgusting after the rape. You daren't make advances to him in case he rejects you. He starts to think you'll never desire him again. You think he'll never desire you again. And meanwhile, all you both want is to hold each other. Try to stop a muddle like this by telling him what you need. And in case both of you are wondering whether you will ever feel sexual desire again, be assured that you will. Don't expect too much too soon, but studies are indicating that women in a good relationship with a partner recover their sexuality. If your sex life does not improve, you might want to seek therapy. See "Your Sexuality" below for more on this.

If your partner is not being considerate about sex, you may have to get away from him for a time. Also, give him this book to read, directing him to the section "How Men Can Help" in Chapter 3. He should also read Chapter 6, "Men Get Raped, Too." He may pressure you to have sex soon after the rape because he wants to prove to himself that you still desire him, that he still desires you, or that you aren't sullied by the rape. He may also believe that the best way for you to recover from the rape is to resume normal sex as quickly as possible. He knows that rape is a trauma that affects sexuality, and this may frighten him into wanting to pretend that it never happened. He also might, on some level, believe that you have been unfaithful and that by making love to you he will repossess you. In one of the first books about rape, *Rape: The First Sourcebook for Women,* a woman was quoted about such an experience.

> I could tell that his reaction was first that I was dirty. Like, he pushed me into the bathroom and handed me a kind of douche thing. He . . . said to me, "Get clean." . . . but he was also excited by the fact that this had happened to me. After I had gotten clean, he was supposed to be comforting me, but he screwed me. It was a kind of fascination with the fact that another man had had me that night. I got the definite impression that what he felt he was doing was retaking possession of me and my body. [26]

A man's reasons for pushing sex on you aren't always this selfish. He may well have the best of intentions, and if he does, you should be able to explain to him why he is mistaken.

If you do not have a steady sexual partner, you won't have the nightly dilemma of whether to try sex or not. On the other hand, you might find the idea of dating and trying new relationships very frightening. For this month don't push yourself. You will probably do better just seeing old friends for a time and leaving romance for later, when you have had more time to recover.

THERAPY

Many women won't allow themselves the indulgence of seeking therapy. Popular lore has it that women are hypochondriacs, that they run to doctors and therapists at the slightest sign of trouble. But for many, just the opposite is true—they won't ask for help even when they really need it. Don't dismiss the rape as something minor just because you aren't actually hurting or bleeding or because you fear being a nuisance. Part of fighting for your recovery is to let people help you. *Ask* for help if you want it.

Another reason you might balk at the idea of therapy is that you see it as a sign of mental or character weakness; you believe you ought to be able to sort out your own problems. Or, worse, you think seeking therapy is an admission that you are truly nuts. But the trauma of rape is not an everyday matter calling for solutions you are practiced at using. It is not like a bad day at work, a fight with your husband, or even a frightening accident. Rape can throw you into a state you have never experienced and for which you have no remedies. Needing therapy is nothing to be ashamed of; in fact, counselors see people who come in for help as being courageous because they are facing up to their needs and doing something about them.

How much therapy you need, or whether you need it at all, depends largely on your emotional state before the rape and on what sort of support you get—or don't get—from your friends and family. The simplest kind of therapy is a few conversations with a rape crisis counselor. This can be done either by phone, a cheap and easy way that can be less embarrassing than talking face to face, or by going in to the rape crisis center. *Crisis counseling is usually free or on a sliding scale.*

You may want more than a few sessions of counseling, however, because you have no one else to turn to, because of other problems in your life, or simply because you feel you deserve it. You may want the longer, more thorough treatment of therapy. Therapists say that if you want therapy, the sooner you get it, the more effectively you can be helped, especially if the rape has caused trouble with your partner. William Miller, a marriage counselor at the University of Pennsylvania who has treated many couples coping with rape, found that those who sought therapy within a few months sorted out their problems better than those who waited a year or more.[27] However, there is no point in rushing off for therapy if you don't feel ready for it. The point of therapy is to help you help yourself, and you have to want to cooperate for it to work.

Whether therapy helps you greatly depends on who the therapist is. Sometimes the therapist you have been using before, who has helped you a lot and to whom you are very attached, is not the right person to help you with the rape. Such was the case for this woman.

> I went to my regular therapist after I was raped, and she told me that I was self-destructive and that the rape was part of that pattern. She said I was punishing myself. I believed her for a while because she'd helped me a lot in the past. She made me think the whole thing was my fault.

Therapists are victims of the myths about rape as much as anybody else, and if they haven't been educated about rape, they may impose their myths and misunderstandings on you, which can be terribly destructive. If they try to blame you in some subtle way by suggesting that you subconsciously sought out the rape, you are being subjected to a violation of the most vulnerable part of you, the part that sought therapy in the first place. You are used to trusting your therapist, to looking up to her or him, and you are more inclined to believe what that therapist says than you are anyone else. Be aware of this if you are planning to go to your previous therapist for help and ask if she or he has had any training in rape and what that training was. The rape has changed your circumstances enormously and you might need someone different to help you recover from it.

Freudian therapists may be especially harmful to you. Freud himself never dealt with the subject of rape, although he did deal with incest and child sexual abuse, but his followers, particularly Helene Deutsch, have created a doctrine ridden with myths. They believe that women are essentially masochistic and that they all fantasize about rape; therefore, they assume that women want and invite rape.[28] This idea is enormously destructive to women, for it lays the blame of rape squarely on their subconscious, which is open to anybody's interpretation, and it lets rapists off the hook altogether. The result is that a woman who goes to this type of psychiatrist might find herself treated like this twenty-one-year-old rape victim:

> I went to a psychiatrist, a man, on my workman's compensation money, and toward the end of the first session, he said, "Did you enjoy being raped?" I got so mad that I got up to leave. He said I owed him money, and then he shouted at me that I was troubled and disturbed, as if my wanting to leave was a sign of madness. He was trying to corner me.

This woman had been the victim of a particularly brutal rape. She had been working late in her office when two men broke in, one waving a gun. One of them held the gun to her head while the other beat her up and raped her. How the psychiatrist could have seriously asked her if she enjoyed that is beyond comprehension, but he did. And he is not the only one. In 1975 sociologist Pauline Bart did a study of how rape victims are affected by psychoanalytic therapy and found that most of the women considered themselves more harmed than helped by it. Bart concluded that this happened because analytic theory fails to distinguish between fantasizing about rape and intentionally seeking it out.[29]

The difference between fantasizing about being raped and actually wanting to be raped or enjoying rape is so enormous that it should be obvious to victims and analysts alike. Many women do have such fantasies,[30] that cannot be denied, for they have been trained to find the submissive role erotic. But in fantasy, *you* are the one in control; you are making up the story, calling the shots. In rape, you have no control, you are part of somebody else's fantasy. In fantasy you never actually feel pain and you never really fear for your life. In rape the pain and fear of death are acutely real. In fantasy you feel desire, you respond to the erotic scene you have created. In rape there is no desire, just terror. In a recent research project on people's sexual fantasies, David Barlow, director of the Sexuality Research Program at the State University of New York at Albany, discovered this about rape fantasies:

> For most people who have a fantasy of rape, it's a very idealized, even romantic act, something like the rape scene in *The Fantastics*. In our research, we find that if you play a tape for them of a realistic description of a real rape, with all its pain and violence, they don't get aroused. The meaning of a fantasy like that may be more symbolic than real; for many women who have guilt about sex, it can be a way of giving themselves permission to enjoy it.[31]

(Barlow's study also found, interestingly, that forced sexual encounters with a member of the opposite sex was the second most common sexual fantasy for both heterosexual men and women. That men should have "rape fantasies" too seems to support Barlow's thesis that a fantasy of rape is a fantasy of sex without any responsibility. For men it may also be a fantasy of sex without performance anxiety—if you haven't initiated it and have no control over it, you don't have to live up to any supersexed image.)

Not all psychiatrists, psychotherapists, and psychoanalysts will have such destructive attitudes toward rape, of course, but it is worth testing them out before you trust them with your story. In their book *Your Children Should Know*, authors Flora Colao and Tamar Hosansky suggest an approach to finding a suitable therapist for a child victim of sexual assault that applies equally well to adults:[32]

• Ask for references from a rape crisis program, Women Against Rape, or a hospital. Such places often have lists of therapists trained to deal with sexual assault. Take at least two names to consult and compare.

• Arrange a consultation with two or more therapists, which should be free.

• Prepare this list of questions to ask when you get there: What is their background and training in sexual assault? How often have they dealt with this problem? How long do people usually stay in treatment? What other sorts of treatment might the therapist use? When do they consult with other therapists? What is the fee?

• During the consultation and questioning, think about how comfortable you feel in the office and how much you trust the person. First impressions are important.

Colao and Hosansky also suggest that, if you prefer to go to a family rabbi, priest, or family counselor for help, asking these questions is still a good idea.

Another form of therapy that many rape victims like is group therapy. Eight women who had been raped within the past year and were attending a weekly group had these comments about it.

> We all felt before as if we were the only ones who ever felt so shitty. The group makes you deal with it, which makes it easier. We know we aren't the only ones now.

> I feel stronger with people around me who are in the same boat.

> One of my goals was to cry. And I did. I wasn't able to before.

It took courage for me to come. I was raped before when I was sixteen and this attempted rape made me feel as if I was going through it again—the first one had never left me. I had to meet other women who'd gone through this. I had to do something because I had it stored away. Therapy gives you guidance to recovery.

Therapy is a relief.

Couple therapy can also be valuable. Several rape crisis centers have female and male counselors for couples now. The usual procedure is that the man talks to your partner alone first and the woman to you, and then all four of you talk together in later sessions. If there is only one counselor, he or she talks to you each individually first and then brings you together afterward. This procedure can help close the gaps in communication that so often arise between couples after a rape. It can also help rid you of the myths that stand in the way of recovery.

A final warning about therapy and counseling: some people are simply not suited to it. Perhaps a counselor said the wrong thing or clashed with you. If this happens, ask for someone else. But it may simply be that you don't respond to this kind of treatment, as was the case for Claire and Larry.

Claire suggested I go for counseling, and I tried it once but I felt I was talking to an empathy robot. I resented having told him about myself. Claire didn't like what her counselor was saying either. It was supposed to be reassuring, but it was so rote that she found it suspect. She was fed stock answers that didn't seem to have much to do with her.

I think people have to hear it from people they trust and who know them. Your bullshit protectors are turned up to full blast after something like rape. The artlessness of friends and lovers is more believable than the pat stuff of professionals.

If the friends and lovers are caring and sensitive about rape, Larry may be right. But if they aren't, a counselor or another woman who has been raped may be the greatest comfort you can find.

Long-term Recovery

The months after your rape are a time of fighting to get back to normal. You not only need to fight the memory and aftermath of rape but, ironically, you may have to fight the very people around you who are trying to help. You are starting to want to be ordinary again, to put the rape behind you and get on with life, but your partner, family members, and friends are often still being protective, still treating you like a fragile doll. Now may be the time to tell them that they have to let go of you, let you be your old, independent self.

On the other hand, you might find your family and friends withdrawing their support before you are ready. They are getting impatient with you, they want you to be better. This withdrawal can be extremely painful, making you feel both at fault and rejected. When Angela found this happening with Clark, she was bewildered and hurt. "How could he abandon me?" she wondered.

If people close to you start to withdraw, remember that they are not doing so out of lack of love but out of exhaustion. Not only are they feeling drained by the support they have given you, but they are feeling the need of some attention of their own. One woman recalled:

> In some ways, I felt that members of my family were suffering more than I had over the rape. I found I was shielding some of my thoughts from my family and friends because I felt they wouldn't be able to cope with them, and at times I felt that I was making a better recovery than they were. This is probably because they fantasized a great deal about "what it must have been like" whereas I knew exactly what happened and was dealing with the problem from a more realistic and informed point of view.[33]

If you feel able, now could be the time to offer some support yourself. Encourage your partner and those close to you to tell you their reactions to your rape and their worries and fears. This exchange may be especially helpful because sometimes people close to you will go into a crisis themselves—a sort of delayed reaction—just as you are getting better. And it could well bring you to a closer understanding of each other and the rape.

If, however, you aren't able to do that yet and the people close to you are showing signs of impatience, try to relieve them for a while. Go to someone else. Pour out your feelings to a professional counselor if no one else seems right. Angela is an example:

> Anybody would have had trouble rising to my expectations after I was raped. If I'd relied more on my family or friends and split the

burden more, it would have made it easier on Clark. But I laid it all on him. Sometimes I think I expected too much from him.

Friends can be a great help during this long period of recovery, too, even if they don't know it. Not all of them will be able to offer the kind of responses you need when you tell them about the rape, but sometimes their company alone can be a comfort. Angela found various ingenious ways of using friends to help her recover.

> I decided I wanted to live through my twenty-second year again and make it okay, as if I'd never been raped. So when my birthday came, I told everyone I was twenty-two, not twenty-three, and no one knew the difference. I'd always felt proud of myself for being younger than other people in my field and getting places fast, so that helped me maintain my illusions.
>
> Then when the next Christmas came, I had a big party for myself. The rape happened just before Christmas and ruined it, so I wanted to recreate it and make it good. The party lasted till 4 A.M. and was great. I felt I'd lived through that night again and the guy hadn't come back and I was safe. This was a big turning point for me, a big source of strength. I recreated that year.
>
> I kept on pretending I was a year younger than I was till I turned twenty-five. Then I was able to really be twenty-five, and that was a recognition that I was over it. I had paid myself back and I was okay.

YOUR SEXUALITY

Most women in steady relationships are ready to start having sex again about six weeks after they were raped.[34] Whether you are ready by then or not until much later, you may have problems. Memories of the rape may intrude on you during sex, especially if you assume the position you were raped in. You may find yourself less able to feel desire, and you might have more trouble reaching orgasm.

Because of the lack of desire rape often causes, you may worry that you have become a lesbian. You may think you feel desire for women after it. There is no evidence at all that rape changes a person's sexual orientation. What might happen, however, is that rape puts you off men completely for a while and you mistake that for lesbianism. You feel safer with women, more relaxed with them, and because part of feeling sexual is feeling relaxed, you feel more sexual with them. This rejection of men is a normal result of a sexual attack and nothing to worry about. Your interest in men will return. On the other hand, if you were already unenthusiastic about heterosexual sex, a rape might be the force that makes you realize an asexuality or lesbianism that was already there. If this is the case for you, you might want to read Chapter 9, "Lesbians and Gay Men."

When you start to make love again with your partner, go slowly, emphasizing all the most gentle and sensuous aspects of sex for some time. You could begin, for example, by just holding each other without having sex for a couple of weeks, not allowing it even if you feel desire. Then progress to just looking and touching. From there you could try other forms of lovemaking, still without penetration. Eventually, try having intercourse slowly and gently, with the understanding that if you feel at all disturbed by it, you will both stop. One of the hardest parts of recovering your sexuality after a rape might be the issue of control. You may, like many women, feel that part of being able to enjoy sex is being able to let go of your self-control, being able to feel swept away. But after a rape you become afraid to lose control. To get over this you need to trust your partner. You need to feel that your desire releases you, not that your partner controls you. Approaching sex gradually, with your needs given primary importance, will help you.

Judith Becker addressed the issue of control in a sex therapy program for rape victims that she conducted in New York. The majority of women who came to her for help were still suffering from flashbacks of the rape whenever they had sex. Others came to find ways of breaking out of patterns they had fallen into with their partners, patterns that were leaving their sex lives a mess. The most successful treatment for both these problems, Becker said, was to encourage the woman to release her anger against the rapist. In one case of Becker's a woman who had been orally raped was unable to eat or drink without her throat muscles contracting involuntarily. She had to be hospitalized and fed intravenously. Once Becker encouraged her to just talk out her fury at the rapist, she recovered.

The other approach Becker used was to encourage the victims to release their anger against their lovers, and to become more aggressive sexually. The women typically had been letting their lovers dominate their sexual habits, which was uncomfortably reminiscent of the rape. Becker said:

We teach women to take back control of their bodies and assert
their sexual needs. We tell the partner that the woman will be doing
the initiating of sex now. If he doesn't like it, we point out that the
old way, with him initiating, hasn't helped her get any better. They
need to try something new.[35]

If you are interested in trying sex therapy, contact your local rape
crisis program and ask to be referred to an appropriate therapist. Meanwhile, have a look at the patterns you and your partner have fallen into
and see if they can be changed. Do you ever initiate sex, or are you
afraid to? Do you have sex when you don't feel like it? Are you afraid to
reject your partner's sexual advances? Do you resent him? Do you feel
that you can't talk about the rape with him? Or about sex? Try to put
yourself first and do only what you want to do. Suggest, for example,
that for two months, you will only have sex when you initiate it, as an
experiment.

If you don't have a steady lover, finding someone with whom you
can ease into lovemaking might be more difficult. You may find that
your sexual behavior has changed, that for instance you are now very
cautious about sleeping with someone new when you used to be relaxed
about it. This fear may well upset you, making you feel that you have
been permanently damaged by the rape. You may not have been damaged, but you probably are changed. The best you can do is take it step
by step, waiting until you find a sensitive, caring partner who is willing
to help you regain your sexuality. Meanwhile, a period of abstinence or
caution about sex might be a good idea. And sometimes finding a new
man who didn't know you at the time you were raped can help you get
over any associations with it.

For more about resuming sex after a rape, see "Problems with Sex"
in Chapter 3.

FINDING HELP

If a few months have passed since the rape, you may think you no
longer have a right to demand or expect help—you should be better,
it's over, and that's that. If the rape happened a few years ago, this
conviction might be even stronger. But you do have a right to help,
always, and if you aren't getting any, you should seek it out. You need
to stand up for yourself around other people. Reject people who make

you feel worse, ask for rides if you don't want to travel alone, and don't feel guilty when you want to talk about the rape to a friend.

Now might also be the first time you are ready to try therapy. Therapy is discussed in detail above, but don't feel that it is only for people in crisis right after a rape. Group therapy seems to be particularly beneficial for women who were raped some time ago, even as long as ten years. Angela went into group therapy eight months after she was raped.

> I joined a group with other women. They weren't even rape victims, but they were professional women whose lives looked very impressive from the outside but who felt that something was wrong. It was comforting to hear that other people have problems—I'd never been in therapy so had never really known that before. I stayed in the group for a year and it helped me a lot.

SELF-DEFENSE

Many survivors of sexual assault find that taking a course in self-defense not only helps them conquer their fears of another attack but improves their entire outlook on life. Rape utterly undermines your self-esteem, but when you've learned new confidence in your strength, your self-esteem can also improve. Self-defense helps you feel more competent, stronger, and even superior, all feelings that rape plays havoc with. You may believe that the rape happened because you were too weak, insecure, or passive to avert it. A self-defense course can get you over those feelings.

Self-defense does not teach you to become a murderer. You might be put off by it because you think of it as training in violence, the very thing you abhor after being attacked. But the emphasis is indeed on *defense.* It is designed simply to make you more able to avoid and escape an attack. It is taught not only to women and men but to children, blind people, and the handicapped.

If you went to observe a beginning self-defense class for women, you would see how wimpy most of them are. They hit with loose wrists, giggle if they succeed in knocking something over, and when it's time to practice an aggressive yell, they come out with a pathetic squeak. This behavior isn't surprising when you consider how women are brought up. Ever since they first played in a sandbox, they were told not to hit, not to fight back, and not to make a noise, no matter what that three-year-old bully was doing to them. But these lessons can be unlearned.

Self-defense teaches you, first of all, how to avoid getting into dangerous situations. The idea is that the best self-defense of all is never needing it. Thus you will learn what to do if you get into an elevator with someone who makes you uneasy, how to reconnoiter a new town so that you don't get lost somewhere dangerous, how to walk down the street defensively and how, basically, to look after yourself. (See "Self-defense" in Chapter 7 for a list of some of these techniques.) No one is suggesting that it was your ignorance of these techniques that got you raped—rape happens to the most cautious of people—but knowing them will lessen your chances of becoming a victim again.

A self-defense class will also teach you how best to respond to the initial attack. If someone approaches you, for example, don't shrink away from him or act intimidated—push him away and shout, "Leave me alone!" angrily instead. It takes practice to be able to do this, but it can be most successful in frightening a would-be assailant off. The class will also teach you how to let out a bloodcurdling yell. The right kind of yell can startle an attacker quite a bit, and often that's all you need to get rid of him. Practice into your pillow—for the sake of the neighbors —and try to yell from the pit of your stomach rather than high up in your throat.

You will also learn how to break out of various grips, including a stranglehold. And you'll learn how to hurt the assailant just enough to give you time to get away. You probably won't ever need to use what you learn from such a course, but just knowing these simple techniques gives you new confidence walking about the streets. Rachel took boxing lessons and found they helped her:

> I feel strong now and not so afraid. Now I know what it feels like to be hit and it's not so bad. You are stunned for a minute and then it stops hurting. I've realized that being hit doesn't kill me. When I was raped, I felt I'd rather get raped than be beaten up, let alone cut or killed. But now if there wasn't a weapon, I think I would fight back. Of course you can never really know, but at least I feel I can.

Self-defense will not appeal to everyone, however. You may not want to be reminded of the rape by dwelling on what to do if it happens again. But if it does appeal, you might find it more beneficial than you expected. Just being in an atmosphere that treats you as a survivor and a fighter rather than a helpless victim is restorative, as Joan, now a karate expert, found out.[36]

> I'd say the best defense is to know thyself. Unless you know who you are and what you are and what you're capable of, you can't take care of yourself. Self-defense helps you find out those things. You have to stop thinking that Daddy is going to save you—he's not and neither are the police. We women have to start fighting back ourselves. We are stronger and have more courage than we know, more than we've been given credit for. We can't take it lying down anymore.

See "Resources," Part Three, for places that offer self-defense classes, and also try calling your YWCA or community center to find out if a course is offered. The most practical type of course to take is self-defense that combines techniques from various martial arts. Pure martial arts courses tend to emphasize the purity of technique rather than teaching you to be streetwise.

BECOMING POLITICAL

Many a woman has found that the best way to help herself recover from a rape is to help others. You can do this by becoming a rape crisis counselor, by forming a group with other women to start a rape crisis program, or to educate your community about rape, or by becoming involved in lobbying to improve the way rape victims are treated by the law in your state. If you are interested in fighting back this way, contact the following:

· Your local women's center or group.

· Women Against Rape. Some such organizations will train you to be a rape crisis counselor. You might work for them as a volunteer, answering calls, counseling on the telephone, and arranging other ways to help the rape victims who call. You might also fund-raise or write or lobby for them.

· A rape crisis center near you that operates as described above.

· The National Organization for Victim Assistance (NOVA), (202) 232-8560. (Address listed in "Resources.") NOVA will help you go about advocating changes in the way victims are treated in your area, put you in contact with other people in the field, and guide you on how you can help.

Victims' Services

Recently a woman's apartment was burgled, and shortly after reporting this to the police, she got a notice through the mail. The notice offered her the following services, *all free:* Emergency assistance for food, rent, utilities, and other essentials. Counseling to deal with the problems of being a victim of crime. Emergency lock replacement, installation of guard plates and window pins. And emergency services for victims of family abuse and rape.

Sure enough, they came and installed a new lock and guard plates right away and for free—during weekday hours. They were not, alas, operative on weekends.

A service such as this can be invaluable, especially when you are bewildered or can't afford to shell out the sixty dollars or so for a new lock. Look under "Victims' Assistance Programs" in "Resources," or in your phone book under "Victims' Services Agencies" or "Victims' Assistance Programs" to see if such an organization is available in your area. You could also try calling the police or Directory Assistance for the same information. If you report the rape, the police may automatically inform a victims' services agency of your plight, but if you haven't heard anything, ask. And if you cannot find any such organization in your area, contact NOVA, mentioned above—they will put you in touch with someone if they can.

CRIME VICTIMS' COMPENSATION

Another victims' service is monetary compensation for the time you have lost from work and for the medical and legal expenses a rape has caused you. The rules about how to file for compensation and whether you can differ from state to state, but most of them include the requirement that you report the assault to the police *within one week* of the crime, and that you file a claim for compensation within the year. The rapist does not have to be caught for you to file a claim. You may also have to prove "a serious financial hardship as a direct result of the crime," and you'll probably have to file in the state you are a resident of, even if you were assaulted elsewhere.

Your ambulance and medical expenses should be largely covered by your insurance, if you have any, but crime victims' compensation should reimburse you for the expenses that are not covered. A typical policy will also reimburse you for loss of wages or support while you are in medical care, the cost of therapy, a job-oriented retraining or rehabilitation program, and attorney fees if you hired an attorney to help you file for the compensation. There will be limits on how much money you will get for all these expenses.

In some places members of your family who were affected by the assault can also apply for compensation, which may be essential if your spouse or children need therapy to help them through the trauma. If you are a minor, your parents will have to file for compensation for you.

Keep all records of the expenses your assault have incurred—medical and hospital bills, prescription receipts, bills from a psychologist, receipts for the cost of travel to hospitals or doctors, and canceled checks. These will be needed to prove how much the assault has cost you.

You don't have to file for compensation by yourself. To find out how to do it in your area and where to get help with the forms, call your local rape crisis center, district attorney or prosecutor's office, the police, or your local victims' assistance program.

For more sources for victims' services, please see the last part of this book, "Resources."

3

How Others Can Help

This chapter is for anyone close to a woman who has been sexually assaulted—her lover, boyfriend, husband, mother and father, brother, sister, children, and friends. How important you are to her after this ordeal cannot be overemphasized. Your reactions can make all the difference to how well she recovers.[1] In a way, you set the tone of the whole experience for her. Will she always feel a failure and at fault, hating herself for "letting" it happen? Or will she feel loved, supported, and strong enough to recover? This chapter will help you guide her toward the latter.

When It Happens: The First Twenty-four Hours

Although the woman you know may have been attacked much longer ago than a day, this section will be useful for several reasons. It will let you know what you did right or wrong. It will assure you of how similar your reactions were to those of other people in your situation. And it will tell you how to cope better if a rape should happen again to anyone you know. Knowing how to help someone who has been raped is as important as knowing how to help someone who is choking or drowning. Consider it basic first aid.

YOUR REACTIONS

The first thing you should know is that the rape is a crisis for you, too. You also feel shock and horror. You find it hard to believe that such a thing could have happened, and you wish to God it hadn't. You are furious at the man or men who did it. You are terrified that this will change her permanently, and you feel bitterly angry at yourself for not having been there to prevent the rape.[2] Clark was overwhelmed when he heard about Angela's rape:

> When Angela called and said, "Clark, I've been raped," I remember thinking, "Oh my God, I'm experiencing one of life's tragic moments." What she said is indelibly etched on my memory. It was horrifying, like hearing about one of your family being in an accident. She said, "I'm not hurt. The police are here."
>
> I pictured the police there and that scared me. I had no idea of the circumstances it happened in. Was it on the street? Did she get dragged off into some bushes? Rape has a horrible connotation, like death.

At the same time you are likely to be thinking that you have no right to be so upset. After all, the rape happened to her, not you. You might even deny that you are shocked and angered by the rape and just try to act perfect and calm. Underneath, however, you are going through so many of the same traumas as the victim that you have become what therapists call a "secondary victim." You have been hurt, too, and you *do* have a right to be upset.

You are, however, in a different position than she. As shaken by the rape as you might be and as in need of comfort as you are, you have to put yourself second. In an ironic way you are unluckier than she in this, for at least she can concentrate on her own needs—if she lets herself, which many women won't. You have to put your needs aside for the time being. This applies to your anger, too. Men in particular tend to get angry, at the rapist and at the victim. Men who are sexually involved with the victim may even feel betrayed by her. Try not to rant and rave against the rapist just yet. You will only frighten your partner and make her feel ignored. And try to forget the sexual aspect of the rape for now—sex was just a tool used by the rapist to degrade her—and just think of her as you would if she's been in a terrible car accident that was someone else's fault. Give her your sympathy, not your rage.

WHAT TO DO

Clark described what he went through after Angela's rape.

> I was one and a half hours away from Angela when she was raped, and during the drive to get to her I kept imagining what had happened. I had very little actual information and my imagination went wild. It gave me a helpless feeling. I was anxious and upset, and I didn't know what I should do when I got there. Mostly, though, I was eager to just comfort her and find out what happened.
>
> When I saw her, she looked like the embodiment of her voice—under tenuous control. We embraced first thing and I felt her shaking, but she was very controlled and speaking in a deliberate, cold voice. She said, "Clark, I'm all right." She seemed very concerned with my well-being, ironically.
>
> The whole scene was nightmarish. The police had drawn chalk lines around her clothes, the place was in a shambles. It scared me. I thought, "My God, it looks like a murder scene."

The first time you see the victim after the rape is probably going to be a shock. She may be beaten up and bruised, her clothes might be torn and her nerves shaken. She might be dazed or withdrawn and seem like a different person than the woman you know. She may well push you away or act cold toward you, or she might look as if nothing has happened at all. Whatever her reaction, it is never quite what you expect, and your own terror will exaggerate any first impressions you have. Try to stay calm, but not cold or indifferent. Now is not the moment to prove to her how upset you are. It is a time to soothe her.

When you see her, your first impulse will probably be to rush over and hold her. You want to cradle and comfort her the way you would a hurt child. You want to make the pain go away. Yet as kind at this impulse is, it is sometimes misguided. Some women do want to be held by someone they love right after a rape, but many don't want to be touched at all. They have just been mauled about against their wills and, like a wounded animal, they want to hold themselves away from any further contact. Yet at the same time, they want to know that you are not angry at them or disgusted by them, that you don't find them soiled by the rape. So when you first see the woman, you have to strike a balance between reassuring her that you are not repulsed by her and letting her decide whether she wants to be touched. The only way to do this is to say something like, "Do you want me to hold you, or shall I wait a while?" or, "I want to hold you, but I'll understand if you don't want me to." Questioning her like this may seem unnatural, but she will appreciate it. If she responds negatively, try not to take it personally. She isn't really rejecting *you*, she's protecting herself.

To help you understand her revulsion toward being touched, imagine that you have just fallen down some stairs and badly twisted your ankle. Most people have hurt themselves in some way like this at least once. You are sitting at the bottom of the steps in agony, dazed and feeling nauseated, when along comes a well-meaning person who grabs you by the arm and tries to haul you to your feet. "Don't!" you scream. "Leave me alone!" You know that being forced to stand will only increase the pain. The very thought of it makes you dizzy. You just want everyone to stay away from your ankle until you are recovered enough to decide what to do next. That is how a rape victim feels; only instead of feeling pain in her ankle, she feels it in her whole body.

The next problem you'll have is what to say to her. Many people have two strong urges. They want to make this whole terrible thing disappear, so they start trying to undo the horror of it. Or they want to whisk her away to safety, and so they start making decisions for her.

As understandable as those urges are, they can do more harm than good. If you tell her what happened wasn't so bad, she'll begin to feel guilty about being so upset and may keep her terror to herself. It's like telling someone with appendicitis that the pain is all in his head and that he's just being a hypochondriac. And if you take over her decisions, you'll be doing exactly what the rapist did, robbing her of her will and dignity. Let her decide whether to go to the police, to the hospital, home, or to someone else's place. She may not feel capable of making these decisions, but let her tell you that. The quickest way for her to get her self-respect back is to start controlling her life again right away. This advice is especially difficult for parents of a victim to remember if they are used to making decisions for her.

If she asks you directly what to do—"Should I call the police? Should I tell my mother?"—still try to leave it to her. Ask her how she'd feel about doing it or not doing it. Her answer will usually make clear to both of you what her real desire is. This technique helps her more than giving her direct advice.

Something else you may do unwittingly is blame her in order to protect yourself. You are looking for a way to make yourself feel safe. Your everyday sense of security has been shattered by the rape, and if you can find a reason why it happened, such as, "It's her fault," you don't feel so frighteningly prone to random catastrophe. Perhaps she did do something careless, and perhaps you did, too, and knowing that you can avoid doing that again might be a comfort. But don't accuse her, because that does tremendous damage. Even if you are thinking, "If only she hadn't gone to that party" or, "I *told* her not to leave the keys under the mat," don't say it. That's the quickest way to alienate her from you. Keys and parties don't cause rape. Rapists do.

Now is the time for you to be kind and loving. *Let her know you believe her*—that is a good start. Refrain from skeptical looks and remarks. Even if she is your teenage daughter and she takes drugs, believe her. Research has shown that the odds are overwhelmingly likely that she's telling the truth. Reporting a rape in our present society is so unpleasant that women simply don't do it unless it's true. The FBI report that the number of false claims of rape is the same as the number of false reports of any other major crime, a mere 2 percent.[3] You might find it easier not to believe her, but she'll only hate you for it. Not believing her will propel her into a maddening nightmare, making her feel punished for being raped. You just can't do that to someone you love.

If the police or hospital staff seem to doubt the woman's story, your assurance that you believe her can be a particular help. Lack of belief on the part of officials is sadly common, especially in small towns or when the rapist is someone the woman knows. Only three years ago, for example, a woman who was brutally raped and beaten in Montana arrived at the police station bloody and bruised only to be met by policemen who flatly refused to believe she'd been raped.[4] How they thought she'd gotten so hurt is anyone's guess.

Tell her you care about her and that you'll stay with her. And ask her what she wants to do next. You can also help her by letting her follow her emotions without check. Let her cry and sob or rant and rail if she wants. She needs to exert her will in whatever way she chooses. As Penny found, it was infuriating to be made to calm down by her husband just when she needed not to be calm. Let the victim cry and let her talk.

Also, don't forget to let her know that you are glad that she survived. She may be feeling a failure because she didn't avoid the rape, but in fact, she is a success. Whatever she did, whether it was to struggle and scream, submit quietly, act friendly, or act cold, it was the right choice because it got her out alive. Tell her you are proud of her and keep telling her that in the days and weeks that follow. As Clark said about Angela:

> Soon after the rape she began to read books about rape. I was overwhelmed by a feeling of pride in her, pride that she was really *working* at getting over it. She was exhibiting a strength and a side of her I hadn't seen, the same Angela I saw standing in the apartment the night of the rape, being so strong.

Perhaps the most important thing you can do for her is simply to listen, even if what she says is painful to hear. Talking is a way for her to face her feelings, share the burden of them, and thus to bear them.[5] It is the basis of all therapeutic treatments and an easy one for you to help her with. Let her be silent, too, if she wants, but make sure she knows that you are willing to listen. Don't just wait for her to bring the subject up; ask her if she wants to talk about it. As Claire said, "The main thing that helped me was being able to talk about it." And when you listen, listen carefully. Usually, the first things a woman who has been raped brings up in conversation, or the things she brings up the most often, are the ones that cause her the most worry. She may keep saying, "He was so dirty," for example, revealing a preoccupation with feeling disgusted and soiled by the rape. Later, you can point out to her how often she said those things and help her to face and examine them.

One of the best times to do this listening is during the wait at the hospital, if you accompany her there right after the rape. She may have to sit there for two hours or more until a doctor can see her, and this is a time when you can act as counselor. If she wants to talk about the rape, listen. If she starts to blame herself, help her not to. If she begins to despair, comfort her. Burgess and Holmstrom tell of a case in which the sister of a rape victim managed to rally her around at the hospital when counselors could not. The victim was desperately upset and kept saying "I wish he had killed me" and crying. When the counselors tried to get her to talk about it, she said angrily, "Everyone who comes in this door wants to talk about it, and I just want to forget it." Stumped, the counselors asked her sister to help, so she walked into the examining room and immediately said, "Now take a deep breath and you'll feel better." The victim followed her advice, and then the sister consoled her in approximately these words.

It is good to talk about it, the rape, to understand why it happened. It was not because of you. You were just the target. If it hadn't been you, it would have been someone else.

    . . . Letting him do it was the way to survive. What you said earlier to me about wanting to die—you can't feel that way. When you get home you can take a bath and that will get rid of the physical part. But then you need to get rid of the psychological part . . . so you won't be choked up inside. . . . [6]

In summary, here are some basic do's and don'ts:

DO:

- Say you believe her.
- Say you care about her.
- Ask her if she wants you to hold her.
- Tell her you are proud of her for surviving.
- Stick by her.
- Let her make decisions.
- Let her cry, yell, or talk.
- Listen.

DON'T:

- Embrace her without asking.
- Get angry at her.
- Blame her.
- Boss her around.
- Rant and rave with fury at the rapist.
- Pretend the rape wasn't serious.

PRACTICAL HELP

On the practical side there is much you can do to help a rape victim right after the rape. You can find somewhere for her to call for help, for instance, because often rape hotlines listed in telephone directories are defunct, not working, or just tape recordings. Ask her if she would like you to help with this, for she may be too easily discouraged by one failure to keep trying herself. You can also go to the hospital and police with her and make sure that she isn't left alone until she really wants to be. She may be feeling timid about asking for your company, so volunteer it. That will be a comfort to her. As one woman said, "A friend can stand up for you if the cops try to push you around or ask inappropriate questions. It can make you feel stronger if a friend offers to stay."

You can also help her figure out what to do once the initial stages of police and hospital visits are over. If she is worried about going to work the next day, tell her she has a perfect right to call in sick if she wants, without explanations. And if, as so often happens, she is terrified of seeing the rapist again, help her work out strategies to keep safe, such as staying with someone else for a while, avoiding the neighborhood of the attack, and getting new locks on her door (see "Victims' Services" at the end of Chapter 2). Remind her that the chances of her seeing the rapist again, provided he was a stranger, are small. Don't, however, ridicule her fears—Rachel did see her rapist on the street two weeks after the rape and got the police to arrest him. Finally, make sure that she has transport and money so that she does not have to take trains or buses late at night after her rape.

A Day to a Month Later

> I was never sure that what I was doing was right. I've never been hurt by anything like that before. It was one of the most excruciating experiences of my life.

As Larry expressed here, the month or so after the rape is a hard time for someone close to a victim. You are trying your best to help her, to keep up your sympathy and support, yet she seems to get no better. Sometimes she even pushes you away impatiently, just when you are trying to be nice. Then when you take the cue from her and leave her alone, she turns around and accuses you of not caring. Other times she takes out her anger on you and blames you for not being supportive, for not understanding, and even for not rescuing her when it happened. Clark had these difficulties with Angela:

> Once Angela said to me, "If you hadn't left, I wouldn't have been raped." But she had a terrible temper and was always sayings things she knew were untrue as a way of hurting me. She didn't really believe that.

Her ups and downs and mixed messages are only to be expected. They reflect the confusion she is feeling and the unsteady process of recovery. Unfortunately, as someone close to her, you often get the brunt of it, but that does not mean she is going mad or that your relationship is falling apart. It's just a very difficult time. The women interviewed for this book had these suggestions for how to help the victim through this period:

• Continue to ask her how she's feeling about the rape. Don't avoid the subject for fear of upsetting her. The worst you'll get is her crying or saying she doesn't want to talk about it, but even if she reacts badly to the question once, you should try again. As one woman said, "Some days I won't talk and other days I want to. It's nothing to do with the friend who's asking; it's me." It is not easy, of course, to bring the subject up if it makes the woman snap your head off or burst out crying, but as time goes by, she still needs to know you are willing to listen.

• Tell her she can call you anytime she feels afraid. This is a great help for women living alone.

• Stick around and make sure she never has to go home alone.

• Realize that recovery may take months, even years.

• Don't take over for her. Penny said, "I remember feeling that I needed to know I could look after myself. I didn't want to be helped. I wanted to feel strong." She may need your help in the form of company and sympathy, but she doesn't need to be treated as a helpless child. One of the easiest mistakes to make is to get overprotective. Parents, older brothers, lovers, and husbands are especially prone to do this. To some extent, it seems natural that you should become a protector, but don't assume that because she was raped, she has proven that she can't look after herself. Here are some other don'ts:

• Don't insist that she report the rape, that she prosecute or not prosecute.

• Don't make her move or change jobs.

• Don't escort her everywhere, keep track of her whenever she goes out, or lock the house for her, as if she can't do it herself.

These protective impulses don't help, especially when they are done without consulting her. They make her feel more helpless than ever, they undermine her attempts to get back to her old self, they show lack of respect for her adulthood, and they give her the feeling that she is being punished for having "let" a crime happen to her. Don said:

I remember fitting bars to hold the windows closed and getting up in the middle of the night to check if the back door was locked. I called Mary more often when I was away, and I'd reach over her in the car and lock her door. Finally, she said, "Why don't you just loosen up?"

One man, the husband of a rape victim, went so far in his protectiveness that he virtually made his wife a prisoner. He hired a full-time maid, he put locks on every door and window in the house, and he wouldn't even let her go out shopping without a member of the family accompanying her. She quickly sank into depression. She found no change in herself, no improvement as time went on, and began to feel as if she must have done something terribly wrong. Her husband was telling her, effectively, that she was no longer capable of being who she was before. He had taken control over her life, just as the rapist had.[7]

Another mistake along these lines is to tell someone about the woman's rape without her knowledge. Don't go rushing off to involve the local rabbi or priest, her teachers, her boss, or her relatives without her permission, for she will feel that you are invading her privacy. You can, however, call a counselor at a rape crisis center and ask for advice about what to do for her and yourself; such a consultation is free.

The question of just how protective to be is not simple. One woman expressed her ambivalence about it when she made these contradictory statements.

> When it first happened, I didn't want to be the strong one. But I also felt I couldn't collapse in anyone's arms. I wanted someone to come with me to the police and then the district attorney's office when I prosecuted, but I also wanted to be independent. Still, I think it's better to have someone be overprotective than not to show support at all.

Angela wanted a tremendous amount of protection from Clark after her rape. Clark said:

> We moved after the rape, but we couldn't afford a good area and she was frightened. She wouldn't go out alone. My whole role as protector was very real. I was her escort and constant companion for the first few weeks. We went to school together and met after class and ate together and went home together. For a while it seemed like the natural thing to do. I didn't feel any resentment about it.

You need to show concern without dominating her. The best way to strike this tricky balance is to keep asking her what she'd like you to do, if she isn't already telling you. Would she like you to go out with her? To leave her alone or not? If you leave it to her to decide how much protection she'd like, then you won't be taking away her integrity.

When you get overprotective, you are not just protecting the rape victim, you are also, however unwittingly, protecting yourself. You may not realize it, but you are terrified, too. Tragedy has thundered into your life and knocked you down, even if only vicariously. As Clark put it, "When someone you are intimate with has been violated, you feel violated, too." Don found that he seemed more terrified of bad neighborhoods after Mary's rape than she was. Women—mothers, sisters, friends, and daughters—feel especially scared by the rape of someone they love, for it reminds them of how easily it could happen to them. Try to remember this and try not to get fanatically protective.

HELPING HER TALK

All the rape victims and counselors interviewed for this book emphasized the importance of being able to talk about the experience to someone. Talking lessens the stress and is the first step to ridding oneself of the horror and memory of the rape. Often, once expressed, horrible things manage to lose some of their horror. These are the kinds of questions you can ask to encourage the victim to talk. Don't fire them all at her at once, and broach the subject gently. Many women feel that anyone who questions them in detail about the rape is being voyeuristic, so make sure you ask her if she wants to talk about it first.[8]

- What is bothering you the most about the attack?
- What did the rapist say to you before he attacked you?
- Did he say anything to you during it, and if so, what?
- What did you say to him?

A lot of women play their conversations with their rapists over and over in their heads, kicking themselves for having said the wrong things or hating themselves for having acted scared or abject. Talking about this gives them a chance to be reassured that they handled the rape as best they, or anyone else, could.

- What threats and violence did he use?
- Did you struggle? How do you feel about that?

Many women hate themselves for having struggled because they think they antagonized the rapist. Just as many others hate themselves for *not* having struggled because they think they should have fought back. Assure her that whichever choice she made must have been right, since she survived, and remind her that no one can second-guess a rapist anyway—struggling may put off one and incite another to kill.

• Was the rapist on drugs or alcohol? How did you feel about that at the time? Disgusted? Scared?

• How do you feel about the attack now?

• What is the most painful part to think about and why?

• Did this attack remind you of any others in your past? Do you feel persecuted?

• Did anyone come to your help or ignore you while you were being raped? How do you feel about that?

PROBLEMS FAMILIES FACE

The first month or so after the rape will probably be a turbulent one for the victim's family. She might go through a period of hating, or at least distrusting, men and associating the men in her family with the rapist. She might also irrationally blame both her mother and father for failing to protect her. This blame may take the form of hostility toward either the whole family or certain members of it. And her fluctuating moods and withdrawal from intimacy will disturb everyone. The atmosphere, therefore, might get tense and hard on all your tempers.

Some families are so concerned with protecting themselves from the horror of the rape that they deny anything is wrong with the victim. Once the bruises have gone, if she had any, they drop the subject and pretend it's all over. This pretense only makes the woman withdraw. If you are denying that she's been hurt, you are making yourself her enemy rather than her friend. You are not helping her recover. Also, you may not be facing up to your own reactions to the rape, which might make your own recovery more difficult.

Try to remember that a woman who has been raped is likely to be suffering from extremely low self-esteem. She needs reassurance from you that she is still loved and valuable. She needs to know that you don't blame her for what happened and that you are proud of her struggle to recover. She needs to know that you still respect her, and she needs you to remember that she is still the same person she was before the rape. All of this is hard for you to give her. Because of her lack of self-esteem, she'll be making constant demands on you, she may be depressing to be with, and her low opinion of herself is dangerously catching—you might find yourself agreeing with her. Remember that she feels this way because the rape has shaken her confidence in her wisdom, judgment, and outlook on life. She feels a failure and she needs you to reassure her that she's not.

If you are the father of a rape victim, you may have more difficulty dealing with the rape than other family members. Firstly, you are more likely to be subject to the myths about rape because of the era you grew up in, and as a result it may be hard for you not to think of your daughter as sullied, as having invited the rape in some way, or at least as having had a nasty sexual experience that is embarrassing to talk about. Secondly, you might feel horrible about not having protected your daughter, one of your primary roles as a parent. As one father put it, "No matter how many years go by, I'll never get over the guilt." And thirdly, you may, like so many fathers, have long since withdrawn from your grown daughter and lost the relationship that once was close. You feel it is somehow taboo to be intimate with a daughter now that she is a woman, and for the same reason, she might have withdrawn from you. All of this makes it very hard for you to help your daughter or yourself. Claire described her father's reaction:

> The first thing my father wanted to do was give me a gun and teach me how to use it. I didn't want to. Then he told me about an injury he'd had in the Army and how he'd kept going. He was trying to tell me I should put the rape behind me and move ahead. But I knew that already. It annoyed me.

As the father or brother of a rape victim, you can help her learn to trust men again. Often the men of the family tend to absent themselves physically and emotionally when a rape happens. Try not to withdraw. Instead, show your daughter or sister that you understand she has been the random victim of violence, that it was in no sense her fault, and that you are standing by her. Read "How Men Can Help" below for more on this.

The support of the women in the family is also, of course, essential to a rape victim. Men are not the only people who believe myths about rape and when you have your own safety to fear for, it is easy to seek reasons why the rape that happened to her won't happen to you— reasons that usually result in blaming her. But as a current study is finding, the support of a mother is one of the key factors in helping women feel safe again.[9] If you keep saying things such as "You shouldn't be living alone," "You shouldn't have gone out with him," and so on, the victim is going to feel that nothing short of locking herself up will keep her safe. But if you show your daughter that you don't blame her in any way, that you believe in her, and that you are willing to listen to and comfort her as much as she wants, you can help her go out into the world confidently again. As a counselor said, "The reaction of your mother is terribly important, no matter how old you are. After all, daughters never quite get over caring about their mother's judgment of them." Claire's experience brought her closer to her mother:

> My mother and I began to communicate for the first time after the rape. The first time I ever remember her hugging me was when I came home after it. And it was hard for her and my father. They are educated, liberal-minded people with sophisticated friends, but they live in a small midwestern town and they couldn't tell anybody about it. Not even their best friends. They couldn't help thinking of it as sexual and therefore as a private and shameful thing. So I didn't even want to tell them at first. But when I did, they were extremely supportive, and it helped me a lot emotionally that I could involve my family. One friend kept saying, "Talk to me about it," but there were certain things I could only tell my family. I had private reactions to the rape that I knew only they would understand.

THE CHILDREN OF THE VICTIM

If the victim has young children, adults close to her can help them. The rape of their mother can seriously shake up their view of sexuality and of their safety in the world; Mother is supposed to be a protector, an authority, someone to provide comfort, not someone who can be attacked and then need comfort herself. If the children were present during the rape, or threatened themselves, they are victims too. Their mother might not be able to cope well with their needs at first. Don't separate them—her children might be her biggest comfort—but be available to answer their questions, talk to them about what happened, and offer them all the reassurance of safety you can. You might also want to consult with their mother about getting the children some counseling. A good book to guide you on how to handle a child traumatized in this way is *Your Children Should Know* by Flora Colao and Tamar Hosansky (Indianapolis: Bobbs-Merrill, 1983).

If you are a teenage or adult child of a rape victim, you will be no less traumatized. A part of you has been raped, too, and your feelings of security in the world shattered as a result. You also might feel extremely uncomfortable about the whole subject because thinking of your mother in any sexual way feels taboo. Again, don't withdraw from her. She may be protecting you all she can by not talking about it, but encourage her to reach out to someone for help, even if it can't be you. And if she is elderly or living alone, don't feel guilty about not having protected her. You can't be with her all the time. Also, avoid taking over her decisions or pushing her to move somewhere safer against her will. (See Chapter 7, "The Older Victim," for more on this.)

How Men Can Help

Penny described the reaction of the first male friend she told about her rape.

> The morning after I was raped, I went into the kitchen and a friend of my husband's, Billy, was there. He was waiting for his girlfriend, Sara, to visit. I was distraught and shaky, but when I told him that I was raped the night before, he just said, "Don't tell Sara or else she'll never want to visit here again."
>
> That kind of determined the way I've felt about telling men ever since. I didn't want to deal with another response like that, just being concerned with how it would affect him, not how it affected me. I haven't had a single good experience telling a man.

Men find it harder to understand what a rape victim has gone through than women. Nobody except someone who has been raped can really feel the horror the victim does, but women can sympathize with it more easily because they are used to living with the fear of rape. They are reminded of it every time they are jeered at, accosted, or leered at in the street, every time they are followed by a man, every time they are pressured to have sex, every time they see magazine pictures of subjugated women, every time they hear a rape joke, and every time they are alone somewhere dark or deserted. So the actual rape of someone they know is simply a confirmation of this fear, a logical extension of the terror they have harbored all their lives.

Most women have been sexually assaulted in some way even if they haven't been raped—by obscene telephone callers, by exhibitionists, by men who feel them up on buses and trains, by child molesters, or by teenage boys who won't accept a no until its sincerity has been proven by a desperate struggle on the couch. One widely quoted study claims that one in four women have been sexually molested as children.[10] This type of experience gives them another reason to understand a rape victim.

Because you, as a man, don't live with this everyday fear, you may think that you can't understand rape, that you can never really "feel" it. You aren't alone in this opinion—most people, men and women, think men are incapable of understanding rape.* But this is not necessarily true. A man can sympathize with a rape victim, but it takes work.

Like every man, you have known fear. You have been bullied as a child, beaten up or chased as a teenager. You may even have been sexually molested yourself as a child—one study found that one in eleven men were sexually assaulted as children.[11] You may have been mugged or held up. Perhaps you have been through a war. When you were little, you were probably terrified by boogeymen and nightmares. And you have known humiliation, too. You have been defeated in a fight, scolded by a parent or teacher, jeered at by friends, or disgraced by a boss. If you just take the time to recall how you felt during such experiences, you can begin to understand how a rape victim feels. You only have to remember that being raped is primarily an experience of fear and humiliation, not sex, and most of your reasons for not understanding it disappear.

There are more specific ways to help yourself understand rape, too. If you want to help the woman, try these, even if they seem like a nuisance. Fathers, brothers, lovers, and husbands do have to put more effort into understanding rape than women, but the work is worth it, for you and the victim.

The following exercises are given to men who wish to train as rape counselors. They are used to help men feel what it is like to be a woman.

* See *Men on Rape* by Timothy Beneke (New York: St. Martin's Press, 1982) for a sad look at how men see rape.

• When you next walk down a city street with a woman, stop and walk ten feet behind her. Watch how many times she is verbally accosted. (One woman counted for herself on a two-block walk. She got ten remarks.) This exercise will help you realize how threatening an everyday walk can be for a woman. Many people think that women find street remarks complimentary. They don't realize how insulting and frightening they can be. The ones that sound complimentary, such as, "Hey, babe, ain't you pretty?" only serve to remind women that they are sexual objects to be assessed by any male, a "babe" to be commented on at will, like a pet poodle. And the ones that are vulgar usually spill over quickly into hostility: "Hey, baby, show us those tits! Oh, too stuck up to smile, huh? Snooty bitch!" As some feminists have pointed out, any liberal would be shocked these days if a black man walked down the street and got remarks about his appearance from whites. Yet women are subjected to this all the time. Behind every snicker, leer, or lustful remark is the threat of rape, sometimes oblique, sometimes blatant, for essentially, he is saying, "I'm judging whether I find you worthy of 'having,' and your dignity, your privacy, and your choice have nothing to do with my judgment." He may not realize that is the message he's giving, but she does, even if only subtly through her discomfort and embarrassment. Understanding this will help you, as a man, understand what actual rape does to a woman; it tells her, "Yes, you are an object of prey."

• Imagine that you are coming home from work at night and you want to do the following chores: go the library, go shopping, go down to the basement to do your laundry, walk the dog, and go running. Now picture yourself as a woman wanting to do those things. What extra precautions would you have to take? Would you run on your own after dark? (What would a jury think if you were doing that when you were raped?) Walk the dog on a deserted street? (What would a defense attorney make of that if you were raped?) Would you go down to the basement late at night? (Angela forgot to lock her apartment door when she went down to her basement to do the laundry. Because of that simple, everyday mistake, the rapist got into her apartment.) How much rearranging of your plans would you have to do to be safe? What feels like paranoia to you is simply the everyday precaution a woman must take. It is no wonder that when a woman does get attacked despite all these precautions, she feels cheated and defeated.

The following exercises are rather unpleasant, but they should help you "feel" what it is to be raped.

· Think of a movie you've seen with a torture sequence in it. (The similarities between rape and torture are discussed in the introduction to the book.) Think of the discomfort that scene caused you and imagine yourself as the victim. A rape victim has been through such torture.

· If you've seen *Deliverance,* one of the few popular films to have shown a detailed scene of an adult man being raped, think of how you'd feel in that man's position. Humiliated, debased, deeply embarrassed, ashamed, angry, disgusted? These are just some of the feelings rape causes in a woman.

· Read Chapter 6, "Men Get Raped, Too," for accounts of male victims of rape. Their reactions hardly differ from women's.

· How would you feel about going to prison, knowing the amount of male rape that goes on there? Imagine feeling that fear all the time. That is how many women feel after they've been raped.

· Many rapists rape orally and anally. You don't have to have a vagina to be raped. You could be raped that way, too. Imagine being held down by a group of men and being forced to suck their penises and accept anal penetration from them. That experience is no different from a typical gang rape.

· Picture this scene: You are coming home from work, somewhat tired and in a slight daze, carrying a briefcase, a newspaper, and a bag of groceries. You are fumbling with the lock to the door of your apartment building when out of nowhere you feel something hard dig into your ribs and a voice says, "Get inside." You whirl around to find a clean-cut man in a suit standing up against you. He lifts a gun to your neck. He pushes you in, his finger on the trigger, and threatens to kill you right there if you don't do as he says. You offer him your wallet and anything else, but he says that's not what he wants. "Take me to your apartment."

No one is around. The gun is up against your neck and the guy seems fidgety, nervous, and unpredictable. You remember a story you read recently of ten people in an apartment building being shot at close range, and you wonder if he's the man who did it. A cold, paralyzing fear starts to creep over you. You just want it all to be over. You want to come out alive.

The man takes you up to your apartment and inside. He locks the door behind him, wrenches the packages out of your hands, and, holding the gun to your head, makes you walk toward the bedroom. You keep waiting for a chance to tackle him or play some other trick, but his eyes and gun are fixed on you. You try to act unafraid and friendly, even offering him a drink in the hope he will fall for it and give you a chance to get to the phone, but he swears at you and pushes you down on the bed. You wonder how you could be so pathetic as to offer him anything.

Still holding the gun at your head, he tells you to undress. You do, thinking only that if you don't anger him, he might not kill you. He tells you to lie face down on the bed, and he sodomizes you. Afterward, he also makes you suck his penis. All the while, he jeers at you, calls you every filthy name you've ever heard of, and insults your looks and your body.

When he's finished, you are crying. He takes your wallet, waves his gun at you, and tells you that if you make a move toward the phone, he'll know. "I know where you live and I'll come back and kill you next time." Then he finally leaves.

This "you" could be a man or a woman.

Another reason you may find it hard to understand a woman's reaction to rape, and one that exercises can't help you with, is that you find it easier to express anger than she does. Men often get frustrated at women's reluctance to show anger after a rape and forget that women have been trained to suppress such fury. If you are threatened or hurt, you have learned to get mad and show it. A woman has learned to freeze instead. She may feel angry, but rather than show it she tends to shrink into herself or cry. Sometimes she just tries to hurry away, or even apologizes. And even if she does burst out in a moment's anger, she may feel afraid as a result and so further humiliated. She does this because she has learned that women are not taken seriously when they get angry. Every time she is infuriated enough by an obscene remark made to her in the street to stop and shout in anger, for instance, she is laughed at or called a "castrating bitch." Her anger is treated as something funny, cute, or at least pathetically inappropriate. Yet if she were a man and she stopped to shout like that, it would be taken as a challenge, not a joke. Thus, she has no faith in her anger or in her ability to fight back. Men go through this kind of thing, too, when they are children. You might be able to remember a time when, as a boy, you got furious at an adult and were simply laughed at for it. Remember the humiliation and burning frustration of that? Women are never allowed to grow out of that stage. So if you are wondering why she doesn't just get *mad* at that rapist instead of sitting there falling apart, remember that getting angry for her isn't so simple.

The difference in the ability of men and women to get angry becomes very important after a rape. The woman will be terrified—of its happening again, of what has already happened, and of what is happening at that moment in her mind. If she's at all able to feel angry about it, she is probably turning that anger toward herself, or just keeping it bottled up. But you, as a man close to her, will be feeling a murderous fury—at the rapist, at yourself for not protecting her, at her for "allowing" it to happen. Her fear and your anger clash. You are reenacting the very anger that has so terrified her, the very violence that made her into a victim. Often men get so preoccupied with their anger that they start ranting and raving about going out to murder the rapist and ignore the victim completely. Counselors are always seeing fathers and brothers, husbands and boyfriends turn from mild-mannered people into vengeful maniacs talking about getting a gun and roaming the streets to hunt down the rapist or about making the woman go to the police or the courts for revenge. If you start behaving like this, she will not only have to deal with fear for herself but with fear of your getting hurt. She may even feel neglected because you are paying more attention to getting the rapist than to comforting her—you've entered a relationship of vengeance with the rapist that excludes her. And she might actually become frightened of *you*, the very person she has turned to for comfort. Larry recalled:

> The first week I wanted to kill or humiliate someone. I wanted to take the rape back, redeem it by humiliating someone. I had fantasies of committing murder. At the time, I thought it was the rapist I wanted to kill, but now I know it really could have been anyone. My fantasies of revenge helped to give me a sense that I'd done more than I really had. I felt I should have done more.

Claire said:

> For a few weeks after I was raped, whenever Larry heard someone screaming in the street, he'd rush out to help. He wanted to help in the way he hadn't been able to help me. I was scared he'd get himself hurt.

Getting angry at the rapist is a perfectly healthy reaction. Everyone does it, women friends and family as well as men, and everyone has those fantasies of gory revenge. But macho displays of revenge are something that belong to the movies, not real life. Keep that anger to yourself for the time being or, better, let it off somewhere else. If you are thinking of her rather than yourself, you'll realize that she needs your comfort, not your lust for vengeance.

THE BURDEN ON YOU

As the days and weeks after the rape go by, the burden on you, as a man close to the rape victim, increases. The worst of it is your continuing fury at the rapist, your hatred of yourself for not having prevented the rape, and your worry that she, and your relationship with her, will never be the same. Normally, when you are filled with turbulent feelings like these, you talk about them to the person closest to you, but when that person is the one who has been raped, you are trapped. She is in no state to sort out your problems; she has too many of her own. You cannot add to her burden. So where do you go? Larry didn't know where to turn.

> I couldn't talk about it to other men. I felt they'd be defensive and say things like, "Hey, we're all on the make," in defense of the rapist. Who wants to know your own sex is bad?

Clark found the same thing.

> Since the rape happened, I've come to feel that rape is the most horrible crime, second only to murder, but most men don't understand that. They just joke about it. I feel guilt by association as a man, being one of the sex that can perpetrate this crime and then make light of it. It seems terrible to me when people joke about it and movies glamorize it. I keep thinking, "Are men really such assholes? Do we all have the capacity in one stroke to humiliate someone and possibly ruin her life?" I saw it happen to someone I love. Her confidence was completely destroyed, her sex life was permanently altered, her relations to men completely changed, and her comfort in the world disturbed forever. People think you're raped and then it's over, but it's not. It touches every facet of your life.

Because so few men understand rape and so many think they have to show some sort of misguided solidarity with the rapist through jokes, you probably feel terribly isolated. Not only are you afraid of the insensitive reactions of your fellow men, but you feel, rightly, that you cannot betray the victim's privacy by going around talking about her rape. Other family members and friends may feel this, too, and often they have no one to turn to for sympathy. When this is the case, you are doing all of the giving and none of the getting, and that is a serious strain. It may even make you resent the victim at times.

Some men solve their need to talk by turning to women friends; others find they can eventually tell a brother or a friend who might be more sensitive. But many, especially fathers, never feel they can tell a soul. If this is your case, try calling a rape crisis center. You can just talk to a counselor on the phone if you want and remain anonymous. Some rape crisis centers are setting up groups and counseling for the families of rape victims or for their partners, and these are proving to be a success. You may find it less embarrassing to talk to others in the same situation as you than to go for individual help, and it can be reassuring to find out how similar your feelings are to those of other men.

An additional problem that may come up for you is if the woman goes through a period of hating men, often an intrinsic part of her reaction to the rape. Angela said matter-of-factly, "For a while I hated Clark and I hated men." Larry found this with Claire, too.

> All the men Claire had been with came in for tough criticism, and I found that hard to take. And it was hard for me, too, because the rape made her examine our relationship with our parents, and a lot of the things she was mad at were male things—and I'm not unique.

Penny also found that she came to resent the men she knew after her rape.

> I don't know why, but I expected in some way that they should have protected me. There's a big feminist thing about how women shouldn't be protected or want to be, but I don't think we can look after ourselves all the time. I don't think a woman should walk around by herself at night in a city. I think we have a right to some protection. It gets men in a bind. We get mad at them for protecting us because that's not feminist and it's condescending, and we get mad at them for *not* protecting us because that's not considerate.

If the woman you are close to expresses a lot of hatred toward men, the best you can do is try to show her that not all men are bad by being gentle and considerate yourself. Also, for your own sake, don't take her vindictiveness too personally. She is perfectly justified in hating the rapist and other violent men, and in hating the aspects of our society that make rapists, but that doesn't mean she hates you.

PROBLEMS PARTNERS FACE

> When you are raped, it happens to your husband, too. At first I wasn't ready for this. I felt, "This is *my* experience." But it was just as important to him.

As the woman quoted above pointed out, the lover or husband of a rape victim goes through trauma, too. Many partners develop the same kinds of symptoms as the victim—nightmares, phobias, rage, guilt, self-blame, self-hate, fear. You need comfort, but she can't give it to you for a long time and she may even resent your needing it. At times, it's hard not to blame her for getting you into this mess. Clark described some of the feelings he went through after Angela was raped. They might sound familiar to you.

> When I first got to Angela, I felt I had to be responsible. I felt, "Here I am, The Boyfriend, and it's up to me to comfort her, to take over here." Once I got there, the police left, so I had to take over their responsibility, too. I saw my role as very paternal, but I was scared.
>
> A few days after the rape she told me in detail what had happened. It was agony to listen to. I could picture it vividly and it made me feel disgusted. I'd think about Angela being attacked by this guy in a stocking mask with a knife who forced her to undergo prolonged misery, and I'd think about this strange guy "making love" to a woman I was involved with. He said horrible things to her, and he held a knife and said he'd cut her. I'd feel her fear whenever I thought about it—the incredible fear of not knowing if her life was going to end the next moment. He could have slit her throat. I'd get involuntary shakes just thinking about it.
>
> For the first two weeks after it, she kept everything suppressed. It seemed like a long two weeks. The rape was there in the air, it was ever present, a pall. The times we could laugh and forget it were very few. She had nightmares a lot and would wake up in a panic, and I'd hold her and say, "It's all right." She was nervous, in a quiet panic all the time, and that concerned me. After two weeks without

an outburst, I felt she was repressing her reaction and it wasn't healthy, but I didn't know what to do to help her express it. I didn't want to bring it up and retraumatize her. That added to my anxiety.

And when I was apart from her, images of the rape would just creep into my mind involuntarily. I'd feel shaky again and I remember thinking I shouldn't dwell on it. I thought I should repress it like Angela was doing.

Then when she did finally let it out, it wasn't what I expected. She expressed it in anger rather than by crying. She started hurling profanities at me at the top of her lungs. She was looking at me with real hate in her eyes. It wasn't pleasant to go through, but I knew she was really mad at the rapist, not me. I was thinking, "This is good." I don't think I said a thing.

But I didn't talk about it. People didn't seem to want to hear about it, so I didn't bring it up, even though I wanted to.

Another man expressed the tortuous self-blame that so many partners of rape victims feel. "It makes me wonder if I loved her enough. I was just fooling around at home and I should have been with her. She was waiting for me when it happened."[12]

You are also likely to be plagued with thoughts of jealousy and betrayal, as Don was.

I'd lie in bed and get in a sweat of anger and not be able to sleep. I kept thinking another man got through that barrier. It wasn't that she'd been sullied, but that my territory had been invaded. And I'd find myself wondering, "Was he better than me?"

Such thoughts are common in the lovers and husbands of rape victims. Even if you are relatively well-informed about rape, you may have deep-seated convictions about "your woman" as property or territory. Also, no matter how much you are assured that rape is primarily violent, not sexual, there still remains the fact that the rapist forced the woman to have sex. It's hard not to feel, somewhere inside, that she has been unfaithful. As one man put it:

I began to have fantasies about the rape scene. I pictured them in all sorts of positions. I found myself wondering if she could have enjoyed it, if she had an orgasm. I couldn't stop thinking about it and was very embarrassed and ashamed.

These sorts of thoughts can cause you to feel a lot of guilt. You know on one level that she couldn't possibly have enjoyed the rape—she was terrorized. You also know that she wasn't being unfaithful, because she had no choice in the matter. Yet you still can't get these thoughts out of your head. You want to set your mind at rest, but if you ask her if she enjoyed it, if she had an orgasm, you are going to hurt her deeply. She will feel that you have betrayed *her* because you will have betrayed your lack of understanding of what she went through. Being asked if she enjoyed it is as ludicrous as being asked if she enjoyed a car accident.

The best cure for these sorts of anxieties, which stem from the myths that have been drummed into you all your life, is to inform yourself about rape. Read the introduction to this book and *Against Our Will: Men, Women and Rape* by Susan Brownmiller (New York: Bantam Books, 1975), go to films, watch television programs about it, and discuss it with people. If you still have nagging questions about what actually happened to her during the rape and how she responded to it, wait until she has recovered enough to handle such questions. Eventually, an open discussion about it might do you both good, but not until she is ready not to feel blamed. If you try to bring up all your anxieties too soon, you might get a reaction like Mary's to Don: "If I expressed too much feeling about the rape, Mary would say, 'What's it to you? What do you know about it?' "

PROBLEMS WITH SEX

In addition to all the issues mentioned above is the tricky one of sex. As the sexual partner of someone who has been raped, you are the most important person to her recovery—you are the one who can help her regain her trust of men and her pleasure in sex. Yet you are also in the most fraught relationship with her; you are constantly wondering, "Will she ever want or enjoy sex again?" and "Does she associate me with the rapist?" Clark wrestled with these worries:

> One time we were making love, and she said, "Don't do it like that. That's the way *he* did it." That hurt me. First I felt, "Ah, I blew it, oh God," and I felt guilty. Then the guilt turned into, "How was I supposed to know?" What I did came from love. The rapist acted from hate. I felt angry at being associated with him. But she said it accusingly. It made me worry about whether we'd ever have a healthy sex life again.

Sex is a delicate subject between most couples at the best of times. Many people don't like to talk about it much; they prefer to leave it to natural impulse. But when sex has been violated by rape and has become associated with pain and terror instead of pleasure, the problems can be tremendously complicated. You, for example, are probably going to want to resume sex before she does. You want to be reassured that the two of you can still make love enjoyably, you want to get back to normal, and you want to regain the relationship you had before. Yet you might be afraid to bring up the subject with her because you don't want her to think you are pressuring her. Or talking about your sex life might mean talking about your fears for your relationship, and you can't face bringing those into the open. What is more, you may feel bad about even wanting sex with her, as if by doing so you are acting like the rapist. It is only too easy to get into mires of confusion about all these things.

Such problems are not, however, insurmountable. In a study of four hundred rape victims, Becker found that the 40 percent who did *not* have sexual problems as a result of the rape had these two factors in common: First, the victim abstained from sex until she was ready for it. Second, these same victims had *partners who said, "I am still interested in you, I still desire you, but let's take things at your own pace."*[13]

The importance of letting your lover know that you still find her desirable without pressuring her cannot be overemphasized. She is in a quandary; on the one hand, she may not be ready for sex—the thought still horrifies and frightens her—and on the other, she is afraid that the rape has made you no longer desire her. This ambivalence puts you in a bind. If you leave her alone, she gets hurt because she thinks you are rejecting her. If you make advances, she gets frightened and angry. It's enough to put you both off sex forever.

The only way to sort out this tangle is to talk. You cannot rely on nonverbal signals alone, because the rape has made things too complicated and distorted. Tell her that you still find her attractive, that you still want to make love to her, but that you understand if she doesn't want to yet. Remember that your desire for her doesn't make you resemble the rapist; he didn't want sex, he wanted to dominate and humiliate. He wasn't concerned with the loving kind of sex you want. And remember that her reluctance to make love is not a rejection of you but a reaction to the rape. Tell her that you are ready when she is.

Not all women are put off sex by rape, and by about one and a half months after it, some are even ready to start making love again. Studies have found that sometimes both partners are ready to resume sex by this time but are afraid to try.[14] The only way to surmount this is to talk about it and approach it gradually and gently. Clark thought he did this with Angela, but even with the best of intentions, he still made mistakes.

> Starting to make love again was out of the question for the first few weeks. I did desire her, but I didn't even want to broach the subject, because she was still healing. Then as our lives began to at least superficially go back to the old way, I began to think about it. Should I bring it up? Was it too soon? Should we talk about it? Should I initiate sex and see how she reacted? Finally, we talked about it in bed and she was willing to try, but she quickly got tense and panicky, so we just held each other instead. The next time we got further, and after a few weeks we did get back to where we were before.

Clark tried his best here but was held back by his fear of bringing up the subject. When he did finally do it, they were already in bed, in a sexual situation, and this made it harder for Angela to say how she really felt without hurting him. Angela recalled:

> I was very worried about being pregnant from the rape, and when I realized I wasn't, I felt relief, and that's when we started having sex again. It was okay, but the position the rapist used or anything that reminded me of him would make me move away suddenly and want to change. Clark wanted to make love again because he was eager to get back to normal, for me to be my old self. But I wasn't able to feel normal yet.

Rape does not have to force you, as a couple, apart. Some people are brought closer together by tragedy and even sex can be better as a result of this closeness. But sometimes rape does have a detrimental effect on your sex life. If you are in a relationship you wish to preserve and your sex life has deteriorated markedly since the rape, it is worth seeking therapy as a couple.

No matter how stable their relationship is, most couples go through a difficult period after a rape. Traumas of any kind shake relationships to their foundations, and if there is already a weakness there, they sometimes exaggerate that weakness to the breaking point. Various studies report a 40–90 percent breakup rate between couples after a rape. No one knows the exact numbers because many rape victims are young and in nonpermanent relationships anyway.[15] But when sexual or communication problems already exist between a couple, or when there is an imbalance of power, rape will bring these problems out.

On the other hand, a strong and loving relationship will usually survive rape and what's more will help the woman recover faster than any other single factor. Angela and Clark broke up after the rape, but they were only twenty-two when it happened, an age when maintaining a relationship is always difficult. For other couples who have been together for some time, handling the tragedy may be easier. Don said:

> Our two friends who were raped stayed in their marriages. It's four years afterward and they're still together. Both women were thirty or older when it happened and had some sense of why they were in the world. And they had good, stable marriages.

If you, as the lover or husband of a rape victim, show her love and care, reassure her that you find her desirable and try not to push her around, you will help her lose her distrust of men and sex relatively quickly. But boss her, blame her for the rape, or make her feel guilty for what happened, and her recovery may be seriously delayed. Above all, don't force her to have sex. If you do, you are becoming a rapist yourself.

Long-term Help

As the weeks and months pass by after the rape, you begin to get exhausted. You have given and given, yet she still gets upset, she still acts strange, and she still demands sympathy, by her actions if not her words. It is very hard on you to keep on giving without reward and it is not surprising if sometimes the strain bursts out of you, as it did with Larry at his sister. Claire said:

> When I told Larry that I didn't want our parents to know about the rape, he turned around and shouted, "Get the fuck out of my life!" I went and started packing. He was devastated that he said that, but

it was too much for him, bearing all the burden. I didn't realize it at the time, but he needed our parents to take some of it, too.

Larry explained how he was feeling:

> Claire talked about the rape all the time, and it was impossible to shut her up. It became a bit much for me after a while. But I felt that no way could I get near the experience except by being a sounding board for her. I wanted to help but I didn't know how. And she felt my impatience with it all. After the rape she came to live with me and my fiancée for two or three months, and the apartment got very claustrophobic. I found myself wanting her to shut up about it and be a good guest.

Your impatience with her isn't just selfishness—you may well be panicking inside about why she doesn't seem to be getting better. You want everything to get back to normal for her sake as well as yours. And then sometimes you begin to feel suspicious of her. Is she just manipulating you with her need for patience and sympathy? Is she using this tragedy to get out of normal responsibilities? Is she simply not *trying* hard enough to get better?

Try to bear in mind that recovery takes time. She wants to get back to normal, too, even more than you, because the fears that are worrying to you are terrifying to her. She is always wondering if she will ever be her old self again, always asking herself, "Will I ever feel all right?"

Another reason you are impatient is that you are probably getting over the trauma of rape faster than she is. Studies have indicated that people close to a rape victim go through the same stages of reactions as she does, but faster.[16] This can mean, sadly, that you and she are out of sync. Just as she is slowly passing out of her initial horrors and getting back to a semblance of normal life, you are beginning to be able to forget about the rape for hours at a time. You may even be ready to laugh and joke about it. Claire said this was true for Larry.

> My brother called me on the phone once and disguised his voice to make it sound seductive and said, "Well, helloooo there." I was terrified. I thought it might be the rapist or some other maniac. I shouted at him, "Don't you *ever* do that again! You don't know what it's like being a woman living alone!" He was real taken aback and apologetic. But little things like that still set me off.

A further difficulty might be her increased dependence on you, especially if she was independent before. This neediness can make you angry at her and then guilty about your anger, and can quickly get to the point of fights or, worse, an ever increasing silence between you. Clark said this is what happened to him and Angela.

> Before the rape I'd been making efforts to encourage Angela to be more independent and self-confident because I was feeling burdened by her need of me. Then after the rape, we had to revert, and suddenly I had to take care of her. I didn't feel any resentment at first, but four or five months later I wanted to go on a trip and she didn't want me to leave town. That was one of the reasons we broke up in the end.

Angela's analysis of what happened between them was somewhat different.

> Clark had always led a charmed existence. He couldn't understand the bad luck I'd had and how low it can get you. As soon as he bought the ticket for that trip, I moved out to a place with two male roommates, so I'd feel safe. I couldn't be alone that summer and he was leaving me. I don't think I would have done what he did, and other people I know wouldn't either.
>
> After he came back, we saw each other intermittently for a couple of months, but we fought over money and all sorts of things. I'd always been the supportive one before and that had changed. The rape led directly to our breakup.

PROBLEMS FRIENDS FACE

There are many, many women who never tell their families that they were raped and so have to turn to friends for their only support. For you, too, the burden of being the confidant of a rape victim can get to be hard to bear after a few months, and if you show impatience, the victim doesn't forget. Several victims said they got wounding reactions from friends:

> I told one guy I was dating about it and I never heard from him again.

> I had many friends who just disappeared.

> One friend said to me, "It happened two years ago, forget it!" I felt
> so bad my voice went funny.
>
> You know, rape victims spend a lot of time just trying to understand
> why the people around them say what they say.

For women friends of the victim, giving support might be especially
difficult because the rape is so directly threatening. It reminds you of
how easily you could be victimized, as if you'd been standing next to a
person who suddenly got shot. That realization can make you want to
defend yourself instead of help your friend. Rachel remembered:

> A woman friend told me that *she* would have been able to resist.
> She said *she* would have been suspicious from the start. She made
> me feel dumb and that just added to my guilt.

Claire had a similar story to tell:

> I had friends who'd go, "Oh yes," and quickly change the subject
> whenever I brought it up. They had the attitude, "It's a terrible
> thing, let's not talk about it anymore." And they were embarrassed
> to hear the details.

You also might find that your friend's rape brings back the memory
of an assault you experienced, perhaps one you had buried long ago. All
of a sudden, you find yourself dealing with your own delayed reactions
on top of hers. Essentially, both of you are going through what therapists call the "rape trauma syndrome" at the same time, which makes
it hard for you to offer your friend help. You can use this common
experience to bring you closer together, however, if you work at it:
you'll have to talk about it, give each other books to read, discuss how
to fight it or even try seeking therapy together. It won't be easy, but at
least you know that you are not alone. Carolyn Craven, a television
reporter, had an experience like this when she was raped in California
by a rapist known as Stinky. She ran home to seek comfort from her
elderly mother only to hear her mother confess that she, too, had been
raped twenty years earlier and had never told a soul. Craven was terribly upset to hear this, yet also comforted, for it meant that her mother
knew just what she had been through.[17]

The women interviewed for this book suggested these ways that you,
as a friend, can help.

• Call every Friday night to see if she's okay and has something to do that weekend.

• Keep asking her how she's feeling, even if the rape was long ago.

• Don't overdo the cheery, bedside manner, pushing her to act "normal." She doesn't need to be rushed.

• Don't treat her like an invalid.

• Show her you understand that the rape can still be with her years later and that you are still willing to help.

• Offer her rides at night or take taxis with her. Make sure the car waits when she is dropped off until she is safe inside. Don't make her ask you for this or make a big fuss about it.

• Understand that sometimes she can't face socializing and might want to change plans at the last minute.

• Don't make her feel guilty if she neglects you for a time.

All of this may sound like a lot to ask, but it isn't really. A few phone calls, a little listening, taking the initiative, and considering her fears is all it boils down to—not that much after all.

4
Prosecuting

If you have reported your rape and pressed charges, you should know that your chances of actually being needed at a trial are slim. Only a small proportion of rapists are caught, identified, and arrested, and only a few of those get all the way to court.[1] There are many stages in between when the case might be dismissed because of legal technicalities or because the defendant pleads guilty to another charge that does not involve you. Also, you might not be needed even when your rapist is put on trial if the prosecutor charges him with other, easier-to-prove crimes. But if your rapist is brought to trial and you are called as a witness, take heart. Nowadays, a rapist's chances of being convicted are quite good; in some areas, such as New York County, the conviction rate is claimed to be as high as 90 percent.[2]

Why Bother?

Many women fear having to go through a trial as a rape victim, with reason. You may be treated with indifference by the district attorney or whoever is handling your case, and callousness by the defense attorney, the one who is representing the rapist. You may have to relive much of the rape during the trial. You'll have to see the rapist again and cope with the terror of that. And you may go through all of that only to see the rapist go free or get off with an insultingly light sentence. Some women, after it's all over, say they wish they had never gone through the trial at all.[3] That is why when someone asks, "Why bother?" it is hard to give a firm answer. No one can promise that prosecuting will be a pleasant or even rewarding experience.

On the other hand, the laws are changing these days in favor of the rape victim. There are also more women attorneys, more enlightened men and women in the law and on the bench, and a wider understanding of rape. Prosecuting can give you satisfaction, for it can provide validation that you have indeed been the victim of a horrible crime. The prosecutor wouldn't even take your case to trial unless he or she believed you and believed that the accused man did it. Prosecuting can also offer you a constructive direction in which to channel your anger and give you the relief of knowing you've done all you can to stop the rapist from harming anyone else.

To help yourself make an informed decision on whether to prosecute your assault, try looking into the legal situation in your area. Contact a rape crisis center and ask about how other cases have gone, about the court's attitude and the specific laws about rape cases in your state. See if the center can put you in touch with other women who have been through a trial, and talk to them. Sit in on a trial, not necessarily a rape trial, to get a feeling for how the procedure goes and how your district attorney's office works. And don't be afraid to ask your prosecutor, district attorney, or any legal advocates working in their office for information, too. If there are no victims' services in your area to help you with this, or the information you get is not satisfactory, you can contact the National Organization for Victims' Assistance (NOVA), which will put you in contact with help in your area or give you suggestions. (See "Resources," Part Three.)

If, after you have made these investigations, you decide that pressing charges and going to trial is not worth your while and that you will only go through more agony for an uncertain outcome, accept that decision with pride. Only you can know how much you have suffered already and only you have the right to decide how much more suffering you can put up with. One young woman, Kathy (who will appear in Chapter 8) explained her reasons for not pressing charges:

> I was raped by someone I went off with willingly. I was buying drugs from him and I went with him, even though I knew I shouldn't. I don't think I'd have a chance with that in court, so I decided not to press charges. If he'd jumped me out of the blue, that would have been different. But I think I did the right thing.

If you do decide to help with the prosecution, you should be proud of yourself. You may go through much pain only to see him get off free.

But should the rapist be convicted, you not only will have brought him to justice for what he did to you, you will have protected other women from being raped by him. Some women say that having persevered through a successful trial has left them feeling relieved and cleansed of the rape.

The Procedures

If you report, your rapist is caught, and you decide to press charges, these are the stages of the criminal procedure you can expect.[4] (These procedures may differ somewhat if the rapist is a juvenile.)

FILING THE REPORT

Reporting your rape is discussed in detail under "The Police" in Chapter 2. *Remember to take the case number and name of the detective assigned to you when you first report the assault.* You may keep getting assigned different police personnel, which is frustrating, so you want to be able to contact your original detective if you see the rapist again or find other clues. You will need the case number for filing for insurance or victims' compensation (see the end of Chapter 2).

Reporting can be made unpleasant in two ways: having to describe the rape in detail to strangers over and over again, and having unsympathetic police or hospital personnel. If you are treated badly by any of these people, report it to their agencies. You have a right to complain. Otherwise, reporting can be satisfying because you are doing something active to fight the rapist. You are also showing that you consider yourself a survivor, not someone who provoked the crime or is ashamed of it.

MUG SHOTS AND THE COMPOSITE PICTURE

If you were raped by a stranger, you will be asked to go through photographs of likely suspects to see if you recognize your assailant. If you don't see him, you may be assigned to a police artist who will, with your help, make up a composite picture of him. Looking through mug shots may be unpleasant for you, especially if you live in a large city and find yourself faced with rooms full of files packed with pictures of criminals. You won't, however, necessarily be expected to do this the minute you first report the rape. Rachel went through both these procedures.

> When the detective on my case asked me to look at mug shots, I had to go through this whole room full of them, but I didn't see the guy who raped me. He was very distinctive because he had high cheekbones and a shaved head. Then I went over it with a police artist who did a composite. He drew the face so well it was uncanny. It was lucky this was two weeks after the rape, when I'd calmed down a bit, because I was really shocked. The picture was so good I said, "Do you know him?" and the friend I was with said I turned white. The artist had just got the expression in the guy's eyes so well. They Xeroxed the picture and put it in patrol cars around the precinct.

VIEWING A LINEUP

When a suspect is arrested, you will be asked to view a selection of men to see if you can identify your assailant. The lineup will be held at either the police station or the district attorney's office. The men won't be able to see you because you will be looking at them through a one-way mirror—on your side it looks like a clear window, on their side it is a mirror they cannot see through. This procedure can be frightening. When Claire was called in to the police station for a lineup, she was not only shaken at the possibility of seeing her rapist again but offended because the police had a *Playboy* centerfold pinned to the wall. But a lineup can also result in triumph. If the rapist is there and you can identify him, it means he is caught! If the rapist is there, seeing him again may retrigger some of the reactions to rape described in Chapter 1, so bring a friend along when you go to look at mug shots or a lineup—you'll need the comfort.

Recognizing your rapist is not always easy. He may have blindfolded you, stayed behind you, or worn a disguise. Sometimes, though, you will have a strong physical reaction to one of the men that may reveal him as a suspect even if you don't recognize him. Other times you will never be sure, and the nagging doubt can be agonizing.

WHO HANDLES YOUR CASE

Rape, like all crimes, is considered a crime against "the people of the state," not just against you personally, so you will officially be only a witness. Theoretically, you can therefore be subpoenaed to testify before or at the trial and you can be charged with having disobeyed a court order if you don't comply. (Rape victims are hardly ever subpoenaed because everyone knows that a reluctant witness can be worse than no witness at all.) It also means that you cannot choose who will represent your case—usually the assistant district attorney does it. The advantage of this system is that it will cost you nothing to have the rapist prosecuted, except in missed worked, travel to the courts, and angst.

Nowadays, the people who prosecute rapists are not so likely to be myth-ridden males who don't understand rape. In New York, for example, there are assistant district attorneys who are trained to deal sensitively with rape victims. Any state that has a sex crimes division in its district attorney's office will probably provide you with an advocate to help you through the procedures. And many areas have special victims' assistance programs. Ask at your district attorney's office to be connected to such a program and look in "Resources" at the back of this book. If there isn't a program near you, try a rape crisis center instead.

INTERVIEW WITH THE PROSECUTOR

Once the case has gone to the prosecutor, you will meet him or her for an interview. You will be asked for the story of your rape in detail and told what to expect through the various stages of legal proceedings. If you have a sympathetic prosecutor, you will probably find this reassuring—after all, the prosecutor is on your side. Rachel was pleased with her interview:

> The assistant district attorney who interviewed me was nice. She coached me through my story and told me to dress like the student I was and not to wear anything sexy. This was for the pretrial hearing, and she assured me I wouldn't be cross-examined.

The main purpose of this interview is to help you get your story straight and consistent. It's very easy to get flustered in a courtroom and start forgetting simple things such as how old you are.

The prosecutor then decides how to proceed with the case. There might be a preliminary hearing or the case might go directly to a grand jury, depending on legal and factual variables as well as on the procedure for your particular state and county. The case must always be prosecuted in the county where the rape occurred.

PRELIMINARY HEARING

If a preliminary hearing is to be held, you will have to be present to testify. The case will be held in front of a criminal court judge or magistrate and you may be cross-examined by the defense. Your assailant and his lawyer will be present, as well as anyone else who wishes, for the hearing is open. Because of this, you should have someone you know with you for support—a relative, friend, rape counselor, or advocate.

The purpose of this hearing is to establish that there are reasonable grounds to believe that a crime has been committed and that the defendant is connected to the crime. At the end of the hearing the judge will decide whether the case should be treated as a felony or a misdemeanor, or whether the charges should just be dismissed. If the case is a felony, it will go to a grand jury. If it is a misdemeanor, it will go to a criminal court.

THE GRAND JURY

The grand jury hearing is actually less frightening than the preliminary hearing, although it sounds worse. For a start, it is a closed proceeding, which means that no one from the public can be present. (Most rape trials are fairly unattended except for the people involved and perhaps some student lawyers, unless you live in a small town or your case was in the newspapers.) Most important, the assailant and his lawyer will not be there, nor will a judge. You will not be cross-examined, either. The people present will be the prosecutor, who will question you about the assault in the way you will have already rehearsed; a court reporter to record the testimony; and the grand jurors, between sixteen and twenty-three people. You cannot bring a friend or advocate into the court with you at this time, but such a person can wait outside for you. Rachel said:

> The grand jury hearing seemed full of people to me, but it wasn't bad. All that happened was that I came in, told my story, and left. I looked at the people and they seemed to believe me. I didn't feel doubted at all.

The grand jury then votes on whether to formally charge the assailant with a felony offense, to return the case to the criminal court to be handled as a misdemeanor, or to dismiss the charges. If the jury decides to make the case a misdemeanor charge, which means a lesser sex crime with a lesser penalty than rape in the first degree, this is no reflection on your credibility. It has to do with how the evidence stacks up and the kinds of legal strategies the attorneys are contemplating. Make sure your prosecutor gives you an explanation of why this decision was reached.

If the case is dismissed, you'll probably feel angry, frustrated, and betrayed. Again, make sure you get an explanation from the prosecutor.

If the defendant is in jail, the preliminary hearing and the grand jury hearing must take place within four to ten days of his arrest, depending on the state, but if he is out on bail or was remanded, the waiting period can be longer. And if he is indicted by the grand jury, which means formally accused of the crime, there can be a long delay before the case comes to trial. It can be months. The prosecutor should keep you informed of the case's progress and let you know if you are needed for any of the pretrial hearings. If you haven't heard any news from the prosecutor for a while, call and ask. This period can be frustrating because the case is hanging over you all the time you are working at recovering.

PRETRIAL HEARINGS

These are held one to two weeks before the actual trial and have more to do with the defendant than you. All defendants in criminal cases are allowed to make pretrial motions about the legal aspects of the case, and some of these will require hearings. You usually will not be needed to testify. An exception to this might be if, for example, a lineup identification was done before the defendant was arrested and you are required to testify about this in court. The issue at hand is not whether you identified the man correctly but whether the police conducted the lineup correctly. If they did, the evidence can then be used in court. A pretrial hearing won't be the ordeal for you that a trial can be, but the defendant will be there and it will be conducted in front of a judge. No jury will be present.

After the pretrial hearings, if there are any, the rapist can give his plea. If he pleads guilty, he will be sentenced by the judge and you won't have to see him again unless you want to attend the sentencing. But if he pleads not guilty, you will be needed at the trial unless plea bargaining results in disposing of the case without you.

PLEA BARGAINING

Plea bargaining can take place anytime after the defendant is indicted and can happen for several reasons. Sometimes if you tell the prosecutor that you don't want to testify at the trial, the prosecutor may negotiate a plea that will get the rapist locked up but will spare you the ordeal. For example, if the rapist is accused of other crimes at the same time, the prosecutor might agree to drop your sexual assault case in exchange for the defendant's plea of guilty to some other charge. Another example is that the prosecutor decides the evidence for your case is not strong enough to win a charge of rape in the first degree. He or she therefore agrees to accept a plea of guilty to a lesser charge rather than risk losing the case altogether. Some cases result in the defendant's pleading guilty to the original crime charged, which means that you won't ever be needed to testify. More often, however, the defendant will plead guilty to a crime other than rape and the rape charge will be dropped. Even if he ends up getting sentenced for the same amount of time, this can be upsetting for a rape victim because the rape does not go down on the assailant's record. Make sure you get an explanation from the prosecutor of why a plea bargain took place and what the result is.

A note about evidence: It is infuriating to see a man you know to be guilty get off because the jury does not believe the evidence of one witness to be compelling enough to convict. In order to be sentenced for any crime from larceny to murder, the defendant must be found guilty *beyond a reasonable doubt.* In a recent New Jersey case of gang rape, for example, the men were acquitted because their victims had been at another house before meeting up with them. Although there was medical evidence that the two victims had had sex, and they claimed rape, nobody could prove satisfactorily that they hadn't had sex before they met the defendants. Almost everywhere now, your word is all the evidence needed to charge rape, but evidence to support your word can be hard to find. Sometimes the methods of getting such evidence are called into question so that the evidence can't be used at trial. Problems such as these might make you feel as if the legal system is letting you down. Try to remember that the law has stiff requirements designed to protect the innocent and that it isn't aimed at destroying your dignity. As John Adams put it in the days of the Boston Massacre:

> We find in the rules laid down by the greatest English judges, who have been the brightest of mankind, [that] we are to look upon it as more beneficial that many guilty persons should escape unpunished than one innocent person should suffer. The reason is because it is of more importance to [the] community that innocence should be protected than it is that guilt should be punished. . . .[5]

On the other hand, nobody can really declare that the law is perfect; there is indeed a great deal of room for improvement in the legal approach to rape.

THE CRIMINAL COURT

If it has been decided at the preliminary hearing or the grand jury hearing that your case must be treated as a misdemeanor, it will go to the criminal court rather than a court of higher jurisdiction. The case will still be handled by a state or county prosecutor, often the same one you've had up until now, and you may still be required to testify in court. The charge will be less severe and the sentence milder, but the procedure about the same.

THE TRIAL

The actual trial before a jury may not happen until months or even a year or two after the rape. This delay is mainly a result of overcrowded courts and a backlog of cases, but it can make you miserable. Often the case comes to trial just as you are feeling able to put the rape behind you, and research has found that going through a trial can make a victim experience all the symptoms of rape trauma over again—nightmares, sleeplessness, depression, and fear (see Chapter 1).[6] For this reason you'll need all the support you can get from your family, friends, rape counselor or advocate.

Your role at the trial will be that of witness, which means that you will probably have to take the stand and be cross-examined by the defense. How unpleasant this is depends on the factors of your case and the personalities of the attorneys involved, but it's never pleasant. In some states now a woman is protected from having her lifestyle and sexual experience dragged into court in a rape trial unless she is currently supporting herself as a prostitute or knows the assailant and he claims a prior relationship with her. If she knows the assailant, she can still only be questioned about her relations with him, not anyone else. In other states, however, the victim's character still seems to be more on trial than the rapist's. To find out how well your privacy will be protected in court, call your local rape crisis center or district attorney's office. The policy on protecting victims depends more on the informal practice of your local court system than on any legal statutes about it. But even when the defense is not legally allowed to question you about your prior sexual experience or lifestyle, they often do. Massachusetts law protects rape victims in this way, for example, but that didn't stop the defense attorneys from questioning the victim of the New Bedford "barroom rape" about her private life.[7] And defense attorneys are expert at making it seem as if you invited or consented to the rape. If, for example, you knew the assailant before, the defense will probably try to claim that you consented to have sex with the rapist and then changed your mind and cried rape. Or they will try to make you look like a "bad woman" whose word is not to be believed. If you didn't know him before, the defense will probably try to confuse and mislead you about whether you have identified the right man. Either way it will be infuriating. The American Bar Association's magazine *Student Lawyer* printed an example of the type of cross-examination a rape victim is likely to get from a defense attorney, only, to show how unfair it can be, they made it of a robbery victim instead:

> "Mr. Smith, you were held up at gunpoint on the corner of First and Main?"
> "Yes."
> "Did you struggle with the robber?"
> "No."
> "Why not?"
> "He was armed."

"Then you made a conscious decision to comply with his demands rather than resist?"

"Yes."

"Did you scream? Cry out?"

"No. I was afraid."

"I see. Have you ever been held up before?"

"No."

"Have you ever given money away?"

"Yes, of course."

"And you did so willingly?"

"What are you getting at?"

"Well, let's put it like this, Mr. Smith. You've given away money in the past. In fact, you have quite a reputation for philanthropy. How can we be sure you weren't contriving to have your money taken by force?"

"Listen, if I wanted . . ."

"Never mind. What time did the holdup take place?"

"About 11:00 P.M."

"You were out on the street at 11:00 P.M.? Doing what?"

"Just walking."

"Just walking? You know it's dangerous being out on the street late at night. Weren't you aware that you could have been held up?"

"I hadn't thought about it."

"What were you wearing?"

"Let's see . . . a suit. Yes, a suit."

"An expensive suit?"

"Well, yes. I'm a successful lawyer, you know."

"In other words, Mr. Smith, you were walking around the streets late at night in a suit that practically advertised the fact that you might be a good target for some easy money, isn't that so? I mean, if we didn't know better, Mr. Smith, we might even think that you were asking for this to happen, mightn't we?"[8]

And of course, a robbery victim would never be asked such suggestive questions. Only a victim of rape is expected to prove that she didn't ask to be victimized.

Someone working for the defense or a private investigator hired by the defendant may approach you outside of the courtroom and try to ask you questions. He might even come to your home. The best way to handle this intrusion is to refuse to talk to him. You could be tricked into revealing something that could be used to discredit you. If anyone does approach you for this purpose, always ask for clear identification, if he won't give it or you feel at all uncomfortable about him, refuse to talk to him or say you'll get back to him later, when you've had time to think. If you have a lawyer, you could say that you won't talk except in that lawyer's presence.

If anyone from the defense contacts you, tell the prosecutor.

Your assailant and his friends and family might try to harass you before, during, or after the trial as well. When you become a witness at a trial your name and address go on public record, so if the assailant doesn't already know where you live he may be able to find out. *If he harasses you in any way, tell the police and the prosecutor right away and move or stay with a friend until you feel safe.* When you tell the police, ask for the officer who originally arrested the assailant or the detective who was first put on your case. If your assailant is harassing you, he is doing something illegal and could be arrested again.

Before you are called to testify at the trial, the prosecutor will talk to you about what to expect and what to say. Again, bring someone with you to the trial. There is no need to go through this alone, and it is reassuring to look at someone you know while you are on the witness stand and to have someone hold your hand while you wait. Indeed, while you are testifying, look at your friend, prosecutor, or a juror who seems sympathetic rather than at the assailant, for watching him may make you feel scared. He will be there in the courtroom trying to look as respectable as he can, and he might even have his wife, mother, girlfriend, or even his children with him to add to his credibility. If you stare at them too much, your confidence will be undermined.

As you testify, don't be afraid to show emotion. Cases are actually lost because the rape victim has been so numbed by repeatedly telling her story that she appears cold and indifferent. And don't feel ashamed, either. The person who should be ashamed is the rapist, not you.

SENTENCING

If the rapist is found guilty, his sentence will be given at a separate occasion from the trial. In some states now, you, as the victim, have an opportunity to influence the judge's decision on what sentence to give the rapist. You do this by writing a Victim Impact Statement, which is given to the judge before he pronounces the sentence. In this statement you write a clear account of the ways the rape has affected your life—any physical difficulties you have had as a result of it, problems with work, emotional traumas, financial setbacks. Writing a Victim Impact Statement can be most satisfying, for it allows you to have a direct influence on how the rapist is punished. Ask the prosecutor for your case, or the legal advocates, whether a Victim Impact Statement is allowed in your area.

You do not have to be present during the sentencing if you don't want, but the prosecutor should let you know what the sentence was. Some prosecutors are more considerate than others about keeping you informed, so if you don't hear, call up and ask. You have a right to know. The sentence for rape differs from state to state and depends on what sort of rape the assailant was found guilty of. In some states the maximum sentence is only a few years, in others it is life. The sentence also depends on the number of crimes he is convicted of at the time, his age, and his record.

If the defendant is found not guilty, the case is over. The decision may be hard for you if you know he is the man who raped you and yet the evidence wasn't enough to convince the jury—you feel humiliated by the trial, betrayed by the law, and probably scared that he might come after you for revenge. But at least you've done what you can. The record for successfully convicting rapists is improving in most states now, but there are always the ones that go free. If you think that the law in your state is unfair to rape victims, you can lobby to change it. Contact NOVA to find out how to do this.

APPEALS

The defendant might try to appeal his sentence after conviction. You have nothing to do with the proceedings at this point, but you still have a right to be informed about what is going on.

CIVIL SUITS

If you are unhappy with the outcome of the legal proceedings or you want compensation for loss of money and health, you can file a civil suit against the assailant for the damages he has caused you. You can do this at any time before, during, or after the criminal proceedings. You may also sue the owner of the premises where the assault happened, such as the landlord of your building, if his negligence in some way contributed to the assault. He may not have locks on the front door, for example.

You need your own attorney to file a civil suit, but if you can't afford one, you can go to a municipal, justice or small claims court, where suits over smaller amounts of money are handled without attorneys. Unlike in the criminal proceedings, when the assailant had to be proven guilty "beyond a reasonable doubt," a civil suit only requires a "preponderance of evidence" for you to win your claim, meaning that the guilt of the accused is not relevant unless you are suing him. To find out how to file, where to get help doing it, and the likelihood of success for your case, call your local victims' services agency or victims' assistance program, a legal aid office, a rape crisis center, or NOVA.

WHEN THE RAPIST IS RELEASED

You have a right to know when your rapist is up for parole and when he is due to be released from prison. In some places you can write to his parole board to give them your opinion of whether he should be released and on what conditions. Ask the prosecutor for your case or the legal advocates you worked with to keep you informed of the assailant's status and whether the parole board would be receptive to your letters. A letter like this should be similar to the Victim Impact Statement. It should describe the practical and emotional effects the assailant has had on your life. The parole board will then be able to consider your side of the story when they are deciding the assailant's fate. Also, the letter will go in the assailant's file and follow him throughout his criminal career.

How Others Can Help

During prosecution the support of others can be of great practical use to a victim of rape. If you are her friend, or a member of her family, you will be needed to provide both concrete and emotional help. Take time off work to go to court with her, let her stay with you during the trial if she's afraid, or if the rapist or his family knows where she lives and is harassing her. And remember that the trial might cause her to reexperience some of the trauma she went through right after the rape. Also, try to support her in whatever decision she wants to make about whether to pursue the prosecution. One woman's mother refused to speak to her for weeks because the woman had been unable to talk during the trial, so she had her mother's scorn to deal with on top of her own guilt. Other families become furious at the victim when she goes to trial because they blame her for the unwanted publicity that results or for "dragging" their name into the mud. She needs you more than ever during this time—don't turn your back on her.

If you are very close to the victim, you might find the court proceedings almost as upsetting as she does. As the husband of one victim said during the trial:

> It's just not fair. We are ruined. Our lifestyle has been totally disrupted. It's just not fair. These people get into courtrooms and just get free. If they let him off, I'll kill him myself.[9]

Anger like this is especially common among victims and their friends after a rape anyway, but it can get worse when the trial is going against the victim. Sometimes you, as someone close to the victim, might find yourself turning your anger and frustration on her and blaming her for the rape all over again. Blaming her will only double the ordeal of the trial for her. Try instead to think about how brave she is being going through this. That way you will be able to choose whether you would rather be like the friend or the husband in this scene of a trial described by Holmstrom and Burgess.

> Upset after testifying, the victim sat down between her husband and a friend. The victim bent over, put her head on her arms, and leaned over across her friend's lap for comfort and stayed that way for several minutes. The husband sat rigid and mute. He kept his hands crossed and did not reach out to touch her or to say anything to her.[10]

PART TWO

RECOVERY FOR SPECIAL GROUPS

Introduction

Young single women are not the only people who get raped. Wives, men, the elderly and the handicapped, teenagers, lesbians, and gay men are victimized, too. Yet it is harder for these people to find the sympathy and help they need. No one wants to hear about the rape of a man, a wife, a lesbian, or a grandmother, and few people know how to help even if they are willing to try. Part Two of this book contains chapters for each of these groups that deal with the special difficulties and prejudices they must overcome to recover from a sexual assault.

Each chapter will follow the stories of individual victims. Carol Coady, a victim of wife rape, tells of her experience and escape in Chapter 5; the story of George, who was brutally raped by a man, is told in Chapter 6; Mabel and Ann, two women raped in their sixties, give their advice in Chapter 7; Kathy talks of her recovery from being raped at age seventeen, and Denise and Shelley describe their feelings as the mothers of two young rape victims in Chapter 8; and Lara explains what it was like when her lover was raped in Chapter 9 for "Lesbians and Gay Men."

Whether you are a man, woman, or child, your reactions and needs after a sexual assault will be basically the same, so the chapters in Part Two are only intended as supplements to Part One. Although Part One is addressed to women, it applies to everyone. Each chapter in Part Two also addresses the victim's friends and families in sections entitled "How Others Can Help."

Finally, it must be said that one of the largest groups of sexual assault victims, if not the very largest—children—are not included in this book. This omission is intentional. The subject is so vast that it can only be dealt with in a book to itself. Some issues that apply to children are covered in the chapter for teenagers, but for a full treatment of the subject please see *Your Children Should Know* by Flora Colao and Tamar Hosansky (Indianapolis: Bobbs-Merrill, 1983) or *The Silent Children* by Linda Tschirhart Sanford (New York: McGraw-Hill, 1980), books aimed primarily at parents, showing them how to teach their children to avoid assault, how to cope with incest, and how to help children recover, and *No More Secrets for Me* by Orlee Wachter (Boston: Little, Brown, 1983), a book for the children themselves.

5

Rape by Husbands

> We were having a fight in the kitchen. He got furious and began
> pushing me around. He shoved me down on the floor and pushed
> my face up against the dishwasher. Then he raped me. Our six-year-
> old daughter was standing there the whole time.

The woman who said this is petite and self-possessed. As she talked, she
was getting dressed after a self-defense class she had taken with her
daughter. Helping the tiny, wide-eyed girl into her coat, she said that
she'd just left her husband because of his abuse. "The police can take
care of him now."

This woman is not as unusual as some might think. There has been
so much talk these past few years about how abused women stay with
their husbands that no one hears about the women who try to escape.
But, according to Diana Russell, author of *Rape in Marriage*, most
women do try to stop rape by their husbands from recurring, and many
succeed.[1] This chapter is for any woman who has been raped by her
husband, ex-husband, or lover, and for her friends and family. Hope-
fully, it will help all of you stop the rapes.

Wife Rape: A Definition

Within a relationship like marriage, there can be confusion between
what is unwanted sex and what is rape. Many a woman will attest to
having had sex with her partner when she didn't want to out of fear of
displeasing or hurting him, of wrecking the marriage, or simply because
she has learned that sex happens when he wants it and her desires are

irrelevant.* Some women feel violated by such experiences and some do not. In her book, Russell quotes two women who described unwanted sex that they didn't like but didn't consider rape.

> Many times I didn't feel like having sex but I did it. With a husband, you feel forced. I have an obligation to my husband which is very bad. It's always been a man's world.[2]

> When I'm sleeping I don't want to be bothered. He didn't force me but if I didn't want it, he'd do it anyhow. I didn't enjoy it. I'd just say "go ahead, but I'm not in the mood."[3]

For other women rape by their husbands is quite clear, for it hardly differs from rape by strangers. Husbands use weapons less often than strangers, but they do use them.[4] Court records show cases where husbands have used guns, knives, tools, and other dangerous objects to force sex and various tortures upon their wives.[5] A case in Pennsylvania involving a separated husband and wife illustrates this.

> He entered her car at a stop sign, pulled out a large butcher knife and forced her to drive to his apartment, where he raped her. He threatened to cut out her insides, to burn her mother's house down and to kill her and her new boyfriend.[6]

Husbands also use other kinds of violence to force sex on their wives, although they tend to be less violent than strangers, perhaps because their wives resist less. Sometimes the violence is a beating, sometimes only pushing and pinning the wife down. Some husbands force sex on their wives by threatening to look elsewhere for it, or to kill, maim, or hurt them or their children.[7]

> It was just like rape. He forced himself on me. . . . One time he came home after he had been out drinking and he wanted to go to bed with me and we had a fight about it. He started hitting on me and finally I stopped fighting. He had sex with me and then went to sleep.[8]

---

* A woman in this situation needs to reassess the pattern of her relationship with her partner, as does the man. Sexual therapy for both of them could be useful if they cannot change things themselves. Read *For Yourself: The Fulfillment of Female Sexuality* by Lonnie Garfield Barbach (New York: New American Library, Signet, 1975).

It was like a rape except I was on the same bed. It doesn't give you much enjoyment. He was more physically strong than I, and I was his wife, so he did it.[9]

As far as recovering is concerned, how wife rape is defined is really up to you, the victim. If you feel forced to have any kind of sex by your husband, whether that force is physical or emotional, this chapter is for you, regardless of how anyone else might define what happens between you. What matters is that rape within marriage is as horrible and degrading as rape outside of it. You deserve as much sympathy as a rape victim who is jumped on the street.

Because of the traditional concept of marriage—that a woman gives her body to a man forever—many people think that there is no such thing as rape within marriage. This belief is reflected in the law, for rape by husbands is only a crime in twenty states at the time of this writing.† In the remaining thirty states rape is defined as "the forcible penetration of the body of a woman, not the wife of the perpetrator."[11] In several states wife rape is not even a crime when the husband and wife are separated.[12] The law's bias against wives is reflected on the federal level, too. The U.S. Department of Justice, for example, defines rape as "unlawful sexual intercourse with a female, by force or without legal or factual consent."[13] The words "unlawful sexual intercourse" and "without legal consent" leave plenty of room for husbands to rape their wives without reprisal. The law says, loud and clear, that once a woman has said yes to a man, she can never say no. Because of this, even if you know that you were forced to have sex against your will, you might feel that it was somehow your husband's right to do that to you.

Rape within a marriage, or within any sexual relationship outside of marriage, is such a matter of shame for women that very few will ever admit it happens or agree to talk about it. A noble exception to this is Carol Coady, a thirty-one-year-old businesswoman who was regularly beaten up by her husband for five years and then raped by him twelve times before she escaped. She now counsels other women having similar experiences, and she agreed to let her real name be used here.

† These states are: Arkansas, California, Connecticut, Florida, Georgia, Illinois, Iowa, Kansas, Massachusetts, Minnesota, Mississippi, Nebraska, New Hampshire, New Jersey, North Dakota, Oregon, Virginia, Washington, Wisconsin, and Wyoming.[10]

Coady said that the first thing every woman who has been raped by her husband must do is face up to what has happened.

> If the man has always called the shots for sex, it's easy to tell yourself that the rape was just another sex incident. You have to get rid of that notion. *You have to realize that when you got married, you did it for love, not violence.*

A lot of women, Coady said, tend to hold on to their marriage vows as an excuse for not facing the fact that their marriage has gone terribly wrong. They tell themselves that they agreed to stick by their husbands "for better or for worse" and that therefore they must never leave. But once your husband has hit you, let alone raped you, he has broken those marriage vows—that promise to love and honor you—himself.

Other women promise themselves that their husbands will change for the better and stop the abuse. Or they believe they must stick it out for the sake of the children. Some women think that forced sex in marriage is simply the norm and that there is nothing they can do about it.

Being able to recognize marital rape for what it is may involve changing your attitude toward yourself and your role as a wife. You need to recognize that you are not a piece of property that belongs to your husband, despite what the laws tell you. No person belongs to anyone anymore—the days of slavery are over. Every woman has a right to her own body and her own sexuality, and no one in the world should be allowed to violate that—it is your basic right as a human being. You also need to recognize that your husband's raping you does not signify that you are a failure as a wife. The introduction to this book discusses how society sees rape victims as failures: they are thought of as failures because they "failed" to protect themselves against an attack. Society sees the victims of rape or battery by husbands as even worse failures because people believe that wives wouldn't be mistreated unless they provoked or deserved it. People also have the attitude, "You made your bed, now lie in it," which makes them unwilling to sympathize. You may be regarding yourself as a failure, too, perhaps without realizing it. Think about your own explanations for why this is happening to you. Do you feel that you are a bad wife, that you've been doing everything wrong and so in some way deserve the rapes? Do you think that if you were a better wife—more loving, more sexy, a better cook, better looking, more competent, etc.—your husband wouldn't be driven to abuse you? Do you believe you deserve the abuse because you "chose" the man who's doing it? Or do you feel that you just don't deserve anything better? Do you believe that leaving him would be an admission that your marriage has failed and therefore that you have failed? Many women who are abused by their husbands feel one or more of these things because, like rape victims in general, they have been taught to blame themselves. What is more, many of the abusing husbands tell their wives that the abuse is their fault. "You aren't doing your wifely duty!" "You never act sexy!" "You always push me away when I want sex!" they shout in justification for "punishing" you. Yet no matter how well you obeyed him, dressed up, or acted sexy, he would only find another excuse to rape you. The reason he is doing it lies within him, not you. It is *his* problem that makes him do it, not your inadequacy.

You may also feel less of a failure if you know how common wife rape is. Russell found in her study of 930 randomly selected women in San Francisco that *one in seven* of those who had ever been married had been raped by their husbands or ex-husbands, and she was defining rape in the most conservative, legal way.[14] Russell estimates that this count is way below the actual numbers, because the survey was done before wife rape became an issue in the press as a result of the Greta and John Rideout trial in Oregon. So the women Russell surveyed had no example to encourage them to admit their husbands had raped them. Another study of four hundred women in Florida, by Louie Andrews and Dianne Patrick of Florida State University, found that one in six say their husbands force them to have intercourse against their will.[15] Some researchers believe that wife rape is by far the most widespread kind of rape of all, occurring twice as often as rape by strangers.[16] So, even if you feel like an unlucky freak because your husband has raped you, you are not alone. Your experience, alas, is not even that unusual.

Why Men Do It

The reasons men rape their wives are not well understood, so explanations tend to be speculative. Indeed, there may be as many reasons men rape their wives as there are men who do it, but these are some theories about their motivations:[17]

• Your husband doesn't see you as a person with a right to say no to sex. He believes the traditional idea of wife belonging to husband, so he thinks sex can occur whenever he wants, regardless of your desires. He does not see women as his equals or as people who have as much choice over their sex life as he does. Nor is he the kind of man who only enjoys sex when he knows his partner desires him as much as he does her. John Rideout, accused of raping his wife Greta, expressed this too. "You're my wife, you do what I want."[18]

• Your husband does recognize your right to say no, but he wants to steal that right from you in order to punish or dominate you. He is willing to stoop low enough to hurt you even in the delicate and sensitive realm of your sexuality.

• Your husband makes you into a symbol of something he hates and wants to get back at. His love is so incomplete that he is able to dehumanize you into a mere symbol.

• Your husband is angry at you, perhaps at all women, and rape is his revenge. Unlike some men, he cannot be at ease with women or like them.

• Your husband is threatened by you—your intelligence, perhaps, or your independence from him, so he wants to get back on top by dominating you. He thinks that raping you will prove that he is boss, that he is superior. Such was the case for Coady. Her husband was so threatened by her superior intelligence and education that he had to resort to beating, then raping, her to restore what he saw as the proper balance between them. A man like this doesn't realize that the most rewarding kind of relationship is one that allows friendship, companionship, and an equal give and take.

• Your husband believes, perhaps fantasizes, that you are interested in other men, so he wants to repossess you by raping you. He doesn't see that women are more than their sexuality and that they cannot be possessed by anyone, especially not through violence. He doesn't know that the strongest bonds between people are love and trust.

• He believes that you deny him sex all the time and that he therefore has a right to take it by force. He is not concerned with helping you want sex with him, with pleasing you sexually. He cares only about his own wants.

• He is unable to separate sex from violence and finds violent sex the most exciting kind of sex. He is either emotionally disturbed or so much the product of society's conditioning that his humaneness has been driven out of him. If sadism is the only form of sex that excites him, he should find a partner willing to play his games and should not victimize you against your will.

• He thinks that getting sex all the time is the only proof of his manhood, regardless of how he gets it. So he feels compelled to take it whether you want him to or not. He is so unsure of himself that he doesn't believe he has anything to offer you as a lover, or, indeed, to offer anyone. He can only take.

• He can't tell the difference between sex and affection. Getting sex means getting love to him, so if you deny him sex, he thinks you are denying him love—so he takes it. Raping you, he believes, is his defense against being rejected by you. He doesn't understand that love involves much more than sex, and that you can't take love anyway— you have to win it.

Many of these motivations are intertwined and most are probably much more complex than is possible to go into here. The subject deserves a book to itself.

Why Women Marry Them

Why women marry and then stay with men who abuse them is a complicated question. The popular and incorrect answer is that such women are masochistic, that they like a man to dominate and beat them, they find it sexy. This unfortunate attitude is reflected in many popular songs, especially in the blues and in country and western. One song recorded by Louis Armstrong, for instance, is titled "You've Got To Beat Me To Keep Me."[19]

Some women and men are genuinely masochistic, but they usually choose a mutually gratifying relationship to fulfill this need. Their sexual activity is not considered rape, as it is not against their will. The punishment-loving woman is a convenient myth for our man-dominated society, as it justifies all sorts of abuse of women, but there aren't many women who buy it. Women know that they don't like to be hurt physically or emotionally any more than a man does, especially by people they love. This is what makes wife rape so particularly painful. When a stranger rapes you, it is easier to feel outraged, to hate him, and to get sympathy from other people. But when someone you are supposed to love and who is supposed to love you rapes you, it is much more confusing. You have been betrayed by someone you hoped to trust, and yet it seems no one wants to hear about it or even to take it seriously.

Coady believes that women accept an abusive husband because they have never learned to recognize that they don't deserve such treatment. Most of her battered and raped clients come from homes where they were abused in some way, where they got the message that they are worthless. Coady said:

> This was true for me. I was never physically abused but I was verbally. I was always being told that I was no good. I felt so worthless that I needed someone to love me desperately, and when this guy came along and was nice to me, I thought I'd found that person. I built up a fantasy about how nice he was that had nothing to do with reality.

As children, Coady said, such women had no way of avoiding or escaping the abuse. They were helpless, trapped in their homes with their abusive parents or guardians, and because they knew no other way of life, they assumed abuse was normal. When they grow up, this assumption continues and they accept their husband's abuse in the same way—they see it as inevitable, as the norm. Coady also said that some women are so starved for love that they interpret any kind of attention, even violent attention, as a kind of love. That is why, she said, it is ludicrous when people say you "asked for it" when your husband hurts you. You no more asked for abuse as an adult than you did as a child. If you end up with man after man who abuses you, as many women do, it is not because you want it. It is because you are unconsciously repeating the same pattern you learned in childhood: you mistake attention for love, you need love, and so you are afraid to lose it by escaping.

Women who marry men who rape but don't beat them, a common pattern in wife rape, may have somewhat different reasons for staying than battered wives. They may not, for example, recognize the rape as abuse, for reasons explained above. Or they may feel so guilty for not wanting or liking sex with their husbands that they don't feel they have a right to object to his rapes. But there are practical reasons women stay, too, and these are equally, if not more, important. They are also likely to be out of a woman's control, so even if she is perfectly aware of what her husband is doing to her and how much she needs to escape, she still may be trapped. These are typical reasons why women don't leave, some of which you may recognize as true for you:

• You have no money because he controls it all, or because there is none, so you have no means to escape with.

• Wherever you go, he can go, too. And if he finds you, he will hurt you more than ever before.

• You have nowhere to go for help. Your friends have drifted away because of him, your family doesn't want to know, and everyone else regards your husband as your problem.

• You can't turn to anyone because either you are too ashamed to tell them your husband rapes you, or they wouldn't believe it anyway. Or, even worse, they would think it's his right.

• You have children and no means to look after them if you take them away, and nowhere to take them anyway.

• Your husband has threatened to take the children out of school if you leave, and have revenge on them. Or he has threatened to hurt your parents or someone else you love.

• Your husband has told you that he'll rape your daughter if you don't give him sex when he wants.

• When you try to turn to the law or government agencies for help, you find yourself ignored or ridiculed. One woman who called the police for help was told by them that her husband was her problem and that she had no right to "inflict" him on the police.[20]

• Your husband lies so well that he turns people against you. One woman who ran away was brought back by the police because her husband told them that she was insane and had to be returned to his custody.[21] This sort of thing happens surprisingly often.

• No one believes your husband abuses you because he appears so gentle, kind, and educated, and he always hurts you when no one else is around. A woman with a husband like this went to counseling with him. She secretly told the counselor about her husband's abuse; then, over her desperate protests, the counselor insisted on telling her husband what she had said. The husband reacted with such sweet concern that the counselor was convinced that the wife was deluded. As soon as the couple got home, the husband severely beat his wife for telling on him. This husband managed so well to convince people that his wife was troubled that everybody she turned to for help ended up blaming her.[22]

A woman with an abusive husband is likely to have a combination of these problems, which can be a trap indeed.

How to Stop Rape by Husbands

The earlier you try to stop your husband from raping you, the more likely you are to succeed. In one third of the cases Russell looked at, rape had occurred only once in the marriage.[23] Sometimes after being raped once, the wife never again refused to have sex with her husband, but often rape occurred only once because she used a strategy early on that stopped the abuse. Here are some suggestions gleaned from Russell's cases and from Coady and her clients' experiences.

LEAVING THE MARRIAGE PERMANENTLY

In Russell's study 42 percent of the women ended the rapes by leaving their husbands for good.[24] Some of these women seemed to foresee that the violence would only get worse and that it was no use hoping the man would change for the better. One woman, who left her husband after he attacked her only once said:

> We were fighting, and I didn't want to have sex. He was almost on the verge of being a wife beater when I left him. He was trying to force me to stay. . . . He tried to force intercourse. He choked me, and tried to throw me downstairs.[25]

Another woman, who had less than a ninth-grade education and couldn't read, left her husband after his one bout of violence even though her options aside from marriage were not great.

> He was jealous because he believed what someone else told him— that I had gone to bed with this other guy. So he told me to suck his peter or he'd beat me up, and I wouldn't do it so he beat me up. He pulled a knife and a gun on me and said he was going to shoot my head off. I walked out and left him. He had no other chance.[26]

It is important to recognize that when a man gets away with hurting you once, he's likely to do it again, no matter what he promises or how remorseful he is. Leaving him, however, is easier said than done. It not only takes tremendous emotional strength, but it takes money. Russell found that economic independence and lack of self-blame were the two major factors that made women able to rescue themselves from their husband's rapes.[27] The Florida study confirmed the importance of economic independence—none of the women who independently earned thirty thousand dollars or more a year were abused, and as a woman's yearly income increased above eighty-five hundred dollars, the incidence of abuse decreased, regardless of the husband's income.[28]

Leaving your marriage can be so difficult that it resembles escaping from a besieged castle in wartime. Because of this it often takes careful advance planning, as Coady found out when she tried to leave her husband.

> He started beating me up in our second year of marriage. It got so bad that I became able to turn off the pain of being punched in the face and thrown against the wall. I was afraid to feel. You have to shut off because you can't cope with the physical and emotional pain at the same time. Being at home then was like being in the middle of guerilla warfare. That went on for five years.
>
> The first time he raped me, I knew he'd kill me soon. I had turned off my feelings for so long that I was numb, but the rape was so traumatic they broke through. I suddenly realized that I was tired of dying day by day. I decided I wanted to take the risk of dying all at once to escape.

It took Coady six weeks to plan her escape. She had to scrape some money together, find an apartment and fix it up to make it livable, all in secret.

> My husband said he'd kill me and our baby if I ever left without telling him, so I arranged for the movers to come just before he'd get home from work. Then I called the police on a pretext and phoned my husband to tell him I was leaving. I had it all fixed so that when he came home, the police and the movers would be there and he wouldn't dare hurt me. Also, I'd told him I was leaving, so he didn't have an excuse to kill us.

Coady's husband found out where she was living shortly afterward and tried to threaten her, but she told him the police knew about him and that he'd be in trouble. "That was a lie. I had to lie. If you go by the rules, the way the laws are now, you never get out. You have to trick the police and anyone else into helping you." He didn't hurt her again because, she says, he knew he no longer had power over her. Many husbands, however, will continue to track down and persecute their wives, so the wives have to keep escaping. "Now my husband is beating up his new wife," Coady says.

GOING TO A BATTERED WOMEN'S SHELTER

Because escaping a violent marriage can be so difficult and dangerous, you may need to turn to a battered women's shelter for protection. There are about eight hundred such shelters in the country, but they are in great demand. If you have an alternative place to run to, such as the home of a relative or friend, do, but never feel that you don't deserve the help of a shelter. Even if your husband has raped you without beating you up, you are entitled to the protection of a shelter, and if by any chance the people who run the shelter give you a hard time because they don't understand that rape is battery, tell them you are in fear for your body and your life. A shelter, however, is only a temporary solution. Most will only put you up for six days. But at least it gives you a respite in which to feel safe and plan your long-term escape.

To find out where a shelter is near you, call your local rape crisis or women's center, National Organization for Women (NOW) office, victims' services agency, or YWCA. If you can't find a place nearby this way, contact the organizations listed under "Shelters for Raped or Battered Wives" in "Resources" at the back of this book. If none of this yields anything, you can write to the National Clearinghouse on Marital Rape (address below) to find out where to go. Send them a stamped, self-addressed envelope and tell them where you live and what you need, so that they can refer you to an appropriate shelter near you. If you don't want your husband to know about this correspondence, give them the address of a friend, make sure the self-addressed envelope you send them looks as if it's from a friend, or get a post office box number. You can do this by going to a post office and paying a small fee. The address is:

> National Clearinghouse on Marital Rape (NCOMR)
> Women's History Research Center
> 2325 Oak St.
> Berkeley, CA 94708

Another reason to contact a battered women's shelter is to meet

other women in your situation. Their companionship can give you the
courage to face up to what is happening and to fight it.[29]

GOING TO A RAPE CRISIS CENTER

If there is no shelter you can get to, or if it is so booked up that there
is no room for you, you can still turn to a rape crisis center for help.
Counselors at the center may be able to find you a place to stay, but if
they can't, they can at least offer you advice, comfort, counseling, and
support. A counselor also might be able to help you plan a way of
escaping your marriage, or stopping the rapes. In states where marital
rape is a crime, the counselors can give you legal advice, connect you
with people to help you prosecute your husband, and tell you how to
get an order of protection to evict him from your home. There is more
about legal recourses under "Calling the Police" below.

As a victim of wife rape you may feel that you have no right to go to
a rape crisis center. Perhaps you think that such centers are only for
women who are raped by strangers and that your rape is your own,
private problem. This is not so. Rape crisis centers are just as much for
you as anyone else.

You may also be reluctant to seek help because you feel ashamed of
having chosen to be with a man who turned into a rapist. Even women
who have left husbands or boyfriends who abused them are ashamed to
seek help sometimes, because they are embarrassed at ever having been
with such a man. Try not to let worries about how other people will
regard you stop you from finding the help you need. Anyone who
understands rape, whether it be by strangers, husbands, or ex-husbands,
should know that you didn't choose the man because he was violent but
because you thought a love was possible.

If you want help in dealing with the emotional reactions to rape, a
rape crisis center will provide it.

LEAVING THE MARRIAGE TEMPORARILY

Some women frighten their husbands into stopping their violence by
leaving at the first sign of it but returning later. Perhaps they go to stay
with their parents, a sister, brother, or friend. The key to frightening
your husband successfully seems to be to take even the slightest sign of
violence seriously and to act on it. One woman in Russell's study went

to stay with her mother after her husband had kicked her. Another woman left after her husband had slapped her. Neither husband repeated the violence. These were, however, relatively minor acts compared to a beating or rape. Whether leaving a marriage temporarily will stop a man from raping you once he has done it is not so clear, but perhaps if he gets the message that what he has done is cruel and horrible and that you won't put up with it, he might change his behavior.

Coady told of a friend who threw her husband out of the house after he'd had a temper tantrum. He hadn't hurt her, but she saw the potential. She insisted that he get counseling before she agreed to take him back. He did, and ever since he has been perfectly gentle. Whether such a strategy will work for you depends on the kind of relationship you have with your husband and whether he really wants to stop being violent. Some husbands, unfortunately, become more violent and vengeful if you try to leave them.

MAKING THREATS

Sometimes threatening to leave, to fight back, or to call the police is enough to stop your husband's violence. In the case of rape, threatening to tell the family might work if it shames him. But you have to carry those threats through if necessary. Once he finds out your threats are empty, they won't be effective at all. Again, threats work best when the violence has only happened once, before a pattern sets in.

GETTING YOUR HUSBAND HELP

All the above strategies can be greatly helped if at the same time you get your husband to try counseling. He has to sincerely want to be helped for counseling to work, but if he does, your marriage may be salvageable. One of the women in Russell's study stopped her husband from raping her by getting him to stop drinking.

To find help for your husband you can call a rape crisis center for references, Alcoholics Anonymous, or a battered women's shelter. Check the back of this book as well for a list of services that counsel men who are violent to their wives or girlfriends.

Some husbands might promise to go for help and even do it, but inside, they resist. If your husband is reluctant, you'll soon find out and then you'll have to decide whether he's worth staying with.

TURNING TO YOUR FAMILY

Being able to summon a parent, brother, or other family member to help you is a great asset. Such a person can not only protect you but may be able to shame your husband into stopping his behavior. In several of Russell's cases the woman stopped her husband's violence in this way.

> We were separated. He came over and said we should get back together and try married life again. I said no. He shoved me, held my shoulder and tried to push me onto the bed. We wrestled back and forth, then he tried to attack me again. He pushed and shoved me, called me names, and was very rude. Again he tried to force me onto the bed, so I got a vase, hit him, and stunned him. Then I yelled for my brother. My husband left because he knew that my family was behind me. . . .[30]

FIGHTING BACK

Most wives who are raped are considerably smaller and lighter than their husbands,[31] so it is very hard for them to fight back effectively. What is more, many a woman who might be willing to smash a stranger over the head with a lamp won't do that to her husband or boyfriend no matter how much he is hurting her, either because she has to face him later or because she can't bear to harm him. But occasionally, a woman like the one quoted above will give as good as she gets, which lets her husband know that she won't submit to bullying or rape. Being able to fight back takes a great deal of assertiveness, however, something that many victims of rape have had frightened out of them. Still, if you get mad enough, fighting back or just resisting may be surprisingly successful, especially if your husband is used to your succumbing without resistance. Whether such a strategy is likely to end the rapes or just put you in more danger, only you can judge.

CALLING THE POLICE

The police are notoriously unhelpful about stopping domestic violence. For one thing, they are afraid—they believe the myth that up to 40 percent of police injuries happen on calls to stop domestic violence, a figure that Ann Jones points out in her book *Women Who Kill* has never been substantiated. In fact, studies have indicated that domestic quarrels cause very few police injuries indeed: Jones quotes one five-year study by Lieutenant James J. Fyfe of the New York City Police Department, who found that almost one third of the incidents in which police fired guns were robberies. Only 12 percent of the firings were connected with disputes of any kind, and those disputes included street-corner fights and barroom brawls as well as wife assault. Calls for robbery, burglary, traffic pursuits, and even suicide are more dangerous for police officers than calls for domestic quarrels.[32]

Another reason the police are reluctant to help is that many officers are of the same prejudiced frame of mind as the abusing husband and don't see much wrong with beating or raping one's wife.[33] Many don't believe that arresting a man helps the situation or even that he deserves to be arrested at all. But recent studies show that arresting the husband *significantly deters* his violence, *even after he is released.*[34] Calling the police is therefore an excellent idea. Not only will you be likely to sober your husband into not hurting you, but you might be lucky and get a policewoman, who is more likely to be sympathetic, or an enlightened policeman. And often the mere presence of the police, even if they don't do anything, is enough to intimidate or shock your husband into realizing what he is doing and stopping it.

In the states where wife rape is a crime (see the list at the beginning of this chapter), it is worth issuing a formal charge against your husband. Prosecution of husbands for wife rape is proving to be highly successful. In California, for instance, the conviction rate for marital rape is 75–80 percent. Nationwide, it is 60–70 percent, much higher than the conviction rate for rape in general, which, in some places, is only about 2 percent.[35] If you do charge your husband with rape, however, don't be surprised if the officials you turn to are initially uncooperative. Most people, including the police and hospital staff, don't keep up with the law enough to know whether wife rape is a crime in their state, so they assume it isn't. Don't be put off by their ignorance. Just make sure that you are treated the way any victim of rape should be—that a full report of the incident is taken by the police, that you get medical treatment, and that medical evidence of the rape is taken. (See "The Hospital" in Chapter 2 for a full description of what to expect from hospitals.) And even if there is no medical evidence, remember that you still have a right to charge rape.

In the majority of states rape by your husband is still not a crime, so you won't be able to get him arrested for rape. If your husband has beaten you or hurt you as well, however, you can charge him with assault. The laws on this differ from state to state, so call a rape crisis center, your local district attorney's office, or a women's center to find out your best strategy. If you don't have time, however, and need to call the police right away, you'll probably find out quickly enough how to charge him.

If there is nothing legal you can do about your husband raping you, except use it as grounds for divorce later on, you can still seek other kinds of help. You have a right to medical treatment and counseling, for example. You don't have to allow your husband to come along when you go to the hospital, and you don't have to say who assaulted you. Also, if you do decide to tell the police about it, then or later, you can ask a rape crisis counselor to accompany you for support. The best way to find help is to contact *both* a rape crisis center and a battered women's shelter. By doing this you are breaking your isolation, an important step toward stopping your husband's violence.

How to Recognize the Danger

There are several ways to recognize a potential wife abuser that are worth noting, especially if you've been through one such relationship and want to avoid another. The key to a nonabusive relationship is an equal balance of love and respect between the partners. The types of behavior listed below show a lack of love and respect, even if they don't mean that the man is 100 percent likely to end up beating or raping you. They are signs to be wary of.

• Has he ever forced sex on you? If a man has raped you or forced sexual acts on you in any way before you were married, he'll almost certainly do it again afterward. He has shown himself to be a man who doesn't care about your needs and desires, only about his. He won't improve.

• Does he seem especially to like sex when you don't? If so, he's a rapist.

• Does he want you to perform sex acts you don't like? Is he particularly fond of bondage or violence in sex? His tastes won't change with marriage, so get out of the relationship before his preferences turn to rape or torture.

• Has he ever threatened you with violence? If during a fight he has threatened to hit you, beat you, or rape you, he'll probably actually do it one day. If he has ever raised a fist to you but not actually hit you, the same applies.

• Does he like to end fights by having sex, even if you are not in the mood? This tactic is not his way of making up, it's his way of winning the fight—he has made you give in to him.

• Is he overpossessive and extremely jealous? Coady counseled a woman whose abusive boyfriend was so possessive that he would follow her around all day, embarrassing her in front of friends and workmates. Someone who is as obsessed by you as this is probably not stable. It may be flattering to be needed so much, but his need is unhealthily great. Such overpossessiveness can flare up into wild, groundless jealousy and quickly into violence.

• Does he have temper tantrums? There are appropriate and inappropriate ways to express anger. If he is angry at someone or something other than you, has no more control over his anger than a child, and takes it out on you, be warned. He is using you as a dumping ground for his fury. If he throws glasses or furniture around, beware. Someone with that little control over himself can be dangerous.

• Are you ever afraid of him? If so, ask yourself what this means for your future together.

• Does he bully you? Is he able to compromise over differences between you or does he always insist on having things his way? If he won't compromise, take it as a sign of his lack of maturity and his lack of respect for you.

• Has he been violent toward previous wives and girlfriends? If you know he has—and he will probably try to hide it—there is little hope that he'll improve with you.

• Does he drink too much and get violent when he's drunk? Drink is frequently associated with domestic violence, and a drunk person is virtually impossible to reason with. He may drink in order to abuse you.

• Does he attack people physically? It is one thing to fight back in self-defense, but if a man is prone to lose his temper and suddenly lash out at someone, he is not to be trusted. Even if you don't think he has hurt women, just other men, the potential is there. Again, it shows that he has an immature control over his temper.

• Has he ever hit or beaten you? Many women believe that once a man has married them, he will change and treat them with more respect. This is not true. If he hits you before you are married, he will certainly hit you afterward.

• Does he want to control your money? This is a serious factor, because the person who controls the money usually controls you. It is traditional for the man to own the money, even if the woman earns it, but for the sake of your self-respect and safety, this is a tradition worth changing. As Coady said:

> My husband controlled all our finances—I even gave him my paycheck. That meant we always had to do what he wanted. Even if I didn't want to do something, I felt I had to because he was paying.

Many women are afraid to say no to sex in case their husbands refuse to give them the money they need to eat and run the house. You can't begin to be equal to someone if you are financially beholden to them. If a man who is courting you wants to take over your money, don't let him. If he insists, claiming that this is his right as a man, perhaps this is not the guy to trust with your happiness.

• How do his parents behave? Take a look at his parents if you can and see if they are abusive to each other. How does his father treat his mother? Is his mother subdued and dominated by her husband and son? Is the father even around anymore, and, if not, what is the history of their separation? Also, look at how well they communicate. If the parents can't get through to each other, the son probably won't know how to communicate either and a relationship with him is likely to be difficult.

• Does he like violent pornography that makes you uncomfortable? This may be a sign that he will want to enact that pornography on you.

Helping Yourself Recover

As with all kinds of rape, recovering is a long and painful process. Read Chapters 1 and 2 of this book, for they apply to you, as a victim of rape by your husband, as much as to victims of rape by anyone else. And don't be afraid to seek counseling if you feel you need it. Counseling can help you get over some of the feelings of worthlessness and despair that rape by your husband may have caused in you.

When you seek a counselor or therapist, be picky. If you feel that you are being blamed, try someone else. Many people, even those who understand a lot about rape in general will tend to assume that it is your fault that you got a husband who mistreated you. You need a therapist who knows that it's not your fault, that you never "asked for it," no matter how much you think you did, and that you are struggling to get out of the whole nightmare. Ask at your nearest rape crisis center or women's center for an appropriate therapist or counselor.

How Others Can Help

If you are the friend or relative of a woman who is being abused by her husband, you can be a tremendous help to her. First, however, you must know certain things about wife rape.

• No husband has a right to abuse his wife, sexually or otherwise. Even though the laws in thirty states still reflect the attitude that a wife is the property of her husband, you must remember her rights as an independent human being.

• Wife rape is not an expression of love. Even if it happens because the wife doesn't want sex and the husband is frustrated, you should ask yourself *why* she doesn't want sex. One of the women in Russell's study hated sex with her first husband but liked it with someone else.

> I couldn't respond to him. I couldn't stand him to touch me. I went to a doctor about it. I had two children, so there must have been sex. But every time he touched me I felt like a snake climbing up at me. Then we divorced and I met my darling and for the first time I knew what sex and love were all about.[36]

This woman was only fifteen when she first had sex with her husband. Incompatibility between partners is not cured by rape, it's exacerbated.

• No woman ever deserves to be beaten or raped. No matter what you think she may have done—been a bad housekeeper, an irresponsible mother, been unfaithful or just a "bad wife"—she does not deserve to be physically abused. Abuse only increases her problems.

• It is not the wife's duty to put up with her husband's abuse for the sake of the marriage or of the children. She did not marry him for rape or battery. If she wants to protect her children, her best duty would be to rescue them from a rapist father.

• Wife abuse *is* your business. Many people feel that because the trouble is between a husband and wife, they should not interfere. But if a woman you know is being raped or beaten, she needs you to interfere. She is probably feeling trapped and alone. She needs a friend.

• An abused wife is not asking for it. It is too easy to dismiss a woman's suffering by assuming that she provokes her husband's violence and even wants it. But it's more likely that she is accepting it because she doesn't know how to stop it.

You can go a long way toward helping your friend or relative feel better by assuring her that you understand these things listed above and that you *don't blame her*. That assurance may be all she is willing to take from you, but if she needs to hide from her husband when he is in a rage, or if she needs help in leaving him, you can do much more. Take her in, if you can, or help her arrange somewhere safe to go. Can you lend her money or help her get some? You can also try contacting a rape crisis center, battered women's shelter, YWCA, or women's center for advice on how she can get help and what she can do. See "Resources" at the back of this book. If she wants to prosecute her husband, you may be able to support her as a witness if you have seen him hurt her or have seen bruises on her. If she has ever run to you distraught over his mistreatment, you can help her in court by relating that incident.

Another way you can help is to let her husband know that you think his behavior is despicable. If you are the woman's father or brother, such a message can be especially effective, as long as you aren't afraid of him yourself. Several men in Russell's study stopped abusing their wives after being threatened by their father or brothers-in-law. Sometimes a mere show of contempt or disgust for what he is doing is enough to shame him into stopping it. One of the husbands in Russell's study stopped his violence when his wife's mother kicked him out of the house. Whether this strategy will work depends on what sort of man your husband is, for some men are so dangerous that they beat or even kill their wives' relatives, too. You'll have to judge this for yourself.

Too many people are afraid to help a woman who is being abused by her husband, or are too lazy to bother. Don't let yourself hide behind excuses—you may be her only avenue of escape. Let her know that you care about her and that you don't consider her a failure. Let her know that you understand that she is a victim of her husband's failure to control his temper and his nastiness.

6

Men Get Raped, Too

George, a professional boxer in his late twenties, telephoned a rape counselor and said he needed help. He arrived uncombed, disheveled, and deeply depressed.

George is powerfully built, a snappy dresser, and proud of his machismo. He usually has several girlfriends at once and doesn't mind boasting about it. One day a friend arranged for George to meet a man about a business deal. George arrived at the plush apartment and was greeted by a man smaller and older than he— call the man Bob. Bob politely ushered George into the living room, sat him in a chair, and offered him a drink. George accepted.

Suddenly, Bob came up behind George, put one hand on the back of his head, and shoved a sharp knife at his throat with the other. Even though Bob had him in a fatal grip, George tried to struggle, but as soon as he raised an arm, Bob pressed the knife into his throat and cut him. Then Bob forced George to bend forward in the chair, tied his wrists to his ankles, and pushed him face forward onto the ground.

Bob undressed George and for the next two hours subjected him to all kinds of abuse, including sodomizing him, cutting him, and urinating on him while shouting, "How are you going to stop me doing this, faggot?" He repeatedly threatened to castrate and murder him. "I was sure he was going to kill me," George told the counselor, "and I kept thinking, what a humiliating way to go. I couldn't even fight him."

When the rapist finally let him go, George's humiliation was by no means over. For four hours he wandered the streets in a daze, noticing neither where he was going nor how cold he was without his coat. At one point he dropped in on a friend, sat around unhappily for a while and, unable to say anything, left. But finally, when

he realized that he was bleeding and in pain, he admitted himself to
the hospital.

When the doctor came in to the room where George was being
examined, the first thing he said was, "You look like you had a good
time." George leaped on him in a fury and had to be constrained.

A year later George was still calling his counselor once in a while
for help. He felt frightened much of the time, was having sexual
difficulties with women, and was still feeling deeply humiliated and
shamed.[1]

That men get raped, too, is a startling piece of news. People know it
happens in prisons, but out on the street? In the community? Many
refuse to believe it. That is why if it happens to you, you'll probably be
stunned. Women at least have always known about the danger of rape,
but most men don't think it is even possible for rape to happen to
them. When you become the victim of a crime you didn't even know
existed, it doubles the shock and makes you feel terribly alone. You
can't believe that anyone else has been through this. But many have.
Emergency rooms and rape crisis centers around the country are seeing
more and more men who have been raped by other men.[2] There are no
official statistics on male rape yet and very few services for its victims,
but the number of reported male victims has risen so sharply in recent
years that some researchers say men make up 7–10 percent of all rape
victims nationwide.[3] At the Sexual Assault Center in Seattle, Washington, for example, 10 percent of their patients are men.[4] Nevertheless,
most people still don't want to think about male rape—many of the
major magazines and newspapers have printed long pieces about the
rape of children but still haven't touched the rape of men.* It is time,
however, for male rape to be recognized, time to admit that rape is no
longer only a woman's problem but everybody's. And you, as a victim,
need to know this so that you don't feel like such a freak.

All rape is vastly underreported, and the rape of men is no exception.
The reasons men won't tell are easy to understand, for being raped does
not fit the masculine image. As Nicholas Groth, who has interviewed
many male rape victims and rapists for his book *Men Who Rape*, said,
"The two major aspects of manhood are strength and sexuality. When
a man's been raped, he's lost both." A male counselor put it another

---

* When I tried to publish an article on male rape in 1982, several publications that had
printed pieces on child rape wouldn't take it. "Too sordid," they said. It was eventually
published in *The Soho News*.[5]

way: " 'I was raped,' doesn't sound too good in the locker room—nor the boardroom or bedroom." And a victim said, "It's a humiliation to get beaten and an even greater disgrace to be used sexually."[6]

Being "used sexually" is, of course, humiliating for anyone, but for you, as a man, it also carries the weight of undermining your masculinity—your very identity—because of the popular assumption that a male rape victim must be effeminate, weak, gay, or all three. A *real* man, people tend to think, would have fought those perverts off. You may be thinking this, too, cursing yourself for your failure to "be a man" and fight your way out of it. Even the film *Deliverance*, one of the only popular movies to depict the rape of a man, contributed to the idea that real men don't get raped by portraying the victim as fat and unathletic. He was smug, too, and there was a strong hint that he somehow got what he deserved. The truth is, however, that any man, like any woman, can get raped, regardless of his size, strength, looks, personality, or sexual orientation. One of the victims Groth interviewed was six feet two inches tall and weigh 220 pounds. George had the build of a trained athlete. What counts is not what you are like, but the circumstances you get caught in.

Men get raped in exactly the same kinds of circumstances as women. It happens to them the most when they are alone in an isolated area, doing something like hitchhiking, swimming at the beach, or hiking in the woods, but it can also happen where they live and work.[7] One man in Groth's study was raped by his boss, who offered him a ride home because he was too drunk to drive himself. He fell asleep in the car and awoke to find his boss sodomizing him. Another was attacked by four men who picked him up hitchhiking. They forced him at knifepoint to perform oral sex on them. Two other men were simply jumped as they were walking down the street. Physical strength is not much help to you when you are outnumbered, held up at gunpoint, or surprised by a sudden, brutal attack, and often rapists use a combination of all these methods to entrap their victims. You did what you could to survive, and you succeeded—there is nothing unmasculine about that.

Male rape is so little understood that the people you turn to for help may treat you with the same kind of snickering disregard that women victims used to get, and still do in some places. Most people assume that a man can't be raped against his will and therefore that the victim must have wanted it. If he wanted it, they go on to think, that means he is gay. The police asked George several times if he was gay, a question that, for him, would have been insulting at any time, but was especially so in the light of his rape. In fact, over half of the male rape victims seen at crisis centers are heterosexual.[8] No one should ever ask you such a question, because your sexuality has no more to do with being raped than it would with being robbed.

If misunderstandings abound about male rape victims, making it hard for you to find sympathy, so do they about the whole concept of male rape. "Male rape? Oh, you mean *homosexual* rape," is the almost universal reaction when the subject comes up, and the people who say this do not usually mean the rape of man by another man, they mean rape by a gay man. They assume that any man who rapes other men is gay and therefore that he does it out of lust. They are making the usual mistake about rape, believing that rape is an outlet for an oversexed, frustrated man tempted beyond endurance by the sexiness of his victim. This assumption allows them to blame you for being a victim of rape by labeling you a tempter.

Groth and Daniel Lockwood, author of *Prison Sexual Violence,*[9] believe that men do not rape other men out of pent-up sexual desire. They do it out of the need to manipulate, punish, or degrade the victim, and for some reason they find picking on men even more satisfying than on women. As one man said, "Beating him up wasn't enough. If you rape him, you degrade his manhood too."[10]

What is more, male rapists are not necessarily gay at all. Of the twenty rapists Groth interviewed who had attacked men, ten of them didn't even care which gender they picked on and had raped women and children as well. Of the ten who had raped only men, some were bisexual, some gay, and some so mixed up that they were impossible to categorize. And all of the twenty men had regular sexual relationships going when they committed the rape, so frustration was not their problem. Even among child molesters, gays are in a small minority—one study found that 83 percent of a sample of child molesters were heterosexual and the rest were bisexual; there were no exclusively gay molesters at all.[11] A rapist's motivation is primarily to humiliate, hurt, and destroy, not to release a normal sexual drive. As one rapist said, "What was really exciting . . . was that all during the assault I felt in total control of him."[12] So any guilt you might feel about having attracted or tempted your assailant, even unwittingly, is misguided. He didn't act out of desire for you but out of the desire to hurt anyone he could happen to get. A man who had raped three men described what made him do it this way:

> . . . The more depressed I get, the more intense my sexual needs become, and the more aggressive my sexual fantasies get, and the thought of actually hurting someone becomes strong. In my fantasy, I'm blowing a guy who's not wanting it, not willing. His reaction is one of fear. He's afraid of me, and then I've got him under my control. . . . Then I hurt him—punch him, stab him, shoot him—whatever.[13]

If you can remember that you were a random victim of this kind of sick thinking, it will help you stop blaming yourself and it will help you resist the blame of others. The victim of a robbery is not told he asked for it, nor should you be.

Your Reactions

> I felt like vomiting—just vomiting—that is all. Like, my insides were destroyed and there was a great deal of pain.[14]

Once the horror of the actual assault is over, you still have to deal with your reactions to it. On the physical level alone this can be an ordeal. Not only may you be injured by the act of rape itself but by other forms of torture the rapist inflicted on you. One study suggested that male rape victims may be gang-raped and brutalized more often than female victims and that they are also held captive for longer.[15] Men have come to hospitals with whip marks, initials carved into their skin, and broken bones from such attacks. If you have been attacked like this, you need medical help.

On the psychological level your reactions to the rape may be even harder to deal with. One of the rare studies of men who were raped in the community, rather than in prison or another institution, found that they had the same reactions as women who are raped.[16] These are described in detail in Chapter 1, but, briefly, they are as follows:

Initially, you will probably feel numb and unable to believe that the rape even happened. You may be in shock, which will make you withdrawn, disoriented, and defensive. These reactions are so common that one doctor suggested in a medical paper that whenever a victim of a gang beating is seen acting sullen and withdrawn, he should be gently asked if he was sexually assaulted, too.[17]

You may have trouble sleeping for a while and be plagued with nightmares. You might also lose your appetite or find that you cannot swallow food without gagging. Your moods will fluctuate, and you might develop phobias for a time that may or may not be related to the rape. Above all, you will probably have to cope with a terrible fear, something that few men are used to. One male victim described this fear in a letter addressed to fellow victims and given out by St. Vincent's Rape Crisis Center in New York.

> I hated being afraid all the time. I didn't feel safe anywhere. I was always bracing for an attack, feeling like a target. I wondered how women live with such fear. How could they stand it? Did they look at me with the kind of terror I felt?

Flashbacks of the assault are likely to plague you for some time, too, and these can seriously disrupt your life. The letter continued:

> I thought about it all the time. In the middle of work, dinner, talking, I would blank out and remember. I tried to push it out. I worked extra hours, filled every minute, but it always came back. I was afraid I'd go crazy.

Another victim, this one in prison, expressed the same agony.

> I started thinking about it and I would get nauseated. I would feel like I had to puke up, but I never puked up. . . . Yeah, tears came to my eyes and stuff like that, but I don't talk about it to nobody. . . .[18]

Throughout these reactions you will probably feel a burning fury—at the rapist, of course, but at yourself, too, for having become a victim. And if you have had to deal with any police officers or hospital personnel who have treated you badly, no doubt you'll be furious at them as well. When George's counselor first saw him, George was like a subdued animal in a cage.

> In the first session he talked for an hour and a half nonstop without ever repeating himself. He let out streams of fury and veiled warnings. He made it clear that mistakes had been made with him and he didn't want any from me.

It is hard to know what to do with so much anger; you want to explode.

Perhaps the hardest reaction of all to cope with is your shame. The man who wrote the letter to other victims described his feelings.

> I was sure people knew or would find out. I was different. They could look at me and somehow see it on my face. I tried to hide all my feelings all the time so they wouldn't find out. I was so ashamed and completely alone.

You feel ashamed not only for the reasons discussed above—for having "failed" to resist an attack, for being the victim of a perverse assault, for having your masculinity degraded—but because you feel soiled. Your body has been invaded in a manner you may find disgusting, by a man you consider perverted. Because of this shame, many men won't even tell their lovers or closest friends about the rape. They are afraid of being seen as a total loss as a man. A victim of prison rape described such feelings when he said:

> I got a girl out there with a kid, and, like, I don't tell her nothing. She don't even know that this happened. . . . I was embarrassed. If I ever told her what happened, I don't know what would go through her mind . . . if I tell her, I am afraid that she is just going to pack up and leave and take the kid and go on their way.[19]

Another reason you might not want to tell even someone close to you is that you have been brought up never to admit to unhappiness, never to express insecurity, and never to allow yourself the emotional outlet you need at a time like this. This inability to open up is a problem for many male rape victims. When George told his story to his counselor, he found himself crying at times and would turn away in shame. The counselor said, "It's okay to cry. Burt Reynolds said one of the most important things he has to do as an actor is be able to cry. It's a necessary release."

If you never release your anxieties and never seek comfort or reassurance, rape can result in years of trauma. A counselor told of one man like this who called him one night and took twenty minutes to get around to asking for help.

> Harry had been raped by two men in their thirties when he was seventeen and had never told a soul for five years. Women didn't interest him anymore and he was scared to death of men. He couldn't bear sexuality in anyone, although before he had been a

normal, lusty adolescent and had liked women. After the rape he just sat at home watching television like a zombie, avoiding his family's questions about why he never went out.

To make it worse, Harry had been assaulted once before when he was only eight. He had frozen in terror that time, turning white and finding himself unable to utter a sound. Luckily, people came along and the man ran away. Whenever Harry saw the man in the neighborhood, he would feel paralyzed again. The rape rekindled all that childhood terror.

If Harry had not heard about the counseling service and worked up the courage to try it, he would have been terrified still.

All of these reactions, and the many more detailed in Chapter 1, are going to make you feel that you are going insane. In fact, you are just reacting normally to an extraordinarily horrible event.

YOUR SEXUALITY

The effect of rape on your sexuality varies. You might, like Harry, react by withdrawing from all sexual contact for a time. You aren't afraid of women the way female rape victims are afraid of men, but you have temporarily lost confidence in your sexual ability, perhaps because you feel so emasculated by the assault or perhaps because you simply can't stand the idea of anything to do with physical intimacy. You may even become impotent for a while, but don't panic if this happens—it is a normal reaction to a major trauma and anxiety in your life, and will pass. On the other hand, you may react by wanting to sleep with as many women as possible. One man told Groth that he was not even enjoying sleeping around so much but that he felt he needed to "score with women all the time" because he needed to assure himself of his sexuality.

You may be deeply worried that the rape has made you gay. Perhaps you think that the rapist was homosexual, and that you have therefore engaged in homosexual sex, even if unwillingly, which "turns" you gay. This worry may be particularly acute if you were brought to ejaculation by the assailant, something that rapists frequently do to their male victims. Rapists masturbate their victims as a way of further controlling and manipulating them. They also do it because it makes the victims so ashamed that they are less likely to report the assault. As one victim said, "I always thought a guy couldn't get a hard-on if he was scared.

When this guy took me off it really messed up my mind. I thought maybe something was wrong with me."[20]

There is no evidence at all that being sexually assaulted "turns" a man gay. Ejaculation can happen automatically and can be quite separate from desire. Forced masturbation, even when done by a man, has nothing to do with homosexuality.[21] You can't "turn" gay overnight, because homosexuality doesn't happen as a result of one experience. It is something that evolves within you over time. If you weren't gay before the assault, you won't be afterward.

If you already have some doubts about your sexual preference, a rape might bring these to the surface and you will probably have to work them out. One man who was outwardly heterosexual but inwardly unsure thought that he was being punished for this by being raped. "What did I do to bring it on?" he asked his counselor. "Was it the way I talk, walk, what I was wearing?" He was afraid to tell his girlfriend what had happened, so the relationship broke up, and it took several counseling sessions for him to finally admit that he was afraid the rape would make him gay. He was tremendously relieved that the counselor didn't scream "Faggot!" at him but instead said, "You're the one who decides whether you are gay, not the rapist."

These worries about homosexuality are often exacerbated because the rapist accused you of being gay. Rapists often do this to justify their own actions to themselves—"I'm raping him because he's gay; he's the pervert, not me" is roughly their reasoning. Some rapists cruise around in gangs purposely looking for gay men to beat up or rape. A lot of male rape is committed by groups of men who are out to prove their machismo to each other, and to do so they have to pretend they are punishing the victim for being gay. Whether he is or not is irrelevant. Any man walking alone or who is in a deserted place is vulnerable to such an attack. A heterosexual victim of gang rape like this was seen in the hospital badly hurt and shaken. He kept saying, "They thought I was gay, they thought I was gay. I thought I was going to die."

Rape by Women

A married man of thirty-seven was attacked by two women with a gun. They made him go into an abandoned building, undressed him and tied him up, then forced him to have oral sex and intercourse with them. Afterwards, they abused his genital and rectal areas until he fainted from the pain. For two and a half years after the attack, he was unable to have sex and became nauseated every time his wife approached him.[22]

Rape by women is, as far as anyone knows, extremely rare, but it does happen.[23] The motives of female rapists seem to be the same as those of male—to overpower, humiliate, and hurt—but the shame of the male victim tends to be stronger when he has been raped by women. After all, a man is always supposed to be willing to have sex with a woman, no matter what the circumstances, so what is he doing crying rape? But rape strips you of your dignity and puts you in fear for your life no matter who does it.

In Dallas, Texas, a man was kidnapped at gunpoint by two women who made him have sex with them in a parking lot.[24] A divorced truck driver of twenty-seven picked up a woman in a bar and went with her to a motel, where he fell asleep. When he awoke, he was tied to the bed, gagged, and blindfolded. For the next twenty-four hours, he was forced to have sex with four women, who held a knife to his testicles and threatened him every time he slowed down.[25] In Los Angeles a man picked up a woman in a bar who took him to the apartment of two women friends. They played strip poker, tricked him into being handcuffed, then sexually abused, taunted, and urinated on him.[26]

Weapons, it is often said, are the great equalizer, and when an assailant has a knife, a gun, or several friends to help, the sex of that assailant doesn't really matter. Children can be murderers and women can be rapists. The effect on the victim is the same.

Rape by women is commonly thought to be impossible because it is believed that once a man has an erection, he has desire—and intercourse with desire isn't rape. But studies are finding that a man can have an erection and even ejaculate without desire. In one of the only studies of men who were raped by women, sex therapists Philip M. Sarrel at Yale University and William H. Masters of the Masters and Johnson Institute found that all nineteen of the subjects had erections during the rape and six of them ejaculated.[27] They suggest that impotence is more likely to be caused by self-consciousness than fear. During a rape the fear of mutilation or death overpowers any self-consciousness about sexual performance, so the erection mechanism can work undisturbed. As explained in Chapter 1 (p. 30), it is also thought that fear, panic, anger, and even pain can cause the body to confuse its sexual reactions with its excitement reactions. Alfred Kinsey of the Kinsey Reports once suggested that fright, anger, and pain can trigger sexual excitement.[28]

Most men don't realize all this, however, so become convinced that their ability to get an erection during rape means that they are abnormal. This, added to all the traumatic reactions that everyone has to rape, can result in years of unhappiness if the man never seeks help. One of Sarrel and Masters' subjects couldn't have sex for four years after he was raped by a woman, another for nine years. Many male victims of women are boys and teenagers and they, too, can suffer deeply.

If you have been raped by a woman, you'll probably be reluctant to admit it to anyone. You may wonder if anyone would take you seriously. But you need the same help as any victim of sexual assault, and if you want to avoid the unhappiness of some of the victims mentioned above, you should not be afraid to seek it.

When You and Your Partner Are Both Assaulted

Sometimes both partners of a couple are sexually assaulted during an attack. Such an attack usually happens only when two or more men overpower you, perhaps in your home, perhaps by kidnapping you in a car. Sometimes assailants will tie a man up and rape the woman in front of him, and sometimes they will rape both of them in one way or another. Either way you, the man, are every bit as traumatized as you would be had you been a lone victim and perhaps even more so, because you've had to watch someone you love suffer as well as suffer yourself.

You might expect an experience like this to draw you closer together as a couple because you've shared the trauma, but this doesn't always happen. You may be feeling so ashamed, for instance, because you didn't manage to rescue the woman that you can barely face her. And she might be blaming you for that, too. Also, because you are both in crisis, it will be hard for either of you to give the other one support; there isn't a stable partner to act as caretaker. You will both be so immersed in your own pain and in such need of help that it will be hard to even contemplate each other's pain.

Joint counseling would be a good idea, but perhaps you should also consider seeking help individually. You should also be able to turn to different friends for help so that you can "spread the burden," as one victim put it. Eventually, you will be able to help each other, too, but that might not happen until you are in a later stage of recovery. If you find yourselves drifting apart, reading this book together may help, as would going to a counselor together. You may need someone else to help break down the barriers that are growing between you and to sort out the resentments.

How to Help Yourself

> When I see what these guys go through and what help they need, I
> feel really sorry for the ones who don't come in for help.
> —A male rape counselor

Trying to cope with rape on your own is an incredibly difficult if not impossible task. Rape is so unlike any experience you've ever had or expected to have that you have no knowledge of how to help yourself recover from it. Yet you owe it to yourself to try. These are some ways to help yourself, but please read Chapter 2 as well. It may be addressed to women, but it pertains to you too.

MEDICAL HELP

Part of surviving is taking care of yourself physically. You may be suffering from all kinds of wounds after a sexual assault, and you are in danger of having caught a venereal disease from the rapist. Go to a doctor, if you have one you trust, or to a hospital. Your wounds will need treatment to prevent infection, and you should be tested and treated for VD.

If you don't want to tell anyone what happened, that need not prevent you from seeking medical treatment. You don't have to explain anything. If you are lucky enough to get a doctor who seems sympathetic enough to tell, however, you could get a reference from him or her for further help. You can also ask if the hospital has a rape program attached to it—more and more of these programs are training counselors to help male victims.

REPORTING

Another way to help yourself is to report your rape, for even though this may not feel as good as fighting the rapist himself, it is a way of fighting back—and that can be satisfying. Telling the police, however, may be frustrating. Most police officers have a hard enough time dealing with female rape tactfully, let alone male rape. You don't have to report right away, although doing so helps your credibility. But it is better to do it late than not at all. Rapists tend to repeat their offenses, and the only way to stop them is to arrest them. George's counselor said that George's rapist was so practiced at rape that he must have done the same thing to at least fifty men before, and that he will probably do it to fifty more—he was never caught even though George knew where he lived. The police couldn't get enough evidence to justify arresting him. Even if your assailant is never caught either, your assault will go down on record and serve to remind everyone that this crime does happen and that it must be stopped.

THE LAW

Prosecuting your rapist can be a great help to your recovery, for it gives you a sense of fighting the rapist. The law about the rape of men differs from state to state. In many states, such as Oregon, rape is defined as a crime that can only happen to women. This definition of rape is true on a federal level, too.† If your assailant is caught, the prosecutor for your case would therefore have to charge sodomy, not rape. Sodomy in the first degree usually carries the same legal weight and penalties as rape in the first degree—the words are different but the effect the same. So don't let the phrasing of the law put you off trying to prosecute.

In the states that define rape as a crime that can happen to women or men, any statutes designed to protect the victim's privacy in court

---

† As of 1980 the jurisdictions where men cannot charge "rape" are Alabama, Delaware, the District of Columbia, Georgia, Idaho, Illinois, Indiana, Kansas, Maryland, Mississippi, Missouri, New York, North Carolina, Oklahoma, Oregon, Puerto Rico, Texas, Virginia, and the Virgin Islands.[29]

(see Chapter 4 about this) will apply equally to you, as a male victim. In other states, however, you may have to put up with suggestions from the defense that you are gay and engaged willingly in the encounter. Insinuations like this are humiliating, but a good prosecutor should be able to dispense with such a shabby defense.

The prosecutor for your case may decide that a conviction is more likely if another type of assault is charged instead of rape or sodomy. In New York, for example, he or she could charge "sexual abuse" (sexual assault without penetration) or "aggravated sexual abuse" (penetration with an object). If you were beaten up, a charge of "bodily assault" could be made. And if you are a minor, a charge of "child abuse" covers sexual abuse.

See Chapter 4, "Prosecuting," for details of the procedure.

CRISIS CENTERS AND COUNSELING

Aside from the medical and legal aspects of helping yourself, you will need some kind of sympathetic support. You may be lucky enough to get this from a woman in your life or a close friend, but if you can't, don't dismiss the idea of counseling. Many men won't go for help like this because they think it's unmanly, an admission of helplessness— men in general go to therapy and doctors less than women. You may also believe that the only way to regain your self-esteem is to avenge yourself on the rapist and that asking anyone else for help is pathetic. But revenge does not usually work. You will probably never find your attacker again and your frustration will only increase, and even if you do succeed in hurting him or even killing him, it still doesn't undo the rape. What is more, it will just get you into trouble.

Counseling can greatly help your self-esteem because it can help you absolve yourself of self-blame and get out all your bottled-up fury. What is more, far from being a weak and unmanly thing to do, it takes great strength and perseverance; counseling can sometimes be painful emotionally. And there is nothing unmanly about wanting to pull yourself back together. As George's counselor said, "When I first saw George, he was unshaven and disheveled and depressed and furious. By the last session he could smile again and was back in his snappy clothes. He had his dignity back."

Another service of counseling is to help the woman in your life cope with your assault. Her support and understanding are essential to your recovery, but she may be too bewildered by what happened to you to give it. She might also fear that you have "become gay" and she is likely to feel that you have failed as her protector. "If he can't protect himself from rape, how will he protect me?" All of this can put your relationship under strain. Going to a counselor together can help educate both of you about male rape and open up communication between you. Giving her this chapter to read will help, too. Give it to anyone else close to you as well—a father, mother, brother, sister, or friend. Not being able to tell the people you love about a major trauma in your life is a very lonely and unhappy feeling, but if they are willing to read this book, they are willing to listen and to help.

To find a counselor, call a rape crisis center, a rape hotline or Women Against Rape and try looking in "Resources" at the end of this book. You may think that these organizations are set up only for women, but this is no longer so. Many rape crisis programs even have male counselors for men now, although you can request a female counselor if you want.

If you don't want any short-term counseling or long-term therapy, you might still be interested in meeting other men who have been assaulted. A rape crisis center may be able to put you in touch with someone, or help you form a group, if you want. Meeting other people who have shared your experience can be most therapeutic.

How Others Can Help

Joe left a restaurant one evening after a light meal and walked toward his van. Suddenly, two men jumped him in the parking lot and pointed a gun at him. They ordered him into his van and drove him off to a remote spot. They took turns raping him at gunpoint, talking all the time about whether to kill him then and there or later. Finally, they let him out and took off with his van.

At first, Joe only told the police about the theft of his van, but eventually he got up the courage to tell them it was a sexual assault, too. He also told Maureen, his wife.

Maureen was devastated. She had never heard of such a thing happening to a man who wasn't gay and immediately became suspicious of Joe. She kept thinking he must be secretly gay and that he had somehow asked for the rape. She also felt that he was dirtied by

it and she didn't want to touch him. "Why weren't you more careful? Why did you park the van there?" she kept saying, as if the rape
were Joe's fault. On top of it all, she felt deeply terrified herself. If it
could happen to him, it could certainly happen to her, and he didn't
seem to be much of a protector. She had never felt so exposed and
vulnerable.

Joe developed all the typical symptoms of rape trauma. He lost his
appetite, he couldn't sleep, and he was plagued with flashbacks of
the rape. Maureen too kept having flashbacks of the scene he'd
described to her. Yet both were so worried about hurting each other
that they wouldn't talk about it. They also couldn't explain to their
two sons what was wrong and found themselves getting fanatically
overprotective of them. By the time Joe and Maureen sought counseling, they were terrified for their safety and furious at each other.

If you are close to a man who has been sexually assaulted, you are
going to face some difficult times. You will have to examine every idea
about rape that sits deeply inside you.

You know women are in danger of being raped, and you may think it
happens to them because rapists are frustrated maniacs in desperate
need of sex. Thinking this, you may assume that the rapists who attacked your friend must be gay and so, like Maureen, you become
suspicious of the victim. What was he doing to be picked out for such a
bizarre crime, you wonder? Is he leading a secretly gay life? You may
also lose respect for him. After all, being raped doesn't seem like a very
masculine thing to do. Instead of protecting you from assault, he got
assaulted himself.

As explained in the introduction to this book, rape has much more to
do with violence than sex. The man who attacked your friend did not
do so out of sexual frustration but out of the desire to hurt someone.
The rapist picked your friend because he happened to come across him
at a convenient time. He probably doesn't even remember what he
looks like—your friend was just one of a string of victims and his looks,
dress, and behavior had nothing to do with it. As for your man's ability
to protect you, that has not been altered. The majority of rapists do not
choose couples to attack, so the presence of your husband or lover is as
much protection as it ever was.

If you are the man's wife or lover, you'll probably feel peculiar about
sex for a while. Try to remember that the assault on him was nothing to
do with his sexuality and that he probably needs the love and reassur-

ance making love with you can give him. If you feel disgusted because a man had sex with him, imagine how outraged you would feel if you were raped and he regarded you as dirty. He hasn't been dirtied by the rape any more than he would have been by another type of attack; he's just been hurt. Show him that you care about him, and if neither of you feel like making love for a while, just holding each other can be wonderfully comforting.

While you are showing the man that you care for him and love him, avoid overcoddling him. If you give him the sense that you are protecting him, treating him like a child, you'll only make him feel more emasculated than ever, and that might make him resent you. Try instead to be proud of him for struggling to get over this terrible experience.

Above all, listen to him. Don't give him the message that you don't want to hear about the assault or his feelings, for he may interpret that as meaning you are disgusted by him. If you can encourage him to talk and show him that you want to understand, you can help him get better. Being willing to listen to him lets him know that you respect him, and he needs badly to feel respected. His self-respect is probably very low as a result of the assault, so he will flourish under signs that other people don't look down on him for it.

During all of this, don't forget yourself. It is exhausting and often shattering to help a person recover from rape, and you need some pampering and sympathy, too. If it gets too much, try to find someone you can talk to about it before you begin to resent him. And if it is all still overwhelming, remember that counseling is for partners, friends, and family as well as for victims. Perhaps you will want to go for counseling with the victim. Don't be afraid to tell the counselor exactly what is worrying you, for as shaming and peculiar as it might seem to you, counselors have heard these problems before and understand why they occur.

7

The Older Victim

It happened two and a half years ago. I was awakened from a sound sleep by a man with a stocking mask on, holding a knife. He had his hand over my mouth and nose and a knife pressed into my throat. He kept saying, "I'll kill you, I'll kill you." The assault lasted an hour. I didn't expect to live. How did I survive? I still wonder.

I was in a state of shock during it. I felt drugged. I built a wall around myself because I was savoring whatever moments I had left of life, knowing I wouldn't survive.

He made me take off my nightgown, and he tied me up with my hands behind my back, and I thought, "This is it." I saw the knife going through me and through me until I was dead. He wanted to tie a gag around me and put me in the closet, but I said I would suffocate, so he didn't. I don't know why he let me live.

I am divorced. I have no children—I'm independent. I used to like to go dancing, I was involved with someone for years, I had a hunger for living. Now everything has stopped. I still wake up trembling. Before I go to bed I have to check all over the house and under the bed and couch. It seems crazy.

You hear about these things and don't think they can happen to you. Now it won't go away. You have to live with it. I've had to accept that. But I don't want to die; you always have time to die. And there is always hope.

The woman quoted above, Mabel, is in her early sixties. That rape happens to such women—women in their fifties, sixties, even nineties —is rarely talked about. Surprisingly little has been written about it, even in sociological and psychological journals. (An exception to this is *Rape and Older Women: A Guide to Prevention and Protection* by Linda J. Davis and Elaine M. Brody.[1]) Because the statistics tell us most victims of rape are girls and young women, the older population has been ignored. Yet middle-aged and elderly women do get raped.[2] Not as often as young women, perhaps, who are more vulnerable because they are out and about more,[3] but one only has to scan the newspapers for a few days to find plenty of reports of middle-aged or elderly rape victims. Often, like Mabel, these women are attacked in their homes when burglaries turn into rapes.[4]

This chapter addressing you, an older victim, is included because you may have certain problems not mentioned in the general section for women, Part One. Men, too, can refer to these pages, for even though there is no available documentation on older male rape victims, they no doubt exist. As some researchers have put it, "Rape is a crime of opportunity."

Your Reactions

Shock is the reaction of anybody who falls victim to a violent crime, but it might be more intense for you if you thought rape could not even happen to you. Rape is so commonly thought of as a crime of lust that the usual picture of a rape victim is a young, enticing woman. "Why me? Why not a younger woman?" is the reaction of many an older victim. The answer to this is that the age of a victim doesn't usually concern a rapist as much as her availability. Perhaps, like Mabel's rapist, he found an accessible apartment—a window left open, a door unlocked—and entering, probably for the purpose of robbery, he found you alone, maybe asleep, easily victimized. Or he was out looking for a woman to rape, and you happened to walk by. To him your proximity meant a chance to exercise his sadistic fantasies. One of the convicted rapists Nicholas Groth interviewed, said he felt an overwhelming desire to "go out and hurt someone" three weeks before he raped a woman of sixty-one.[5]

Other men, however, pick older victims on purpose. Some such rapists told Groth that they saw older women as representing authority, something they wanted to get back at.[6] The man who raped Ann a year ago, when she was sixty, seemed to have revenge in mind.

> The man who raped me was very talkative. He said he was twenty-eight and that he picked me because I was an older woman. He

ranted and raved for a long time and told me that his mother used
to beat him up. It was pretty clear who I stood for.

Whatever a man's reason for raping, it has nothing to do with you
personally; you are just a symbol. This is one of the reasons rape is so
degrading, but it also explains why you are in no way to blame for it.

Pain during and after the rape is of special concern to you because
you may be more easily hurt and take longer to recover than someone
who is young. As you mature, your bones become more brittle, your
flesh bruises more easily, and your vaginal walls become harder and
thinner.[7] The result is that you might sustain genital and urinary tract
injuries from a rape and find it more painful than a younger woman,
even if no other violence occurs. If the rapist also beats you or uses
other violence, you may have a long period of physical recovery, for the
older body mends slowly. A long physical recuperation can be extremely depressing, not only because the injury is a constant reminder
of the rape but because it brings out all your fears for your independence. "Will I be strong enough to get about on my own?" is a worry
many elderly women already have; after a rape that worry only increases. For all these reasons it is essential for you to seek medical help
after a rape, even if you don't have any obvious injuries. The only small
comfort here is that overt injuries tend to get you more medical attention and sympathy than the invisible injury of rape.

As well as shock and pain, you are likely to feel more shame than a
younger woman because of the myths about rape you grew up with. "I
can't even say the word," is the feeling of many an older woman. If you
grew up during a time when talk about sex was considered vulgar, you
are not likely to feel at ease talking about rape. Also, rape may be
something you thought only happened to "bad" women, so you don't
want to tell people in case they gossip about you or look down on you.
If the rape included oral or anal penetration, you might see this as a
disgusting perversion that doubles your shame and shock. And if the
rapist has also given you a venereal disease, as happened to Mabel, you
might feel cheapened and humiliated in every way. Mabel recalled:

> At the hospital, they shot me full of penicillin, both buttocks, be-
> cause the rapist had gonorrhea and it showed up in my culture. I
> didn't develop the disease after that, but it was all terrible and ugly.

All of this shame may make you isolate yourself. It's hard to go against a lifetime of habits and beliefs to seek help, no matter how much you may need it.

Being a victim of crime is being a victim of the ultimate unfairness, and everyone feels cheated by it. But when you've already been through a long, hard life, this feeling is worse. "I've been through so much already, why this now?" is the thought of many an older victim, along with "I don't deserve this. I've always been good, I've always been careful." If you are already thinking about your life being mostly in the past, about death, a blow like rape can seem particularly unjust. "Why can't the elderly be spared? Haven't I been through enough already? I have so little time left—why did it have to be ruined?" are questions that may occur and recur. Such questions are justified, for nothing is more riddled with gross injustice than rape and its aftermath. Yet that very long life and hard experience you lament can stand you in good stead. You may have already suffered great difficulties—the death of people you love, traumas, maybe war—and you have experience coping with crises. A young woman might not know whether she can cope; she has never been put to the test and has no knowledge of herself in the face of crisis. But you have the strength and wisdom of age. These very factors helped Ann when she was raped at the age of sixty. She was in a unique position to compare her reaction to rape with that of the young because she had also been raped thirty-five years earlier, in 1947.

> I was raped when I was twenty-five by someone I knew socially. I took it terribly hard. For six months afterward my body was puffed up with water retention, and I had to go to the doctor for it. I was having an hysterical reaction to the rape. I had to go to a psychiatrist, too. I was a mess.
>
> This time was entirely different. My husband had died only a few weeks before and I was grieving. It was a Saturday night and I had gone out to buy a newspaper. I was preoccupied and didn't even notice when the man slipped in the door behind me. The door locked behind him and there was nobody around. He told me to go up to my apartment with him. I said, "You're going to kill me, aren't you?" because I just had the feeling he was. But he said, "No, I ain't gonna kill you."
>
> I took him upstairs because I didn't want to get killed. He was jittery, obviously full of drugs. I was afraid to resist him. While it

was happening, my mind was fixed on coming out alive. I felt disgust and all that, but mainly I didn't want to get dead. And, in a way, I did talk myself out of it because, even though I got raped, I slipped him a kind of Mickey. He was jittery and I told him I had a pill that would calm him down. He agreed to take it. It was a powerful pill I had left over from my husband's illness, and it knocked him out. I called the police and they came and arrested him.

Afterward, I felt mostly relieved that I'd gotten out of it alive. I was angry for a few days, but I wasn't even afraid to go out by myself. The trauma about my husband was uppermost in my mind, so the rape seemed secondary. Now I hardly ever think about it except for the odd flash of revulsion.

So I think it is an advantage to be older. Last time, I was terrified of getting pregnant from the rape, and this time I didn't have to worry. And that time I hated myself more and was more physically disgusted by the rape because of my lack of experience. Also I had more guilt that I had brought it about because I trusted the man. But I can't work up a good hatred of this sick man as I did of the first one.

A common reaction to the shame that rape causes is to want to barricade yourself in your home. Some elderly and solitary women are already prone to do this anyway, being afraid of crime, of crowds, of coping with the outside world, and a rape will make such fears worse. If the rape happened in your home, you can end up in the paradoxical position of imprisoning yourself in the very place that causes you terror. Mabel was raped in the apartment where she had lived for many years.

I'd like to move and not have the feeling I was eating up my last dollars by doing so, but I can't. I'm on Social Security disability and I can't afford it. But I've lost my sense of my apartment as a haven. It's become a jail. No matter how beautiful your home is, it can become a prison.

Mabel stays at home because she has lost the desire to go out and she is afraid of going about by herself. She spends her days watching television and reading, an existence she partly resents, partly enjoys. Mabel is doing this mainly out of choice, for although she cannot afford to move, she can afford to go out occasionally and does have friends who invite her. But some women are confined by physical disabilities, financial constraints, or a crippling fear.

You might regard your age as a hindrance to recovery. You may think, "What can be done for someone my age? What's the use?" and feel too tired and overwhelmed to make the effort it takes to overcome trauma. But there are hidden advantages to being older that are worth remembering, even beyond the ones mentioned above: other people are less likely to blame you for "seducing" the rapist and more willing to see you for the innocent victim you are; your sense of self is less easily shaken by trauma than it is in someone younger and less self-aware; and if you have a husband, lover, or close friend, your relationship is more likely to be stable and strong enough to survive the disruption of rape—indeed, a long-term, stable relationship is one of the most helpful ingredients in recovering from rape. Also, no matter how old you are, you are still alive, and that alone is worth struggling for. As Mabel put it, "I thought I was going to die when I was raped, and in that I discovered how much I wanted to live." Surviving rape, she now says, gave her a second chance at life. "And," she added, "there is always hope."

How to Help Yourself

MEDICAL TREATMENT

The first thing you owe yourself is to find medical treatment. Making yourself seek treatment is not always easy, especially if you want to maintain your privacy and dignity by keeping the rape secret. But rape is not an ordinary crime, and you may have received injuries that you are not even aware of.

Whether you go to the emergency room of a hospital, to your doctor, or a clinic, you will get a pelvic examination to check for venereal disease, internal injuries, and to take evidence of the rape. (See "The Hospital" in Chapter 2 for more detail.) A pelvic examination is never pleasant after a rape but especially not if you haven't had one in years and are not used to them. If you cannot get a friend or relative to see you through these procedures, to escort you to and from the hospital, to explain things to you, and to stick up for you, call a rape crisis center before seeking medical help and ask for a counselor. You could also ask at the hospital, for some have their own rape crisis programs.

The hospital staff should see to it that you are put in touch with people who can help you with such matters as getting your locks changed, stolen items replaced, and finding you financial and emotional assistance; but if no one volunteers such references, ask for someone who will or call a rape hotline in your area, a rape crisis center, or a victims' assistance program (see "Resources," Part Three). Some people feel that going to an organization like one of these is seeking charity. It isn't. Getting help after a crime like rape is your right and one that you have been, at least indirectly, paying for all your life in taxes.

REPORTING AND PROSECUTING

You may, like many older victims, be wary of reporting your assault and pursuing it through a prosecution because you are acutely embarrassed about it or afraid you will not be believed. Since popular myth has it that only young women are raped, you may fear being met with such remarks as, "You just imagined it," "Who'd rape *you?*" or, "Wishful thinking!" In addition, if you are elderly, you might fear slights to do with your hearing, sight, and memory. Although prejudices like this do exist, most police officers are aware that older women get victimized, and they will be willing to take you seriously. In court, however, a defense attorney might well try to claim that your impaired faculties have led you to identify the wrong man. This defense can be insulting, but try to remember that the attorney isn't thinking about your feelings or even the truth of what he is saying. He's just trying every way he can to get his client off the charge. The prosecutor should be able to handle such imputations. Also, if the trial is causing you stress, the prosecutor and probably the judge will do what they can to spare your having to appear often. When an eighty-two-year-old woman appeared at the trial of a man who had sexually attacked her and robbed her at knifepoint, the defense attorney interrupted her testimony several times to claim that she was incompetent because of her age, that her eyesight was bad, and that she was hard of hearing. After being cross-examined for about two and a half hours by this man, the woman finally turned to the judge and said, "How long are you going to torture me?" The judge held a hurried conference with the prosecutor and the defense attorney, then ruled that the questioning should be closed and that the woman had presented a "valid and full picture of her testimony."[8] The prosecutor is on your side, and no one wants to put you through more agony than is strictly necessary.

Another reason you may be unwilling to press charges is fear of the travel involved, should the case go to court, and of being exhausted by the process. You can find help with transport and emotional encouragement by requesting a legal advocate from a local victims' assistance agency or from the sex crimes division of the law courts in your county. You may be assigned an advocate automatically. (See Chapter 4 on "Prosecuting.")

Prosecuting can be rewarding. It is exhausting and at times upsetting and frustrating, but by doing it you are not only vindicating yourself, you are doing a service to all the other women your assailant might have attacked.

YOUR SAFETY

Your next most important concern will be your safety. If the rape happened in your home, or the assailant stole your purse with your address and keys in it, be sure to get new door and window locks *immediately.* You can have this done for free in many places by calling your local victims' assistance (or services) bureau (see "Victims' Services" in Chapter 2 and "Resources," Part Three). These agencies should also help you claim Social Security disability, if you need it, and help you pursue a legal course, such as suing your landlord for negligence.

Rape makes you feel afraid and shaky for a long time, so if you live alone, it is a good idea to arrange for a friend to call you at a certain time every evening to make sure you are all right. You could even designate a code word or phrase to use if something has gone wrong, such as, "The dog's not feeling well today."

If the rape happened outside your house, you may feel afraid of going out. If so, try to have family or friends come to pick you up when you want to go shopping. If that is not possible, take your trips out at various times of the day and vary your routes. If you think that someone is watching you, and many rape victims fear this for a time even when it is not likely, breaking routines can foil him. Again, rather than locking yourself in, reach out to places that can help you. Telephone a rape crisis center, a victims' assistance agency, or a rape hotline and explain your dilemma. They may be able to find you help—even a brief visit from someone once a day can get you through the worst time after the rape until you begin to feel safer and calmer again. Also, if you already belong to a group like a YWCA, a community or senior center, a church or a synagogue, don't neglect that as a resource for company and comfort.

SELF-DEFENSE

A further way to help yourself recover your sense of safety is to take self-defense classes. Many people think that older and handicapped people cannot learn self-defense, but programs held in community centers and the like are meeting with success. Much of self-defense has to do with how you carry yourself and with knowing how to avoid danger, not with actual fighting, so there are techniques that everyone can learn regardless of their physical capabilities. Taking such classes has been found to be psychologically therapeutic for victims as well, because it increases their self-confidence, makes them feel safer, lessens their fear of another attack, and puts them in touch with other people who have been through similar experiences.[9]

Here are some basic tips on good self-defense techniques:[10]

At Home

• Don't just *have* locks on your doors and windows, *use* them.

• If you are alone when the doorbell rings, call out "I'll get it," as if someone is with you.

• Never open the door to strangers, even if you have a chain on it. Ask who is there through the door and use the peephole. If you don't know the person, ask him to slip his ID under the door, and if you aren't expecting him, call the company to check who he is. Several case studies of older rape victims found that 43 percent had voluntarily admitted their attackers into their homes.[11] The Boston Strangler got his victims by posing as a repairman.

• If someone wants to come in and use your telephone for an emergency, tell him to wait outside while you call for him. Do this even if he claims his wife is about to give birth, his mother is having a heart attack, or someone has had an accident. You can help in a genuine emergency just as quickly by calling the police or an ambulance yourself.

• Beware of the following commonly used ruses to get into your home: "I'm collecting money for my mother's funeral." "I'm collecting for a charity." "I'm from security."

Going Out

- Vary the time of day you go out to do shopping or go to the bank.
- Deposit your money in the bank by mail if you can.
- Vary the route you walk to and from the bank and shopping.
- Try to walk with other people in deserted areas or after dusk. Arrange to meet friends whenever possible.
- Walk with your head up, eyes scanning the street casually as you would when driving. Look alert and confident.
- Give the impression that you know where you are going, not that you are in a daze.
- Try to avoid carrying a purse. If you must, a clutch purse is safest unless you need your hands free. Don't wind a purse strap around your arm or shoulders—you can be too easily pulled to the ground.
- If someone does grab your purse, let him have it. If you try to fight, the violence may escalate.
- Always carry your keys separately from your purse and ID. You don't want to give a mugger the chance to get in your home and rob or rape you.
- If you see someone approaching who looks as if he has mugging in mind, open your purse and dump the contents on the ground. He then won't have to attack you to get your money.
- If you see someone coming who you think might try to mug you, drop your purse in a mailbox. As long as it has the proper ID in it, it should be returned to you by the Post Office.
- Don't overload yourself with packages, and be prepared to drop them if you have to. A smashed bottle is better than a mugging.
- If something does happen, yell as loudly as you can. This is more to startle the assailant than to attract help, although with luck, the yell will accomplish that, too.
- If you are near people when attacked, yell "Fire!" or "Police!" rather than "Rape!" or "Help!" People respond better this way, perhaps because they feel less afraid to help.
- If your voice is frail or you cannot trust yourself to scream, carry a shriek alarm or loud whistle instead. Don't put it around your neck, however, for you could be strangled with it. These alarms are meant to

frighten the assailant and attract attention, but don't let them lull you into a false sense of security. (See "Resources" for where to get shriek alarms and whistles.)

• Don't rely on weapons or tear gas to defend you unless you are an expert at using them. Tear gas often doesn't work, especially against men who are drunk or on drugs, as many rapists and robbers are, and weapons can be seized and used against you.

• When you are waiting for public transport, keep alert and look around you. Stay out of hidden bus shelters and dark corners.

• When you get on a bus, always try to sit near the driver. On a train, choose cars that are not empty.

• When you are on a bus or train, hold your purse firmly on your lap, making sure the clasp is fastened, and don't count your money in front of people. Also, try not to fall asleep!

• When walking at night or in deserted areas, walk in the street rather than along the sidewalk near hidden doors and alleys.

Coming Home

• Get your keys out before you reach your front door so that you won't have to fumble for them.

• Avoid standing in the foyer or hallways rummaging around in your bag. Foyers are where most attacks take place.

• Check behind you as you enter your house or apartment building. Many attackers push themselves into your home just as you open your door—that is how Ann's rapist caught her.

• If a stranger tries to enter an elevator with you, either wait for the next one, use the stairs if you can, which are safer, or stand near the buttons. If he acts threatening, push all the buttons at once and get out as soon as you can. You want to avoid letting the man take you up to the roof or down to the basement, or letting him follow you to your apartment. It is always safer to be out of the elevator.

• If you arrive home and find that your door is open, *Don't go in.* Go to a neighbor, the superintendent of your apartment building, or outside to a phone booth and call the police.

• If someone wants you to admit him to your apartment building, don't let your politeness overrule your safety. Tell him or her to ring the bell of the people he is visiting.

• All these precautions also apply if a woman is trying to follow you or get into your home. Women are robbers, too, and may be part of a team, even of a rapist team.

If You Are Attacked

• Take a few deep breaths and concentrate on staying calm. If you breathe too fast, as people are prone to do in a panic, you could get dizzy or even faint, which will make you more vulnerable. Deep breathing calms your body.

• Do as the assailant says, calmly.

• Look him in the face, unless he orders you not to. Looking at him makes you seem less afraid, which may make him less afraid and thus less likely to hurt you in a panic. It will also enable you to describe him later.

• Don't stare panic-stricken at the weapon—that makes you seem more vulnerable.

• Try to talk to him, meanwhile looking for avenues of escape.

Some of these techniques are easy, but others require breaking a lifetime of habits, which is difficult, and often sad. But it is just your politeness and consideration that an assailant will use to victimize you. Being careful doesn't mean you can never help a neighbor in distress again. Agree to help, but only in ways that won't put you in danger.

Self-defense will also teach you how to defend yourself physically using the everyday objects you carry with you, such as a book, pencil, cane, or umbrella, but these techniques must be taught properly and practiced in a class to be safe to use. (See "Resources" for places to take self-defense classes.)

There is an unfortunate attitude in American society toward the elderly these days: they are seen as helpless, weak, and rather silly. The wisdom and dignity that other cultures have recognized in the old have been forgotten in favor of the narcissistic culture of the young. It is hard not to absorb some of that prejudice and thus become used to regarding yourself as absentminded and incapable. The core of self-defense is doing away with such an attitude and seeing yourself as powerful instead. That is why walking assertively and being firm instead of meekly polite helps, too. Such behavior goes so counter to the stereotype of the old that it might well astonish a would-be attacker into trying someone else instead.

RECOVERY

Most older women in America have living relatives.[12] Family members can be an enormous help to your recovery if they are appropriately sympathetic and readily available. The problem is that many older women don't want to tell their families about being raped, especially when their only living relatives are their children and grandchildren, because they don't want to shock and upset them. You are the only person who can judge how your family will be affected by the news, but don't sacrifice yourself too much over this. They may be upset, but they will also probably like to feel needed and will be pleased to help you. Sometimes, a crisis like rape can even draw a family closer, because it gives everyone a chance to show how much they care for one another.

The essence of recovering from a sexual assault lies, studies are indicating, in one's attitude. If you see recovery as getting back to the person you were before, as if the rape had never happened, you are bound to be disappointed; you can't undo a rape. But if you see it as being able to cope again, being able to feel happy, then your goal is possible. It is hard not to feel defeated and hopeless after such a trauma, but you can help yourself by thinking of all you have survived so far and by feeling proud of yourself for surviving again. Think back to the ways you coped with other crises in your life, and use those methods. And allow yourself to release all the outrage that is bottled up inside you. Mabel described her struggle to recognize her fury:

> Soon after the rape I was told I should get angry. My counselor said I wouldn't get better until I did. But I couldn't. All I could feel was grateful that I was alive, that he'd let me live. I was bewildered.
>
> I couldn't get angry until one and a half years after the rape, but now the anger is helping me. Now I feel, "How *dare* anyone do that to another human being—impinge upon their privacy, molest them, kill part of them?" What I'd really like to do is get on top of a mountain and scream and scream, but I don't have a mountain and I'm too inhibited, so all that screaming is locked inside my head.

A recent study has found that crime victims who unlock that screaming—who release their fear, anger, horror, and disgust—actually recover faster than people who put on a brave front.[13] Don't torture yourself by trying to act brave all the time. Let the fury out, whichever way it wants.

The Disabled

Unfortunately, a disability does not disqualify you from becoming a victim of a crime, including rape. When a rapist wants someone easy to get at, he doesn't worry about their physical state of being, only their accessibility. If you've been sexually attacked, you'll not only have the same trauma to deal with as other people—phobias, nightmares, shock —but you'll have the burden of feeling doubly unlucky, doubly victimized. Your hard-won independence seems to have brought punishment instead of reward and you may find yourself feeling more helpless than you have in years. Also, when you are already dependent on the kindness of others, having your trust violated is deeply, horribly disturbing. On the other hand, you already have important survival skills and strengths that may well stand you in good stead.

To help yourself get over your sense of isolation and helplessness, consider taking a self-defense class. Rape takes away so much of your sense of autonomy that it's important to restore it as quickly as possible and to experiment with ways in which you can increase your strength and power. Such classes have been offered to people in wheelchairs, to the blind and the deaf, and they have proved successful.[14] Contact your local YWCA, community center, or organization for the handicapped and find out if they have such classes. If they don't, request one. (See "Resources" for places that offer them.) Here are some examples of the kinds of things you can learn:[15]

· When you have to ask someone for help, do it directly and firmly, not apologetically.

· When you don't need help anymore, tell the person firmly. By doing so you will show that you are alert and self-confident, not such an easy target.

· If the person won't go away but insists on staying with you, holding your arm, taking your packages, don't be afraid to be rude. If he still won't leave, stop someone else and say clearly, "This man won't leave me alone," or, "Someone is following me," or even, "Get the police!"—whichever pertains. You could shout one of these sentences loudly and clearly if you can't attract any one person's attention.

· Carry a shriek alarm or whistle, but not around your neck.

· Practice a loud, angry scream into your pillow.

· Move purposefully when you are out, whether you are in a wheelchair or use a cane or a walker. That means holding your head up, knowing where you are going, and looking alert.

Like the elderly, disabled people are seen as helpless and befuddled, even as childlike. You know better. By appearing sure of yourself, even tough, you can do much to make yourself feel and look more confident and to dissuade people from harming you, even if inside you feel it's all bluff. The people who pick on the disabled as victims do so because they don't want resistance and assume they won't get it. If you can show them how wrong they are, you have a good chance of frightening them off.

How Others Can Help

If you know an older woman who has been sexually assaulted, you are likely to feel deeply shocked. People tend to think of older women as invulnerable to sexual attack, and it violates some deep-seated taboos to realize they are not, perhaps because people aren't used to thinking of older people, especially their mothers and grandmothers, as sexual.

Your reaction of shock and subsequent tendency to withdraw from the victim may make her feel worse. You cannot help feeling that way, of course, but do try to keep from showing it at first, at least to her.

If the woman is your mother or grandmother, or another close relative, you may suffer almost as much as if you'd been attacked yourself. You are probably used to thinking of your older relatives as authorities —they're supposed to look after you. When they get hurt, especially raped, it makes you feel uncomfortable and betrayed. You might even get angry at the victim for letting you down, for getting herself hurt, for needing rescuing instead of being the rescuer. Also, if spending time with her is already a sticky issue in your family, you may find yourself silently accusing her of manipulating you for sympathy. As "bad" as such feelings are, don't feel too guilty about them—they are only natural. But try to let off steam at someone else, not the victim.

There is much you can do to help the victim, both practically and emotionally. Most of this is discussed in Chapter 3, "How Others Can Help," but if the victim is older, especially elderly, these suggestions might help, too.

• If she is willing, take her to a hospital or medical center, to the police, and later to the courts if necessary. She may be afraid of traveling, especially if she is already frail or if she has been badly hurt by the attack. Don't bully her into going to these places, however. She must make up her own mind.

· Help her get her locks replaced if the attack took place in her home or the assailant took her keys or address. Call a victims' assistance program or a locksmith.

· Help her replace stolen goods—credit cards, checks, ID, television, etc. She might not be feeling up to doing these small, bothersome tasks herself.

· Suggest telephoning her every evening at a certain time if she lives alone.

· Encourage but don't pressure her to get in touch with agencies that will help her. There are many services for the elderly as well as for rape victims; call around until you find one that specializes in crime victims' needs.

· Don't get overprotective. If she is frail or disabled, you might feel particularly tempted to cosset her and treat her like a child. She may welcome this at first, but she needs to regain a sense of independence and autonomy as soon as possible.

· If she tends to isolate herself, try gently to prevent that. Arrange to visit her, check up on her. It won't work to push her into going out or seeing people before she's ready, but let her know you are there if and when she needs you.

· Encourage her to seek therapy. Older people are sometimes reluctant to do this, perhaps because they see therapy as something only for the mentally ill, but it can be an invaluable help.

· Talk to her and try to overcome your discomfort with the subject.

There is another circumstance in which you, as an older victim's friend or relative, can be of essential help: if she lives in an institution such as an old people's home and was assaulted there by a member of the staff or a fellow patient. Sadly, such occurrences are not uncommon, and the administration of the institution is likely to want to cover up the assault by denying it happened at all or refusing to investigate. The victim will need you to reassure her that you believe her, to remove her from the place, and to make the necessary complaints. Fighting an institution by yourself is difficult and intimidating, so you might want to contact a rape crisis center, victims' assistance program, or your district attorney's office for help.

If you become overwhelmed with the burden of being the victim's sole confidant during this crisis, if she is becoming increasingly dependent on you and demanding, enlist the help of others. As someone close to her, you are suffering too, and you too need to lean on someone. Allow yourself a break before you blow up at her, and find a friend or relative who can take turns being with her. And if it all becomes too much, call a rape crisis center for advice or to arrange a meeting.

8

Teenagers

I was with my cousin, my boyfriend and a friend—all guys—that night. We were high, drinking. This guy came up and said he'd get drugs for us and I went with him. Three guys and I, the only girl, went with him! But I agreed to 'cause I wanted the ego trip of coming back to my buddies with all these drugs I'd gotten. And I was too drunk to think straight.

So he took me into the park and got this lead pipe—I don't know where he got it—and said he'd kill me if I didn't cooperate. I tried to run away and I screamed, but he caught me and said he'd kill me. So I just began to beg and plead and stuff. He probably loved that, that's probably just what he wanted.

I was seventeen and I was still a virgin.

Like Kathy, quoted above, most rape victims are girls between sixteen and twenty-four.[1] Many are even younger.[2] One widely respected study found that one in four American girls were sexually molested before they turned thirteen.[3] Boys aren't much better off; some researchers believe they are victimized just as often.[4] As Groth, who has done much work with child molesters and victims, once put it, if we were to count all the incidents of child and teenage sexual abuse that actually go on, we'd realize that we have "a major epidemic on our hands."[5] If you are a teenager who has survived sexual assault, or the relative or friend of such a teenager, this chapter is for you.

Who Rapes Teenagers?

Most of the people who assault teenagers are the same kinds of men who assault adults, men who get a kick out of humiliating and terrifying people. But some rapists like to pick on young people for other reasons: they like "easy" victims—people who are small and naïve and perhaps less "streetwise" than adults—or they are particularly attracted to the young. They may feel this attraction because they never grew up themselves, because the vulnerability of the young is erotic to them, or perhaps because they hate young people; one imprisoned rapist explained why, at age thirteen, he had tried to rape an eleven-year-old girl by saying that he had a "hatred for young girls."[6]

Many of the people who assault teenagers are teenagers themselves, for young rapists tend to pick people of about their own age who live in their own neighborhoods.[7] Gang rapists are usually teenagers, and their victims are commonly in the same age group, perhaps even at the same school.[8]

The other group of people who rape teenagers are people the teenager knows—boys at school, friends of friends, fathers or brothers of friends, camp counselors, teachers, or dates. Boys are raped by people like this, too (and the men who rape boys are not usually gay[9]). Most rapists are men, but women sexually assault boys and girls as well.

No matter how many explanations you hear about why people rape, however, it is always hard to believe that anyone would do such a thing to you. Try to remember that you weren't picked because you did anything wrong but only because the rapist figured he could get you.

Your Reactions

After it happened, I went to my mother's. It was three in the morning but I told her I'd got lost on the train. I didn't tell her what happened. Then I didn't go out of the house for months. If friends called, I told my mother to say I wasn't home. I wanted to be hypnotized to forget it all.

During that time at home, I gained fifteen or twenty pounds. I didn't want anyone near me. I wasn't beaten really badly when I was raped, but he said demeaning things to me. Told me I was ugly and fat and stuff. Then when I got fat, that made my self-esteem worse. I felt worthless and ugly and fat.

I was always passive and happy-seeming before I was raped. Then I became paranoid and I hated people. I wouldn't go around the corner to get a paper for five or six months because it meant I'd have to walk past the park and guys there always made remarks. I used to think it was cute, or if I was in a bad mood to think, 'Give me a break,' but after the rape that just twists your insides around. And if someone brushed up against me in a crowd, I got shivers. I wanted to push people in front of trains. I wanted to get a gun and kill the guy who raped me.

I realized eventually that I was becoming like the person who attacked me—aggressive and stuff, so I had to sort of forgive him. I wouldn't be friends with him or anything, but I had to not let his sickness make me sick.

Whether you are thirteen or eighteen, a boy or a girl, your reactions to being sexually assaulted will be very like those that Kathy describes above: shock, disgust, a terrible fear, fury, and an inability to believe it really happened at all. Please read Chapter 1 for a description of all the complicated feelings you are likely to have and Chapter 2 for ways to help yourself. You need to know that no matter how crazy your reactions seem, they are normal. As Kathy put it:

For a year I was really out of my mind, depressed. But it's important to know you're going to hurt a lot and be depressed—it's part of healing to feel that pain and go through it.

You may have certain worries, however, that are different from those of adults. These are discussed here.

WORRYING ABOUT PARENTS

One of your biggest anxieties may be whether to tell your parents about the assault. Will they be able to handle it? What will they do to you if they find out? You might not be on the best of terms with them in the first place, and you probably don't usually discuss your private life with them; to talk to them about anything to do with your body or sex may embarrass you. But rape isn't really about sex, it's about violence. You need the help your parents can give if they are willing to be kind and not angry, so don't let a relatively unimportant feeling like embarrassment get in the way of finding comfort.

You may also be reluctant to tell them because you're afraid they'll get mad at you. Maybe they'll say something like, "I *told* you not to go out with him," or, "That's what happens when you run around with that crowd." Perhaps they'll be so angry at you for what happened that they'll impose curfews or withhold money to punish you. If you were actually breaking a rule when the assault happened, such as going somewhere your parents disapproved of or pretending you were staying with a friend when, in fact, you went out with a boyfriend, you may feel especially afraid to tell them in case they say, "That serves you right" or even, "So, it's your fault." And if you think the assault happened because you did something stupid, you may be doubly ashamed and afraid of telling them. Some parents do react to the assault of their child with anger. They don't understand rape and think you "invited" it, they are mad at the rapist but take it out on you, or they are generally angry that you got hurt and blame you for it. Only you can judge whether it's worth telling your parents. But you can help by asking them to read the section especially addressing parents later on in this chapter and by telling them that their anger isn't helping you get better. Also, think carefully about whether you are right in expecting them to get angry.

Another reason you might not want to tell is that you don't want them to know certain things about your life. Perhaps you are no longer a virgin, for instance, and you don't want them to find out, especially in the context of something as violent and horrible as a rape. Or perhaps you are taking drugs and you know they'll discover this if they are told about the assault. You'll have to decide whether keeping your secret is worth foregoing their help.

Many teenagers won't tell their parents because they simply want to be independent. Your privacy is so important to you now that you believe it would be better to keep the assault as a terrible secret rather than run to your parents for comfort. Yet, even though telling them will mean giving up some of this privacy and independence, the strain on you will be less in the long run, as Kathy discovered when she eventually told her mother.

> I didn't tell anyone about it for months, not even my mother 'cause I was pretty sick in those days. I'd left home when I was fifteen and was living with a girlfriend, and I was into drugs and drinking. And I kept everything in. People used to say, 'You're always so happy, you

never have any problems!' Nine months after I was raped, I went into AA [Alcoholics Anonymous].

When I did tell, it was kind of a Freudian slip. I had all this medication because I'd got an infection from the rape that kept coming back—that's another thing that freaked me out. I had to hide that, too, so I kept the medicine in my underwear drawer. One night I left the drawer open while I took a shower and my mother went in my room and saw it. She's a nurse, so she knew what it meant. She came into the bathroom and said, 'Is there something you're not telling me?'

So I finally told her I was raped. I watched her pupils get huge and then small again. Then she hugged me.

If I'd been able to tell my mother earlier, it would have made it easier. It was hard hiding it all those months.

Another, more frightening reason you won't tell might be that you were threatened. Most rapists claim that they will magically "know" if you tell, and threaten to rape you again or even to murder you for revenge. Perhaps your attacker threatened to hurt your parents, brother, or sister or to shame you in some way, such as showing nude pictures of you to your family. One man frightened his victim into silence by telling her that he was having an affair with her mother and that her mother approved of what he was doing. Others use lines such as, "Your mother will die of shock if you tell her." Many a teenage and child victim has been kept silent for years by such threats and lies. If you aren't telling because the rapist has threatened you, consider these points:

• How much information about you does the rapist really have? Does he know where you go to school or where you live? And how likely do you think he is to carry out his threats? If you think you are in real danger from him and you can't tell your parents, are there other trusted adults you can tell so that you don't have to live with this fear alone?

• He probably has no way of knowing whether you "told" or not until he is arrested, and then you will be safe from him.

• Although he may have convinced you that you are the one who was bad and who deserves punishment, that is not the case. He knows that if he really showed pictures of you or told "dirty" stories about you to anyone, he would be the one in trouble because he is the one breaking the law. He probably wouldn't even dare carry out this threat.

• You should not believe anything he says about you, your family, or what he will do. He's lying to keep you quiet.

• Anyone who loves you will be more concerned with rescuing you from this man, getting him caught, and helping you get better than with being angry at you.

• If you tell, you will be able to help get him arrested and you will be making yourself safe from him.

If you aren't telling your parents because you don't want to upset them, try to remember that almost any parent would rather be upset and yet be able to help than be kept in the dark while their child suffers alone. And if you won't tell them because you think it's none of their business, ask yourself what you mean by that. Is that what you truly believe or are you covering up for another reason? Are you underestimating their love for you? Or are you, for example, really ashamed of having been raped and that's why you won't tell? If so, you should never let shame stop you from getting help, for you have done nothing wrong. Only the rapist has.

SHAME

Feeling ashamed that you were assaulted is just about universal among rape victims and is discussed in Part One, but as someone living at home, you might feel especially ashamed of having disrupted the family with your tragedy. You might then find yourself trying to make up for it by becoming a perfect daughter or son. You stop going out, you help at home with all the chores, you cling to your parents, you study hard, and you never lose your temper. Denise, the mother of a thirteen-year-old who was raped, said her daughter acted like this.

> The month after the rape, Sara became almost overachieving. She was competent all the time, good at school, she stopped talking to friends for hours on the phone, and she began looking after me. She acted as if *I* was the victim. I felt bad and upset, and she probably thought the trouble with me was her fault.

You may be acting like this not only to make it up to your family but in the unconscious hope that if you are very good, no more bad things will happen to you. This thought might be comforting for a while, but don't depend on it too much. Bad things happen to you regardless of how good you are, just as good things can happen even when you've been bad. There's nothing wrong with wanting to stay around at home for a while and get closer to your parents, but don't punish yourself for the assault by denying yourself friends you want to see or a burst of temper you know you need.

Your shame may, on the other hand, have the opposite effect; you feel that having been raped means that you must really be "bad," so you start to act bad. You drink, take drugs, fight at home, play truant, even run away. Acting like this may be a way of punishing your family for failing to protect you, but it is also a way of punishing yourself: you are taking all the anger you should have toward the assailant and directing it toward yourself and the people you love. But punishing yourself for having been a victim only adds to your suffering. Maybe you did break a rule or do something careless, maybe you were already being "bad" when it happened, but you still didn't deserve or invite the rape. The only person responsible is the rapist and he's the one who should be punished.

Acting bad can also be a way of calling attention to yourself, of asking for help. Often rape victims feel they aren't getting enough sympathy, so they develop other symptoms such as sickness or aggression. Instead of hurting yourself, try looking for sympathy elsewhere. If nobody at home is adequate, try friends or a rape crisis center, where the people are trained to understand better.

DISILLUSIONMENT

> I leave the lock off my door when I'm expecting my boyfriend sometimes, but whenever I do he gets real mad and shouts at me, 'You don't learn!' It kills me when he says that because I want to live life the way I see it in my head. In the life in my head, I can leave my bike out without locking it, I don't have to lock doors . . . When you're a teenager, you're very idealistic. You want to be wild and have a good time and trust everybody.

As Kathy found, being raped stole much of her idealism away. She was just discovering the world, embracing it, when she was raped and it all seemed to be spoiled. Rape lets you know in the hardest way that there are scary things out there, things that no one can avoid, and this discovery may well depress you for some time. It may also make you feel resentful that you can't just go out and take the world on your own terms, or be as adventurous as your friends are. Kathy said:

> Once, soon after I was raped, I was walking down the street with my best friend when these two guys pulled up in a car and asked directions. I got suspicious, but she went right over. One guy had a bottle in his pocket like a gun and said he'd kill us if we didn't do what he said.
>
> I was like, 'Oh no, kill me first, don't let this happen again!' And I started screaming and yelling. She stayed real cool and called over this security guard walking by. That scared the guys off. Later, she couldn't understand why I reacted like that. I used to be so cool. She made fun of me.

ANGER

You are going to be furious at yourself and your attacker, something that is discussed in detail in Chapter 1, but you might also be angry at your parents for the rape—you feel that they have let you down. They are supposed to be your protectors, the people who look after you, so where were they when you got attacked? Or you might think that if they hadn't been so strict, or so neglectful, you wouldn't have had to seek relief with other people, maybe people who led you into dangerous situations.

There might be some truth in these accusations, but it still isn't fair to blame them for the rape. Even if they tend to neglect you, it doesn't mean they want you hurt. But such rational explanations probably won't help your anger go away, for anger isn't rational. You just have to let it out so that it doesn't burn inside you, making you full of hate. If you can, tell your parents that you are mad at them, that you think they've failed you or that they are blaming you or not helping you enough. If that doesn't help to open a discussion and clear the air, suggest to them that you all go to a rape counselor together. A counselor may be able to explain things to them that they won't take from you. Also, try beating up a pillow, letting yourself scream, or breaking some flower pots if it all gets too much. Another good way to let your fury loose is to join a self-defense class (see the self-defense section below and in Chapter 2). This suggestion might sound silly, but martial arts experts have long understood the value of redirecting and using pent-up rage. Anger is a powerful force, one that you have a right to feel and one that you can use constructively.

WORRYING ABOUT SCHOOL

A major reaction to rape for many teenagers is to worry about how it will affect their lives at school. Schools are enclosed, gossipy societies, and it can be hard to keep news like a rape quiet. You may dread going back—you are terrified of the looks you'll get, the whispers and the taunts. Girls tend to worry that they'll be regarded as "sluts," boys fear being labeled cowards and homosexuals, and both are afraid of being seen as freaks or objects of pity.

It is best to return to school as soon as possible after the assault because the longer you wait, the harder returning will be. But if worries like those are borne out, you may want to change schools. This isn't always easy, especially if you go to a public school and your parents can't afford to change neighborhoods or pay for a private school. An alternative is to tell someone you think will be sympathetic, such as your parents, the principal, your adviser, or a teacher, about the way you are being treated and discuss what can be done about it. In one high school where a girl was raped by a schoolboy on the campus, the school officials were so shocked by the rape and the students' unenlightened attitude toward it that they arranged for a rape prevention program to be given by experts to the students and teachers on campus. Before, the victim had been isolated by her friends, the girls were scared, the teachers bewildered, and the boys were making rape jokes. Afterward, everyone had learned to take rape more seriously. They had also learned how to protect themselves.[10] So if you do complain, you might even be able to help your whole school learn more about rape. See Part Three, "Resources," for places that will send experts on rape and self-defense to schools.

If you are able to keep the assault quiet and only tell a trusted friend or two, then school might be a source of relief. The sooner you can get back to your normal life, the quicker you will feel normal yourself. It is comforting to know that other people don't see you as different.

WORRYING ABOUT FRIENDS

You may be lucky enough to have a friend who understands about the assault and who says the right things, but this is fairly rare. You are more likely to be getting angry at your friends because they aren't reacting the way you want. Instead, they are embarrassed and awkward with you or they make insensitive remarks such as, "Well, why didn't you just fight him off?" Some of your hitherto best friends might even withdraw from you. Reactions like these are hard to bear. It's happening not because your friends don't care about you but because they don't really understand rape. They see it as sex, so they are embarrassed by the subject. And they are shocked and scared by it. Also, they don't know how to make you feel better and are so afraid of saying the wrong thing that they say nothing instead. Perhaps you've experienced the awkwardness of coping with someone else's tragedy yourself—if a friend's relative died, for example. If someone you particularly care about is acting like this, give him or her this book to read, especially Chapter 3, "How Others Can Help."

Telling boys can be even more difficult. Teenage boys have rarely had much education about rape and are apt to have all the old-fashioned ideas about it that television, movies, and their parents perpetuate—that rape is sex, that all women like it, and that a woman who is raped is just a slut. If you hear comments like these from anyone, you don't have to take them. Tell the guy he's wrong, that what happened to you was more like being beaten up, and no one wants that. And if you can't do that, just leave. You don't have to listen to such stuff.

Boys who have been raped may have an even harder time with friends than girls, because most people don't even realize that boys can get raped. In a book about the sexual assault of children and adolescents called *Your Children Should Know,* the authors quote a boy about his rape.

> I was on my way home from a party when I was jumped by four men. I thought they wanted to rob me. . . . One of them started laughing and said, "No, Pretty Boy, we want you." I tried to run, but I wasn't fast enough. Then I tried to fight, but there were four of them and even though I was fifteen, I was pretty small. I couldn't tell anyone afterwards, because the only thing that kept going

through my head was that everyone would keep calling me "Pretty Boy."[11]

Boys might find it easier to confide in a girlfriend than another boy.

WORRYING ABOUT SEX

Like all rape victims, you are going to worry about how the rape will affect your sexuality. If you have not had much, or any, sexual experience, you may find it especially hard to understand the difference between rape and sex. "If that's what it's like, how will I ever enjoy it?" You may also feel bitter that you were initiated in such a brutal, terrifying way. And if the rapist made you do things you never heard of before, that may add to your shame and embarrassment. Kathy, who is now twenty, talked about her reactions to being raped when she was a virgin.

> When I was growing up, I was mostly friends with kids older than me. I saw old friends get pregnant and have abortions when they were teenagers. I was running around in a cool, fast crowd, doing drugs and drinking. So I had to keep something special for myself and my virginity was it. I wanted to fall in love with someone and really know him and trust him before I had sex with him. Then I was raped. It was taken away, and I hit bottom after that.
>
> I met my boyfriend six months after I was raped, and he's still my boyfriend. I didn't sleep with him for the first six months I was with him and I told him about the rape before because I wanted him to know it was part of me. But I don't think it was stopping me making love, because they are two completely different things.
>
> When I was raped, I had my arms over my face and he was clawing at my neck with his nails and I was thinking, 'No, no, don't do this to me.' But if you care for each other, you might be clawing and stuff but it's different because you want it to happen, however it is. You get turned on in your head and your heart first.

Chances are that you will discover, like Kathy, that you can enjoy lovemaking, provided that you have a partner who is loving and considerate. But it may take you a while to feel ready for it. Just remember that rape has nothing to do with love, while sex, at its best, is an expression of love. Or as one teenage victim put it, "Comparing rape to sex is like comparing a punch in the mouth to a kiss."[12]

RAPE BY FRIENDS OR ACQUAINTANCES

When you are assaulted by someone you know or went out with, as often happens, your reactions may be very strong. For a start, you'll probably feel bitter. After all, you trusted the guy, you thought he was nice, maybe you even had a crush on him, then he turned cruel, selfish, and violent on you. What, you wonder, does that say about your judgment of people? You feel betrayed and stupid.

You have been betrayed and that is undeniably awful, but you shouldn't hate yourself for making a mistake. He's the bad one, not you. He's the one who broke the rules of trust and kindness and used your trust against you. He's the one to hate.

You might also feel responsible for the rape because you were kissing or petting with him. Many people believe the myth that once a man gets aroused, he can't control himself, but that is utterly untrue. If he respected you at all, he would have stopped when you wanted to. And the sexual drive in men isn't so powerful that it takes over their bodies like some magical, irresistible force, no matter what they claim. Agreeing to go out with someone, to kiss, to pet, is never agreeing to have sex. Your body belongs to you and only you, and you have the right to decide what to do with it, at all times.

In a recent survey of 432 teenagers from a Los Angeles, California, high school, 75 percent of the boys and 55 percent of the girls said they believed a man has a right to use physical force to get sex from his date if he'd spent a lot of money on her or if she gets the "guy sexually excited."[13] How vividly these high school students imagined what "physical force" entails when they were asked these questions (screaming, struggling, hitting, crying) is open to doubt, but the fact that teenagers can believe rape is okay in any circumstance shows the sad fact that, even in the 1980s, education about rape is seriously lacking. Slavery was abolished a long time ago and you'd think people would realize that human bodies are not to be bought and sold, especially for the price of a dinner! If a boy pays for a meal or a movie, you don't owe him a thing, except a thank you.

The man or boy who assaulted you is likely to use some or all of these excuses to justify what he did: he'll say you led him on by agreeing to go out with him, by being alone with him, by flirting, kissing, letting him pay for a hamburger—whatever he can think up. He's pretending to himself that he's not a rapist. Don't believe him.

After a rape by someone you know, you may find it hard to trust men again. When you are ready to try dating, you could start by going on double dates or seeing boys with groups of friends until you've developed enough of a relationship with a guy to trust him alone. Most males are not rapists, and your judgment isn't so terrible. You were terribly unlucky, but even that isn't so unusual. Almost everyone has been conned in some way.

How to Help Yourself

In case you think you should try to act like being raped is no big deal, believe me—it is. Don't ignore it—take care of yourself.
—A teenage victim[14]

CHOOSING WHOM TO TELL

You will find it hard to recover from a sexual assault if you never tell anyone about it. The memory of it tends to burn within you, making you feel different and separate from other people. What happened to you is terrible, but it isn't so unusual that it makes you weird or an outcast. Plenty of people get raped, and because of that, there are others out there who can understand.

If your relationship with your parents allows it, the best thing to do first is to tell them. They can give you the support and comfort you need to see you through going to the hospital, reporting the rape, and recovering emotionally. Whether you can trust them to be more helpful than harmful is something only you can know, but if you think they need educating and might respond well to it, give them this book to read. There is a section later on in this chapter that tells parents how they can help you without making you feel overprotected, blamed, or a burden.

If you know that you can't trust your parents to help, do at least tell a friend, sister or brother, or another adult you trust, such as an aunt or the mother of a friend. You can also call a women's or rape crisis center to talk to a counselor, for they are there just as much for you as for adult victims. Even though Kathy couldn't tell anyone she knew about

the rape, she did call a rape hotline two days after the rape and she
went to the hospital for help.

> I talked to a social worker and she was great. She got me a woman
> doctor and told me I could use a phony last name.

If you are a minor, some officials may insist on informing your parents and the police about the assault. If you don't want this to happen,
you can call various places first and ask them about their policy. Some
places will allow you to use only your first name without a last name or
address; other places will keep your confidence except in cases of incest.

A rape counselor can help you tell your parents about your assault.
She can tell them things that you feel too embarrassed or emotional to
talk about, and act as a cushion between you and your parents, stopping
them from getting mad at you and explaining away the myths about
rape. And if the police are informed, a counselor can stay with you to
provide support throughout the questioning and other legal procedures,
something adult victims need as much as you do.

Choosing which friends to tell depends on how well you know them
and how you think they'll respond. Sometimes a trauma like rape can
change the type of friend you value, making you reassess who is important to you and who is generous enough to be able to help you through
difficult times. Don't feel bad if you start wanting to reject certain
friends and turn to others—that's natural. And in the end, you'll probably end up with kinder, more loyal friends anyway.

At some point you'll probably have to explain to whomever you tell
about the rape that you don't want to be treated as somebody special or
different any longer. Because you are young, they might tend to baby
you, to want to shelter and protect you. At first, being treated this way
may be nice, but after a while it is smothering and it interferes with
your independence.

HOSPITAL

Unless you have a private doctor you want to go to, going to the
hospital as soon as possible after the rape is essential for reasons described in Chapter 2. If you feel frightened, you can have your mother,
friend, or a rape counselor stay with you throughout the hospital procedures. If you are female, a female nurse should always be present during
the examinations—you are not supposed to be left alone with a male

doctor. Most hospitals and doctors of either sex will automatically have a nurse present, so you shouldn't have to fight anyone about that.

You may also want to go to an adolescent clinic, such as The Door in New York, if you are concerned about keeping your assault a secret (see "Resources").

The pelvic examination, when the doctor looks in your vagina, and perhaps your rectum if you were raped anally, is necessary to check for injury and to collect evidence of the rape. If you are a virgin, or haven't had a pelvic examination before, you might feel frightened by it. Insist that someone you trust stay with you, and hold her hand if you want. If the doctor hurts you, say so and tell him or her to stop. It may hurt a little but it will be over quickly. If you go to the hospital without a parent, at least take a friend for comfort, especially because you might have a long wait before anyone can see you.

REPORTING

If you didn't call the police right after the assault, you may be made to by the hospital staff. You probably won't want to see the police alone, so if a parent or friend isn't around, ask a rape counselor to help you report. Just call a rape crisis center or Women Against Rape to send someone to help. (See "Resources" for a place near you.)

The police may want to interview you without a family member at some point, especially if they suspect the assailant was someone you know. They believe you might feel freer to tell them what really happened alone. If you are scared, insist that a friend or the rape counselor stay with you.

A lot of teenagers are scared of the police and sometimes with reason —in some small towns, there seems to be constant warfare going on between the police and the teens. But you are the victim of a crime now, not a suspect, and the job of the police is to help you. If you don't like the way a police officer is treating you, complain and ask for someone else. You have a right to be treated with respect and kindness.

PROSECUTING

If a suspect is arrested and put on trial and you have pressed charges, you, as the victim, will be called to testify as a witness, even if you are a minor. At some point you'll have to testify without your parents present. However, most court systems will have a legal advocate to help you and explain things to you. What exactly you will go through and how to find support is described in detail in Chapter 4 on "Prosecuting."

SELF-DEFENSE

Self-defense should be taught to boys and girls in schools the way gym is. Children are taught how to cross roads, how to behave if there's a fire, and to avoid strangers, but, ironically, they aren't told how to defend themselves from the most likely danger of all, sexual assault. In school, boys practice fighting all the time, but girls aren't supposed to, even though they need to defend themselves just as much, if not more. The "ideal" girl is expected to be "feminine"—polite, soft-voiced, quiet, pretty, and unaggressive—not someone who can raise a blood-curdling scream and punch a rapist in the balls. Unfortunately, the "ideal" girl is also the ideal victim, the one who will be easily intimidated into not screaming, not fighting, not running, and not telling. But knowing how to defend yourself doesn't mean becoming gruff and menacing. It means becoming confident.

If your school doesn't offer self-defense classes—a combination of judo, karate, and basic fighting techniques—you can probably take them from a YWCA, Boy Scouts or Girl Scouts, or from various private associations. You could also talk to people at school about arranging for a self-defense teacher to come and give a few lessons. See Part Three "Resources" for self-defense and rape education groups.

Not only is taking self-defense fun and good exercise, it gives you a chance to release your pent-up emotions, to regain some of the confidence the assault took from you, and to learn how to avoid, as well as defend yourself from, future attacks. It can even help you if you are a victim of incest. One girl who took classes in self-defense managed to stop her father's assaults by this simple method: when he turned the doorknob to enter her bedroom at night as usual, she said in a loud voice, "What do you want, Dad?" He was so embarrassed that he crept away and never tried it again.[15] Please see "Self-defense" in Chapter 2 for more on this.

Incest

The sexual assault of teenagers cannot be discussed without mentioning incest. Child protection organizations estimate that between a hundred thousand and a million American girls and boys are sexually molested each year[16] and that one third of the molesters are members of the victim's immediate family.[17] In other words, a large proportion of the sexual assault of teenagers is incestual.

For some children the incest starts when they are young and ends with puberty; for some it doesn't begin until puberty. For some it goes on throughout their childhood and teens until they leave home. The ingredients of incest that make it particularly traumatic for victims are (1) it is committed by somebody older than the victim, someone whom they love in some way and who has authority over them, and (2) it involves some sort of physical or emotional force. Because these ingredients determine the trauma to the child, experts in the field no longer define incest as sexual relations between family members related by blood. If a stepfather has authority over a child, his sexual assaults on her are just as emotionally disturbing as those of a biological father.

Incest is committed by fathers, mothers, stepparents, foster parents, brothers and sisters, uncles, aunts, and grandparents of all classes and races. The vast majority of offenders are male, but women do it, too. Often the sexual contact is forced on the child violently, but sometimes he or she is coerced into it by a set of tricks, promises, deceptions, or threats.[18] With children, the sexual contact does not usually involve penetration, but with teenagers it does.

There has been a lot of publicity lately given to incest victims who claim to have enjoyed their "special relationship" with the offender, but such a reaction is rarer than popular myth would have it. In a study of teenage girl prostitutes conducted in San Francisco, it was found that over 60 percent of them had run away from home specifically to avoid incestual abuse.[19] The *Runaway Newsletter* reported that incestual abuse was one of the three primary reasons children of both sexes run away from home.[20] One only has to listen to childrens' accounts of the terror, disgust, and pain they felt to see how far from pleasure such an experience is for most of them. And even if they aren't repulsed or hurt by it as young children, once they become teenagers, they feel trapped and disgusted by it and feel like outcasts when they see how other families behave.

Most incest, about 90 percent according to some studies, is between fathers and daughters,[21] and is accompanied by a cloud of secrecy. The father convinces his daughter that her mother will not be able to stand knowing about it, that she will break up the family if she tells, and that no one will believe her anyway, and so binds her to live in terror alone. This terror can go on for years.

Often a victim of incest won't be able to rebel until she is a teenager and is old enough to realize that she has the power to change things. She'll probably find herself in a trap, however. Her father may regard her as a lover or substitute wife, as if she were a grown woman, and be extremely possessive of her. He may forbid her to go out with friends, especially boys; insist on driving her to and from school; and get whiny, threatening, or even tearful every time she tries to break away. She will resent this, yet perhaps feel sorry for him. Some girls like being this important to their fathers, but most hate it. They want to be daughters, not wives; teenagers, not responsible women. But once a victim gets a little older, she might find it possible to tell another family member and she might be able to make herself go to authorities to seek help. (Often this is when it is discovered that the offender is molesting other children in the family as well.)

If the offender is someone other than a father, such as an uncle, the victim is still liable to be terrorized and confused into silence by him. Sometimes when children try to tell their parents what is going on, they are pooh-poohed into silence; no one wants to hear the bad news.

If you are in a situation like any of these, here are some tips that you might find useful:

· You are not bad. The incest is not your fault and you didn't invite it, no matter what anyone might have told you. You were forced into it, even though you may feel that you did it willingly. There are many subtle ways to force a child, and you were the victim of some of those.

· You can love normally. You may feel bitter, for what began as innocent love got turned into something nightmarish, but that doesn't mean you can't love someone else on your own terms, in the way you want. It may take time and you may need help, but many, many people in your position have recovered and gone on to have normal, happy lives.

· Your father/uncle/brother, whoever he is, may not be an utterly evil person. He may need help; he may need to straighten himself out and realize the harm he is causing. But that doesn't mean that no part of him is good or loving.

• Your mother is not to blame. Often a father will tell his daughter that her mother is a bad wife and that's why he had to turn to her. But his impulse to turn to his daughter is born of other problems than a bad marriage: if he needs to turn to someone else, it should be another adult, not his daughter. And although there is little doubt that the marriage is bad, that is never one person's fault. Your mother may never have guessed what was happening, even if it seemed obvious to you, or she may have known on some level but was unable to face up to it. She can be your ally, however, if you and she can trust one another.

• You can find someone to believe you. People in the family may be so shocked by incest that they refuse to believe you, but you can turn elsewhere for support. Are you close enough to the parents of a friend to ask them for help, for instance? You can also call a rape crisis center, where you'll find people who have come across many teenagers in your situation and know that you have no reason to lie about such a thing.

See "Resources" for a rape crisis program near you.

The subject of incest is too vast to do it justice here, but excellent books on the subject, written for both the victim and the victim's family, are: *I Never Told Anyone* edited by Ellen Bass and Louise Thornton (New York: Harper & Row, 1983); *Father's Days* by Katherine Brady (New York: Dell, 1979); *Conspiracy of Silence: The Trauma of Incest* by Sandra Butler (San Francisco: Volcano Press, 1978); and *The Best-Kept Secret* by Florence Rush (New York: McGraw-Hill, 1980). Also see the books on children recommended in the introduction to Part Two.

How Others Can Help

The people close to a rape victim can help her or him tremendously with recovery, but this is never so true as with a teenager or a child. Young people look to adults for models of how to react and cope. They also look to adults for protection. If you are close to a teenage victim, and especially if you are a relative, you are in a unique position to help her.

HOW PARENTS CAN HELP

Denise talked about how she felt after Sara's rape:

> If I'd had my choice, I would have walked Sara to and from school for the rest of her life. Sometimes she'd be late home from school and not call, and I'd be in agony. I wanted to be by her side forever, to follow her all the time, but she said, "You always *look* at me." I was obviously bothering her.
>
> In the first month after the rape, I started to fall apart. Sara watched me disintegrate and she was very strong. I felt she needed me, but I was a vegetable—I couldn't feel anymore.

One of the saddest things about rape is that it makes so many people victims—not just the person who was raped, but her or his parents, siblings, friends and perhaps even the whole school. Everyone will feel frightened and angry. As the parent of a rape victim, you are a victim, too, and you will probably suffer almost as much as your child. But you are also the most important influence on her recovery. Frankly, you can either make her or his recovery relatively smooth or you can make it hell. Here are some do's and don'ts to help you choose the first path. These apply equally to the parents of girl or boy victims.

DO

• When she first tells you about the assault, tell her you love her, you care about what happens to her, and that you are glad she told you.

• Reassure her immediately that you believe her.

• Tell her that you are angry not at her, but at the rapist.

• As her symptoms gradually come out, assure her that she isn't going crazy. Tell her they are normal reactions and that she will get better and stronger.

• Tell her that it's okay to hate the man or men who did it, but not to hate herself.

• Keep reassuring her that you love her.

• Tell her you are proud that she got out alive.

• Tell her that from now on you will pick her up in the car or by foot whenever she wants, no questions asked. It is a good idea to say this to any teenager, assaulted or not, for many put themselves in danger because they are afraid their parents will be angry at them for calling them late or being somewhere they aren't supposed to be.

· Tell her you trust her to let you know when she needs you, no questions asked and no punishment even if she's broken the rules. If she knows you trust her and that she can trust you, she can better protect herself.

· Ask her if she wants to go to the hospital right away or later, and if she wants to go to the police. Let her make these decisions herself.

· Ask for her permission before you tell anyone else about the assault.

· Tell her exactly what you are doing about the assault, whom you are calling, and what arrangements you are making. She needs to feel in control.

· Ask her if she wants counseling but don't force it on her. Tell her to say when and if she wants it later.

· Tell her that getting help is a sign of strength, not weakness, but that she has to feel ready for it to work.

DON'T

· Get angry at her—for getting hurt, for not telling you sooner, for getting conned, for not resisting, for inviting the rape.

· Curtail her independence by keeping her in, insisting on accompanying her everywhere, tightening rules.

· Punish her. She didn't do anything bad, the rapist did. Even if she broke rules, she's been punished enough.

· Blame her, even if she was taking a foolish risk when it happened.

· Keep treating her as if she's different. Special treats, presents, extra leniency might only reinforce her feelings of being changed by the rape. At the same time, if she needs a light on at night or you to drive her places, allow her that. A rule of thumb about this is to let her be treated differently in ways she wants, but not to impose.

· Refuse to discuss the assault.

· Pretend it will go away if you don't talk about it.

· Assume that she wants to move if the assault happened at home. She may already be feeling bad about disrupting the family. Leaving the family home may just make her feel worse.

While you are trying to be perfect, following all the do's and don'ts, you are bound to make mistakes. Every child is different and every rape victim is different, so even if you follow all the suggestions here perfectly, you might still do something wrong for your particular teenager.

Don't hate yourself for it, just try to keep communication with her or him open.

Serious harm coming to a child may be the most painful sort of experience a family can bear. Partly to help herself endure that pain, Denise started working for a rape crisis center after her daughter was raped. She also wrote a letter to be given to other parents in her position, in which she described that pain.

> When my daughter was assaulted, the pain I felt was deeper than I ever could have anticipated. I felt overwhelmed, afraid and filled with a sense of loss beyond what I could understand. . . . The shock is over [now] but there will always be a certain sadness that she had to endure that trauma.[22]

Another mother put it even more succinctly: "I wish it could have happened to me instead of her."

This pain will infect your whole family. You, your spouse, and your other children will suffer from it. Sometimes the pain will make family members turn on each other, so it is important to keep communication as open as possible. Talk to your other children, don't shunt them aside in your eagerness to help the victim. Explain as much as you can to them about what has happened and what it means. Treating your other children considerately is a way of helping the victim, too, for she doesn't want to be resented by her siblings. And be prepared for some of this stress to cause conflict with your spouse. Denise said:

> My husband reacted to Sara's rape by burying himself in his work. I was frightened and needed him. I was scared to take out the garbage, to get in the elevator alone. So there was trouble between us.

You and your spouse will be mourning the part of your child that seems to have been killed by the assault, the part that used to be free and trusting. You will also be constantly wondering if she'll be permanently damaged by it, if her sexuality will ever be normal, and you won't even know anymore which behavior changes are due to age and which to the assault. Everything will become exaggerated and full of depressing significance.

You will probably be riddled with self-blame. "How could I have let this happen?" is the almost universal reaction among parents of rape victims. You feel that you've failed in your most essential role as a parent, that of protector. If your child was out somewhere dangerous or late when the assault happened, you might blame yourself for being too lenient, for not knowing what she was getting up to, for not having a close enough relationship with her for her to tell you what she does, or for not teaching her to protect herself better. If she was out as an act of rebellion, you may blame yourself or your spouse for "driving her to it." You might also be afraid that your friends and neighbors will regard you as bad parents for "letting" this happen. But even the children of the most perfect parents are raped. You can't watch teenagers every minute of the day, you can't keep them prisoners, and you can't expect them not to try to live a life of their own. As Shelley, whose daughter Lynn was raped when she was only eight, said, "I felt I wanted to put Lynn back in my womb. I wanted to surround her with protection." But you can't. And you shouldn't.

You will have to cope not only with all your own worries but with the complicated and often extreme reactions your child is having to the assault. Please see Chapter 1 for a description of what these are likely to be, so that you aren't too shocked or worried by them. She may not have these reactions at first, but after two or three months her nightmares, fears, shakes, and crying may begin. Shelley said this happened to her daughter.

> For the first three months after the rape, Lynn didn't show much reaction to the rape, except that if she saw a boy in the street who looked like her attacker, she would cringe. But afterward, great clots of fear began to come out. One night I had to hold her wrapped in a quilt on my lap because she was shaking so hard her teeth rattled. Then she couldn't sleep if I was asleep, and she'd wake up with screaming nightmares.
>
> After she'd had some counseling, the nightmares stopped, but if she ever heard a word like "attack" or saw something that reminded her of the rape, she'd get upset all over again.

Denise described similar reactions in Sara.

> After about six months Sara wanted to see a counselor. By then she was crying and grieving and having nightmares—it had finally really hit her. But she was also able to talk about it when she chose, unlike before.
>
> It was strange having my child go to therapy. I felt I was losing her as a confidante. She had secrets with someone else. The bond between her and the counselor was almost visible.
>
> Now, fourteen months after it happened, she still has nightmares

a lot. Some are symbolic and some are real. She dreams she captures him, for instance. They are scary dreams. She cries for her father to come get her.

But she's also got a kind of maturity she didn't have before, which is a kind of payoff, I guess.

Letting go of your child, allowing her to be independent, is very hard after an assault. But it is essential. If she wants to go to a counselor without you, you must respect her wishes, for she may need to discuss your reactions and her feelings about you.

Part of helping your child recover is also allowing yourself some relief. Turn to friends for support, but when you do, choose them carefully. Not everyone will be helpful, as Denise discovered.

Some of my friends felt threatened by Sara's rape and so didn't want to hear about it. Others didn't know about it but saw that I was acting odd and so thought I didn't like them anymore. I think it's a good idea to tell your friends that you are dealing with something difficult and ask them to be patient with you.

A Note for Fathers

As a father, you are terribly important to your child's recovery from sexual assault. You can provide a daughter with a model of a man who is good, gentle, and not a rapist, and you can assure a son that his assault doesn't compromise his sexuality or make you think less of him. If you feel embarrassed by the subject, or are full of self-recrimination for not having rescued your child, don't let that make you withdraw from the family, get mad at your child, or dismiss the rape as a "woman's problem." Your child needs you, and even though you may feel a failure for not having protected her, you can make up for that by helping her now. Please read the section on "How Men Can Help" in Chapter 3.

If Your Teenager Won't Tell

No matter how good your relations with your child may seem, he or she may not tell you about an assault for fear of your anger or out of shame, embarrassment, or a stubborn pride. There are certain symptoms, however, that might indicate that something like a sexual assault has occurred. If you see any of these in your child, don't immediately jump to the conclusion that he or she has been raped, but it is worth asking gently if something is wrong. If you ask with the promise that you won't get angry, your teenager might trust you enough to tell. And if you still aren't getting any information, try asking directly, without anger, if she or he has been attacked in some way. Here are some common symptoms of sexual assault:

• A sudden change in behavior, such as depression, an overt obsession with sex, unusual quietness, or bursts of anger.

• An abrupt onset of a phobia or fear of school, a certain person or place.

• Sudden reluctance to go out.

• A change in dress, such as wearing unflattering clothes or lots of layers.

• Self-mutilation, such as burning arms with cigarettes, cutting the skin, pulling out or chopping off hair.

• Crying spells.

• Washing excessively or not at all.

• Boys suddenly asking lots of questions about homosexuality.

• Running away or playing truant.

• The teenager contracts VD or the girl gets pregnant. Don't assume that she had voluntary sex, especially if she's very young or naïve or has never had a boyfriend. Don't make a big, punitive deal of it either. You could just say, "Did this happen with a boyfriend, or did someone make you have sex?" Reassure her that you are not disgusted or angry with her and that you want to help. The pregnancy or VD is frightening enough.

Perhaps the problem is not an assault, but you will want to find out what it is anyway so that you can help. If it is an assault, then exercise the do's and don'ts listed above, especially letting your child know that you are very glad he or she finally told you.

HOW SIBLINGS CAN HELP

Denise said her other children were seriously affected by Sara's rape:

> Sara's older sister went through a stage of putting herself in danger after the rape. She started traveling alone, taking late night walks by herself. I think she felt guilty about not being the one who was raped.

Her older brother wanted to get some counseling about it. He found himself getting less sociable, and he was confused about what kind of man rapes, what rape really means.

Then her youngest brother, who's just a little older than Sara, became very arrogant. They used to be close, but he bullies her now. He gives negative responses to her questions and statements and says, "If you do that again, I'll kill you." If she cries, he feels remorse and then he gets punished by us—that almost seems to be what he wants. He complains that we're always easier on Sara than on him. He's making himself the villain of the family, when he used to be the most popular.

As the brother or sister of a rape victim, you are closely affected yourself. You probably feel scared, vulnerable, and angry. You may also feel jealous because, all of a sudden, the victim is precious and delicate and special; then you feel terribly guilty for having that jealousy because, after all, she was the one who was hurt. On top of this you might, like Sara's older sister, feel guilty because you weren't hurt and she was. Brothers also often feel confused about their role as sexual aggressors—"Am I a rapist? What is a rapist?"—and sisters feel extra vulnerable. Try to talk about these feelings to each other, your parents, or friends. They are normal reactions and you shouldn't feel too bad about them.

If you are the older sister or brother of a victim, you won't escape feeling threatened and confused by the rape, but you can still be an enormous help. If she doesn't want to tell your parents about the assault, for example, she might feel able to tell you. If she does, you'll have to cope in the way parents will, so be sure to read the section "How Parents Can Help" above. Especially remember to assure the victim that your rage is at the attacker, not her. Also, don't betray her trust. If she is adamantly against telling your parents and you think she is wrong, you can try gently to persuade her to, but don't push it and don't tell them behind her back. She needs to keep a sense of control over her life right now because the rapist tried to rob her of that. And she needs to know she can trust someone.

If you agree not to tell your parents, you can still help by contacting a rape crisis counselor, if the victim is willing, and by going with her to the hospital, the rape crisis center, and the police. Also, if your parents notice that something is wrong and try to pump you about it, tell them that the victim is upset about something but that she doesn't want to talk about it yet. And reassure them that you are helping meanwhile.

It is quite possible that when your sister or brother tells you about being assaulted, the culprit will be someone you know, even your own father. This news is terribly upsetting for you, but the very fact that he or she told you is the most important step on the way to stopping the abuse. Please read the section on "Incest" above.

HOW FRIENDS CAN HELP

If you are the friend of someone who has been sexually assaulted, the best you can do is show her that you still respect her, that you don't blame her, and that you care about her. If she wants to talk about the assault, don't try to shut her up, and don't be afraid to ask her how she's feeling about it once in a while. She might want to talk about it. Read Chapter 3 for more about what you can do.

If you are a friend of the victim's parents, you can also be a help or a hindrance to the family's recovery. Denise complained about the reactions of her friends.

> Some friends said all the wrong things to me. My mother-in-law said, "Well, you're strong, you can handle it," and that wasn't comforting at all because it made me feel as if I wasn't allowed to show how upset I was. I didn't feel strong.
> Then another friend said, "There's something more in it than the rape. The rape shouldn't be so upsetting." She tried to delve into my psychology to prove something was wrong with me for being upset that my thirteen-year-old daughter was raped! And someone else said, "If you'd been working, you would have handled this better," as if my being a housewife was making me a weaker person.

Try as you might, it's hard to avoid making at least one tactless remark, but you can make up for it in other ways. Mainly, you'll have to exercise patience and do a lot of listening, which is quite a test of your friendship.

You may find yourself more affected by the rape of your friend's child than you expected. If you have children yourself, you will be terrified for them, and you might be disturbed by seeing your friend so upset, especially if he or she is usually confident and capable. You'll probably also grow impatient over time, for your friend won't get better quickly. You may even feel sick of the whole subject while simultaneously being horrified by it. A trauma such as rape spreads out to the people the victim knows like ripples in a pond, each person having to be sympathetic to one person and then needing to let off steam at another. But as it spreads, it diffuses, and a network of support can result.

HOW TO HELP WITH PROSECUTING

Parents and friends of a teenager going through the trial of an assailant will be needed badly. The courts are always intimidating places, but especially to young people who may distrust the police and not quite understand what is going on. Also, having to describe the assault over and over is traumatic for the victim and may elicit a recurrence of her rape trauma symptoms (see Chapter 1). The victim needs your assurance that you believe her, that she is doing a strong and noble thing, and that you are proud of her.

If the teenager is becoming disturbed or traumatized by the legal procedures of viewing a lineup, being interviewed, having to testify, or being cross-examined, inform the prosecutor on her case immediately. You should also arrange for a rape counselor or victim's advocate to talk to her. They can reassure her and find out what she needs to make her feel better. If you have any complaints about how the case is going or how the child is being treated, make them to the prosecutor.

Your first priority is the victim's recovery, and if you and she feel that she is suffering too much, you may both want to withdraw her from the case. If so, tell everyone concerned as soon as possible so that they can work out how to save the case without her.

Please see Chapter 4 for more on prosecuting.

Rape doesn't have to ruin a person's life, and the young are especially resilient and optimistic. If you can show the victim that you love her and respect her for her struggle to recover, you are helping her recover. As Shelley said:

> About one and a half years after her assault, Lynn decided to try staying with some friends for three days, the longest she'd been

away from me since the rape. In the middle of packing, she stopped and came in and sat down next to me and said, "Mom, am I going to make it?"

I said, "Yes," and for the first time, I knew it was true.

9

Lesbians and Gay Men

If you are a female or male victim of sexual assault and you are gay, you will have special difficulties to face. Feeling like an outcast because of your sexual orientation is bad enough, but when you have the stigma of being a rape victim added to that, it can isolate you even more. This chapter will discuss the problems unique to you, but it is only intended as a supplement to Part One for women and Chapter 6 for men.

Women

Perhaps the most damaging reaction to rape for many lesbians is the sense that they are being deservedly punished for their sexuality.[1] Lesbianism is considered so aberrant in our society that it is a rare woman who doesn't feel guilty about it on some level. Lara, whose lover was raped by a male friend, said:

> When my lover was raped, she was in her first lesbian relationship. The man who raped her was her best friend, and he said he did it to show her that she really wanted men. He kept saying "This is what you want, isn't it?" during the rape, and he tore a bracelet I'd given her off her wrist.
>
> Afterward, she felt terrible that she hadn't tried to fight him off. I think it was because she felt, deep down, that she deserved what he was doing to her. She took it as a kind of punishment.

This attitude just compounds the guilt most victims of rape feel anyway; you are guilty not only because you think the rape was your fault but because you think your lifestyle has brought on the rape. You might even decide, "That's what I get for leading a deviant life." You might be afraid that your lifestyle puts you in more danger because men are threatened by lesbianism.

When the rapist knows you are a lesbian, as happened to Lara's lover, he may well have contributed to your guilt by telling you that he raped you "for your own good." He is subscribing to the myth that all a lesbian needs is "one good screw" to start wanting men. In fact, he raped you as an expression of his own fantasy, and only used that myth as a justification for his actions. On the surface, you probably know this, but if you have only a seed of doubt about it, you can torture yourself with it. Try to remind yourself that you are not bad, you do not deserve punishment, and that no one has a right to punish you for your lifestyle anyway. Above all, remember that the rapist was using you for his own ends, whatever his excuse, and that the rape really had nothing to do with who you actually are.

If the rapist was a stranger, or someone who didn't know that you are a lesbian, be careful not to slide into the paranoid thought that somehow he *did* know and picked you out because of it. Rapists don't care about what your life is like or what you do. They only care that you are available.

When you are not openly lesbian, a rape can make you question your life in painful ways. By hiding your sexuality, you have kept a distance between yourself and others, so you aren't likely to be close enough to them to confide in them about the rape. And even if you can tell, you still can't express your deepest fears about how it relates to your sexuality. Faced with this dilemma, you might find yourself withdrawing into further isolation, or you might have to risk your job and your relationship with your family by coming out. Neither choice is wonderful.

Families present a special problem. A supportive family can be a tremendous help to your recovery, but a condemning one can make you feel worse. The last thing you need to hear is, "What do you expect with your lifestyle?" or, "Now maybe you'll like men," which is about as logical as saying to the victim of a car crash, "Now maybe you'll like driving." Many lesbians are already estranged from their families, and the rape just further separates them. If you can't turn to people you've known all your life for help, don't just give up. Try to find someone to talk to, for talking is the best way to sort out all the pain and confusion caused by rape. If no one you know seems right, try a professional counselor.

Lesbians who are already uncomfortable with men may become over-whelmingly angry at them after a rape. But your increased hostility is not unusual. Just about all rape victims go through a period of hating or at least distrusting men afterward. One study that compared 225 lesbians with 233 heterosexual women found that the lesbians tended to reject all men as companions after a rape and the heterosexual women tended to blame themselves more for not being careful.[2] If you want to overcome your distrust of men, being friends with them can help—as will the passage of time. Knowing men, straight or gay, can also help you conquer a crippling fear of them.

There is a myth that rape won't cause sexual problems for lesbians because they don't have to make love to a member of the sex that attacked them. This myth has led to the expectation that a lesbian should recover from rape more easily than a heterosexual. But a lesbian has as many sexual problems as any woman and is affected by rape in the same ways, too. One study found that lesbians had the same sexual problems as a result of rape as heterosexuals—low sex drive, no arousal, and difficulty achieving orgasm.[3] Feeling sexual has so much to do with a sense of confidence, with liking yourself, and with being able to relax that a trauma like rape, which attacks these qualities, can adversely affect you regardless of your sexuality or of who did the rape.

This last point brings up another problem—when the assailant is female. Women do occasionally rape other women, usually as part of a gang of men or women. The shock and betrayal a woman feels on being sexually assaulted by another woman can be so enormous that some block out the memory of it altogether. In one case, related by Tamar Hosansky, an instructor at the Safety & Fitness Exchange in New York, it took two years of therapy before a victim remembered that the leader of the gang who had raped her was a woman and that, worst of all, that woman had inflicted more injuries on her than anyone else. When you are a lesbian, you may especially tend to see women as nurturing, sup-portive "sisters," so when one turns around and mugs or cons you, let alone rapes you, it can make you feel as if your last bastion of safety has been violated. If you were assaulted by a woman, your trust of everyone you know, men and women alike, has probably been deeply shaken. You might feel that you'll never be able to trust or love anyone again. You will, but it may take time.

HOW TO HELP YOURSELF

Lara talked about the ways being a lesbian can help you recover from rape. "We can't go home for holidays or walk down the street holding hands with someone we love without getting harassed, so we're used to having to stick together. We can use that as a strength." She also mentioned that a lesbian might be able to get more sympathy and understanding from a lover than a heterosexual woman would. A man has to work hard at understanding what it is like to be raped, but a woman can imagine it quite vividly if she's willing to try. Also, your lover will probably understand more readily than a man that you need to be held and comforted without sexual pressure for a while.

Lara suggested that lesbians might feel safe enough with their lovers to really open up and let all their terrors out in a way few heterosexual women can, but this openness has a bad and good side. It can help you find relief, but it can also terrify your partner. Try not to be offended if she doesn't seem to want to listen sometimes—she's traumatized, too.

If you can, use these strengths to help yourself: If you are hating yourself for what happened, for example, think about how you came to terms with your lesbianism and use that as a model for dissipating your self-blame. If medical and legal personnel are giving you a hard time about your rape, blaming you and so on, remember how you coped with discrimination about your lesbianism and use those skills. You might have become involved in some political action concerned with lesbians, for instance, something you can do on behalf of rape victims, too. And if you find yourself hiding your feelings and withdrawing from people, think of the friends who stuck by you in the past and turn to them.

The first piece of advice anyone knowledgeable about rape gives a victim is *"Don't blame yourself,"* but this is easier said than done. As many lesbians are feminists, they are likely to know that they shouldn't blame themselves for rape, but just knowing you shouldn't feel something doesn't stop you from feeling it. You may not only be blaming yourself, but feel guilty for doing so because you know you shouldn't. So you end up guilty for feeling guilt. The best you can do if this happens is to examine what exactly you feel guilty about and why. If, for instance, you are blaming yourself for not fighting back, look at why you didn't. Was it because you were afraid for your life or health? If so, you did the right thing in not fighting, because you survived, and that's nothing to be ashamed of. Are you ashamed of not fighting back because you feel that, in the face of crisis, you just buckled under to years of feminine conditioning and therefore that all your feminist ideals and struggles were for naught? Yet ideals are always hard to live up to and may be downright impossible in the face of a life-or-death decision. Or did you not fight back because you felt you had no right to—that you were getting what was coming to you? If so, ask yourself why you feel that way. This kind of questioning might bring up some painful realizations concerning your sense of self and your sexuality, but it can help you sort them out, too. Sometimes just facing up to a nasty secret such as "I'm ashamed of myself" can help you defuse it. If you need to talk over these types of issues with someone—and they are not easy to deal with on your own—don't be afraid to try a counselor if no friend seems appropriate. You can ask at a rape crisis center or women's center for a lesbian counselor if you want. They may not have one, but they should understand and honor such a request if they can. (See "Resources" for places to call.)

HOW OTHERS CAN HELP

Lovers

If you are the lover of a woman who has been raped, you have become a victim, too, not only because the person you love has been hurt, but because you feel frightened for yourself. The rape of a woman you have a sexual relationship with is so close that it almost feels as if you were raped, too. Sometimes your victimization is even more direct than this, for when rapists find two women in one place, they often tie one up and force her to watch while they rape the other (if they don't rape both of them). If this happens, you have a triple burden to bear— having had to witness horrible violence being done to your lover, the guilt of having been unable to rescue her, and the guilt of not being the one who was raped—the guilt of the survivor.

Whatever the circumstances of the rape, as the victim's lover you will probably have the same kinds of terrors, nightmares, and depressions as she. You also might find yourself thinking all kinds of ungenerous, unsupportive, and unfeminist thoughts about her. Go to another friend to let off steam so that you can avoid hurting her more. Lara had to do this.

> When my lover was raped, I was furious at her. I knew I shouldn't feel that way and that it wasn't her fault, but I couldn't help it. I was so afraid that I'd say all kinds of harmful things to her that I went to a friend to let it all out.
>
> I screamed all the most awful things I could think of, things lesbians and feminists know better than ever to say, like, "Why didn't she fight back? What kind of lesbian is she, anyway? Why are women so weak?" It's as if all the myths and prejudices about women I'd been fighting against had to come out. But that really helped. Afterward, I could give her what she needed.

Because you are a woman and a lesbian, you might think that you know more about rape than most people and so will be able to give your lover the appropriate kinds of help. But even with knowledge and the best of intentions, you can still make mistakes, as Lara found out.

> After my lover was raped, I decided that she wouldn't want sex. So I waited for her to approach me. Meanwhile, she thought I wouldn't approach her because I considered her contaminated by having been raped by a man. So I was walking around feeling pleased with myself for being so considerate while she was walking around feeling like a leper. If we'd talked about it, that misunderstanding need never have happened.

The sense that the rape victim has been contaminated by a man is quite common among lesbian lovers. You might not only feel this but that you have been betrayed; she has been unfaithful both to your love and to your sexuality by having had sex with a man. This sense of betrayal may be very strong, even when you know it is illogical and unfair, and it can make you angry with the victim. If you are angry at her, try to talk about your anger with someone other than the victim at first, because she might not be able to cope with your feeling betrayed by her for an act she had no control over. If you are disgusted that she had sex with a man, remember that the sex was more akin to a beating than any form of lovemaking. Try to direct that disgust where it belongs—toward the assailant.

Relatives and Friends

If you are related to the rape victim or are a close friend but not her lover, your ways of helping her will be the same as those mentioned in Chapter 3. But remember that she will need extra reassurance that you don't think she deserved the rape because she's a lesbian and that you don't despise her for being a double outcast. If you haven't come to grips with her lesbianism before, this is the time to do it, for otherwise you won't be able to help her much. Read books such as *Loving Someone Gay* by Don Clark (New York: New American Library, 1977); *Sappho Was A Right-On Woman* by Sidney Abbott and Barbara Love (New York: Stein & Day, 1978); and *Now That You Know: What Every Parent Should Know About Homosexuality* by Betty Fairchild and Nancy Hayward (New York: Harcourt Brace Jovanovich, 1979).

If other issues come up, such as her increased alienation from men, the best you can do is make her feel loved. If you are a man, you can help her with this by proving that men can be loving and sensitive.

Victims, their lovers, friends, and family might find comfort in these words written by a lesbian whose lover was raped.

To a Gay Woman Whose Lover Has Been Assaulted

You will wake up in the middle of the night and realize you almost lost her. . . . If you are lucky and she is not in the hospital, but lying beside you, you will lean over to make sure she is breathing. You will think perhaps she did die.

You will imagine that you were there and that you killed him. He will bleed, scream, plea for mercy; you will have no mercy.

You will want to hear all the details, and then you won't want to. You will imagine more details. You'll wonder if she's telling you everything.

In the middle of conversations, of work, of socializing, you suddenly blank out. You remember she was almost killed.

You hate him.

You go numb, you cry uncontrollably, laugh hysterically.

You will feel terrified. Your life is ruined. He will come back and murder both of you. If you weren't gay this wouldn't have happened. If you had done this or that, it wouldn't have happened. If only . . . if only, if only . . .

You can't change what happened. You're glad she's alive. You're afraid the relationship is ruined, that she'll never laugh again, that you'll never have fun, go to a movie, make love.

Every time you touch her, you think of what he did. The parts of her you love so much, that mean tenderness and warmth, suddenly mean violence and death. You are afraid to touch her because you will start to cry or scream.

You're not being supportive enough, you can't meet all her needs. If it had happened to you, she would act better. You should, you should, you should . . .

No one understands. You feel totally alone and you can't depend on her because she's in crisis. The world has been pulled out from under your feet. You are alone and you are lost.

Remember—

If your love is strong, nothing can destroy it. He may have tried but he couldn't take her away from you.

She will act strange. It may feel as if she's angry at you and is leaving you, but that's not true.

You are not crazy to be so upset.

It will get better. It will seem as if it's getting worse.

Try not to shut off your feelings. They will help you mend.

Somewhere in the experience there will be something positive; you will have learned something.

You'll realize just how strong and caring you are.

You don't have to be perfect. You are going to make mistakes.

It's not your fault, it's *his* fault.

Don't expect yourself to rise to dazzling heights of endurance; you are going to be exhausted, irritable and scared.

You are brave to be facing this.

You don't have to tell everyone and you don't have to keep it to yourself.

Allow yourself to fall apart when you need to.

All the anguish means that you love each other very much. The love was not killed. You are the same two people with a crisis that you will get through.[4]

Men

As a gay man who's been sexually assaulted, you are likely to feel the same sort of guilt lesbians do: "He attacked me because I look/act/am gay," which quickly leads to, "If I weren't gay, this wouldn't have happened."[5] The assailant may have made this guilt worse by telling you that you were getting what you deserve, but men who rape other men almost always say this to their victims, gay or not. By pretending to themselves that they are punishing you for being gay, they can pretend that they are acting like a macho straight man in assaulting you, instead of being the sick men they are.

If the rapist did know you were gay, it may bring up some agonizing problems for you. "This is what I get for being different" is a common reaction of gay victims, and it easily leads to the reasoning, "And because I'm different/gay," or, "because I lead a decadent life, I deserve to be punished for it." If you already feel ashamed of being gay on some level, being gay and a victim of rape is doubly shaming, as if you've failed in all possible ways of being masculine. This shame is only too understandable, alas, for society holds gays in contempt for not being masculine and male rape victims in contempt for the same reason, so you become doubly stigmatized. Also, if you keep your sexuality secret, you may see the assault as a punishment for leading a double life. This kind of reasoning makes many men hide away after an assault, cutting themselves off from any possibility of being helped. It also might even make you feel afraid to be gay anymore.

Like women, gay men are usually raped or assaulted in one of three ways: they are jumped, lured into a trap, or attacked by someone they agreed to have sex with. In the first case your reaction won't be much different than that of any rape victim—you'll be stunned by the suddenness of attack and experience symptoms of shock afterward. In the second case you'll be shocked but also feel betrayed by the friends who set you up and probably hate yourself for being tricked. In one such instance, a man had been invited by friends to a party. He went, not knowing that he had been set up as their "chicken," someone for them all to "enjoy." He was passed around, sodomized by instruments, mocked, and insulted. Afterward, he was not only deeply shaken, but he despised himself for having fallen victim to such a trick—he felt stupid.[6] In the third case, when you were assaulted by someone you'd agreed to have sex with, you'll not only feel shocked and betrayed but completely responsible for having been assaulted at all. You'll probably hate yourself for your lack of judgment and feel that you will never be able to trust anyone again.

Being attacked by a sexual partner happens unfortunately often to men and women. Sometimes the attacker is a robber taking advantage of the easy pickup system among some gays, but sometimes he's a torturer or someone who cannot have homosexual sex without having to exorcise his guilt about it by beating or hurting his partner afterward. Something like this happened to a twenty-two-year-old painter.[7] He had been introduced to a man by friends, and they went out and had a good time, afterward agreeing to go back to the man's apartment for the night. Once they got there, the man became brutal. He tied the painter up and kept him captive for two days, torturing and beating him and forcing him to perform sexual acts against his will. When the painter was finally released and able to go to the hospital, he was not only physically hurt but so disoriented that he couldn't even remember his address for a while. In another case a man went home with someone who tied him up and waited for a friend to come over so the two of them could abuse him together. These sorts of assaults are devastating, yet many gay men won't complain about them, perhaps because they assume this sort of behavior is usual for a certain kind of gay lifestyle. They may also be afraid to contribute to the myth that gays rape innocent boys by publicizing that gay rape does happen. This myth should be laid to rest here: research has found that gay men are a tiny minority of child molesters. Most child molesters are either heterosexual in their adult sex life, or are pedophiles, people whose sexual life is entirely directed toward children, a disorder that has nothing to do with homosexuality.[8] Whatever the reason, gay men have complained that rape is talked of very rarely in the gay community—it is almost a taboo subject.

Rape should be taken as seriously by gays as everyone else, however, for it is a horrible experience that severely affects the self-confidence and self-esteem of its victims. You should feel that you have a right to bring it up, get help, and make as much of a row about it as you can.

One of the reasons gay rape is so little understood is that there is a myth that all gays are sadomasochistic and want to be gang-banged, sodomized with instruments, and so on, and that rape is just the ultimate pleasure to them. This attitude is even prevalent among some gays. When a counselor was telling a gay friend about a brutal rape, the friend said facetiously, "Ooh, that sounds good. Can you introduce me?" The people who think like this don't even understand the first principle of rape, that it is a life-threatening assault. Whatever form of sex you like, you have to want it to enjoy it. When you are forced against your will to engage in sexual acts, especially under the threat of being maimed or killed, you are being terrorized, not seduced. Even if your taste tends to run toward the masochistic, you still have limits and you still have a form of control—some people say the masochistic partner actually controls sexual encounters more than the sadistic partner.[9]

And if you often fantasize about being raped—a recent study found that a forced sexual encounter with a man is the second most common sexual fantasy among gays[10]—that still doesn't mean you actually invited it. (See the discussion about the difference between fantasizing about rape and wanting it in the "Therapy" section in Chapter 2.) As a counselor said, "Play rape isn't real rape. Anytime you say no and mean it, yet that no isn't honored, that's rape." Anytime your control over your own body is taken away against your will, you are in the kind of danger that is not fun.

Another reason that rape should be taken seriously in the gay community is that the rape of men tends to be brutal and medically dangerous with the spread of AIDS. Emergency-room staff have told of men they've seen coming in with initials carved into their skins, whip marks, and other injuries caused by torture. Unfortunately, victims of this sort of thing are often too embarrassed to go to hospitals, which can result in festering wounds, badly damaged psyches, and untreated sexual diseases. If the community were more supportive of gay rape victims, the victims would find it easier to get medical help.

HOW TO HELP YOURSELF

If you have been raped or assaulted in other ways, the first thing you must do is attend to yourself medically. Unfortunately, because you are gay, seeking medical help can mean opening yourself up to derisive remarks from hospital staff and other officials. In Chapter 6 there is a description of what happened to George, a straight victim of rape, when he went to the hospital bleeding and in pain. The doctor greeted him by saying, "You look as if you've been having a good time." The doctor assumed that George was gay and masochistic, but even had that been true, it still would have been an insult—here was a man badly hurt and upset and the doctor calls it "a good time."

If you live in an area where there are centers for gay men and lesbians, try calling them for a referral to a hospital or medical service where you might be treated with more respect than at a traditional place. (See "Resources.") Even if you weren't physically injured, you should go to the hospital for a VD checkup and treatment. You don't have to tell anyone that you were assaulted or even that you are gay.

The next thing to consider is whether to report the assault. Once more, this is especially tricky when you're gay. Most police officers will have the attitude that gay men want to be raped so have nothing to complain about. The National Gay Task Force is trying to change this attitude and to set up centers to help gay victims of violence. To find out about such a center near you, check Part Three in this book and try calling these numbers:

National Gay Task Force
Outside of New York State (800) 221-7044 (toll-free)
In New York State   (212) 807-6016

If you can find a center for gays near you, you may be able to get support for both reporting and prosecuting. (See the end of this chapter for more on prosecuting.)

On the psychological level you'll probably have to grapple with at least a degree of self-blame. When someone is raped, they tend to look for reasons why it happened—everyone needs rational explanations for random events to make them less frightening. Because there isn't a reason except that you were terribly unlucky, you tend to look for those reasons within yourself. So you may decide that you were raped because you were careless, stupid, weak-looking, because you gave come-on signals to the wrong man, because you have bad judgment, or because you are gay. Then you begin to wonder why you made the mistake, whatever it was, that lead to your assault. If you were abused by a prospective lover, for example, you may think, "I went home with him and I wanted sex, so maybe I wanted that too," and then you go on to, "Maybe that means I'm subconsciously seeking abuse." And before you know it, you've absolved the assailant altogether and plumped all the responsibility on yourself.

These thoughts are hard to bear. Sometimes they even have a grain of truth to them. But, nevertheless, the rape is never your fault. If you went home with a man you don't know, yes, you took a risk, but that is very different from asking for abuse. If a woman agrees to go on a date with someone at a party, that doesn't mean she wants him to knock her unconscious and rape her. You may meet a man you want to make love with, but that doesn't mean you want to be raped or tortured, nor does it mean that you don't have a right to be outraged, shocked, and murderously furious about it afterward. *You* know when something feels like violence, not sex, so you know when you've been assaulted. And you have a right to mind.

You may have the additional problem of needing help yet only having the straight world to turn to for it. If you need medical treatment, for instance, the odds are that you'll be in the hands of straight men and women, and the same applies when you go to the police. Having to rely on straights can be frightening, especially if you were the victim of antigay violence by straights. And if you were assaulted by a man you agreed to have sex with and you haven't come out yet, you are in particular trouble, for to seek help you may have to reveal your sexuality. These difficulties are why seeking help at a rape crisis center is wise. Even if the center is primarily run by women, they should be more sympathetic than traditional hospital staff, and many of them will know what it's like to be sexually assaulted. Don't be afraid to ask for a gay counselor if you want; if the center has any, they will oblige.

If you are in a steady relationship with a lover, your assault may bring up difficulties between you—jealousy, estrangement, shock, confusion. Please read the section on lovers under "Women" in this chapter.

If you are single, you have to face the problem of how to go on to have sexual relationships. A sexual assault is so terrifying that it leaves you with no confidence in yourself, with a terror of strangers, and a fear of sex. One study found that heterosexual men tend to react to rape by overcompensating and sleeping with as many women as possible, but gay men often withdraw from sex altogether for some time.[11] They become scared of men and therefore scared of sex with men. If you are in a steady relationship, you can be helped over this by an understanding and gentle approach by your lover, but when you are single, you might not have such support. The best thing to do in this case is give yourself time to recover. Spend time with people you trust and love, and approach sex again cautiously, when you feel ready. Don't feel you must push yourself to it in order to get over the rape faster.

Talking your fears over with a friend or counselor helps as well. Too many men tend to carry the burden of their assault in secret, which just erects a wall between them and other people that leaves them feeling alone, vulnerable, and, often, a little crazy. When you bring the subject up with selected friends, you may be surprised at how many have shared your experience in one way or another—it is thought now that as many male children are assaulted as female.[12] Talking to women can help, too, for they tend to be more willing to discuss rape and more understanding about it than most men. They may also be more ready to sympathize.

The New York City Gay/Lesbian Anti-Violence Project has these suggestions on how to protect yourself from future assaults and antigay violence, sexual or otherwise:

· If you pick up a stranger in a bar, introduce him to a friend or the bartender. Get a good look at him in the light. Some people work bars as teams and rob patrons and their apartments.

· Be wary of "knockout drops" around strangers—get your own drinks.

· If harassed, avoid verbal exchanges or gestures that might lead to violence against you.

· Be cautious of come-ons from drivers.

· If you are suspicious of the way a driver is acting, such as following you along the curb, write down the vehicle's description and license number.

· Walk assertively—with brisk, confident strides—and look alert.

· If you are tired, stoned, or just feel vulnerable, take taxis or use main thoroughfares.

· Carry a whistle or shriek alarm.

· Learn some simple self-defense techniques. (See "Self-defense" in Chapter 2.)

· Be prepared to scream and run.

HOW OTHERS CAN HELP

If you are the straight friend or relative of a gay victim, this is the time to face up to your prejudices about homosexuality and try to conquer them. See the books recommended on p. 221. For a gay victim of rape to be helped by others, he must first know that he is not secretly despised or derided for what he is.

If you are gay, the rape of a close friend or lover will be highly threatening—you'll feel so vulnerable yourself. Because of this, you might find yourself denying him the sympathy he needs and blaming him instead. One man who was beaten and robbed by a blond he'd picked up went to a counselor for help and found himself getting the blame. "I like blonds, too," the counselor said, "but I never pick up *that* type of blond." The counselor was protecting himself from the fact that he, too, could be a victim by pretending that he had better judgment than his client. Finding reasons why it happened to him and wouldn't to you might make you feel comforted, but it isn't going to help him. Keep such thoughts to yourself for the time being, and examine them while you are at it. Are they true?

As the lover of a rape victim, you may feel betrayed by him and even jealous. You might catch yourself tending not to believe him, thinking he's making up the story to cover an infidelity. You have these suspicions partly because you don't want to believe such an awful thing could happen, partly because you feel vicariously assaulted yourself and partly because your thinking can't be rational at a time of crisis. His assault will not only hurt and depress you, but might make you furious at him—for not protecting himself better, for bringing this tragedy into your lives, for upsetting the balance you'd achieved, and for simply getting himself hurt. You are what is called a "secondary victim" now and you are having many of the same traumatic symptoms as the victim, so try to tend to your own needs as well as his. Let off steam at someone else.

Reporting and Prosecuting

In twenty-eight states, at the time of this writing, homosexual sex—specifically oral and anal sodomy—between consenting adults is still illegal.* The awareness of this may make you, as a gay man or a lesbian, afraid of going to the police about your assault. You should know that this law is hardly ever used to prosecute consenting adults anymore, and that you should not be afraid because of it. It is used instead to prosecute child molesters, perpetrators of forcible sexual abuse, and gay prostitutes. To find out how the law tends to be used in your jurisdiction, consult your district attorney, local gay rights organization, or your local branch of the American Civil Liberties Union (ACLU).

If you are not openly gay, prosecuting your assailant may mean making some difficult decisions. On the one hand, if your sexuality becomes known, it might jeopardize your job and your relations with your family and friends. On the other hand, if you try to keep it hidden, you may

* As of April 1983, the states which hold consensual sodomy to be illegal are Alabama, Arizona, Arkansas, Florida, Georgia, Idaho, Kansas, Kentucky, Louisiana, Maryland, Massachusetts, Michigan, Minnesota, Mississippi, Missouri, Montana, Nevada, New York, North Carolina, Oklahoma, Pennsylvania, Rhode Island, South Carolina, Tennessee, Texas, Utah, Virginia, and Wisconsin. This is also true in the District of Columbia.[13]

have difficulty answering medical and legal questions truthfully. How important this is depends on the circumstances of the rape. If you were raped in circumstances that had nothing to do with your being gay, then your sexuality should never come up in court—it is an irrelevant part of your private life as far as the case is concerned. If you were raped in a gay bar, however, or by someone you picked up while cruising, covering up may prove virtually impossible. To be a strong witness in a rape case, you need to present a truthful and consistent story. Before deciding whether to be a witness—a decision you *don't* have to make before reporting the rape—think about whether you are willing to have your sexuality become known and how that might affect the case.

If you are openly gay, or decide to become so in order to prosecute, you may worry about how you will be treated by the attorneys in court. Federal guidelines have established that a woman's sexual history cannot be used against her by an attorney defending a rapist unless she is a currently active prostitute or had relations with the accused before. This protection extends to men, except in the states that define rape as something that can only happen to women (see the list on p. 164 in Chapter 6). If you were raped in circumstances that are connected with your being gay, you are male, and you are in a jurisdiction that doesn't protect your private life, your lifestyle probably will be used against you by the defense. "He's gay, so my client didn't rape him. He consented to the sex." How this attitude affects your case depends on the prejudices of the jurors. If you aren't sure whether you want to press charges, you might want to consult your district attorney or local gay organization about how your sexuality might affect the case and about your rights to protection.

The points against reporting your assault to the police are that you may be ridiculed and insulted, you may not be believed, and the chances of your assailant getting both caught and convicted are slim. The points in favor of reporting are that you may be able to get financial assistance (see "Victims' Services" in Chapter 2), you will get the satisfaction of doing what you can to fight back, and you may help prevent the assault of others if he is caught. Above all, by reporting the violence against you, especially when it is antigay violence, you help inform the public that it happens and you help the gay community learn not to accept violence as part of their fate.

PART THREE

RESOURCES

Rape Crisis Programs
Victims' Assistance Programs
Self-defense Training Centers
Shelters for Battered Women
Counseling for Violent Men
Self-defense for Older People
Where to Get Safety Devices
Teenage Programs
Gay and Lesbian Services

RESOURCES FOR PART ONE

Rape Crisis Programs

This list of rape crisis programs and centers around the country is not utterly complete—there are so many that it would take a fat directory to list them all. If there isn't a program listed that is convenient for you, try the following:

• Look up "Rape" in your telephone directory.
• Call your local YWCA and ask for a rape crisis program or battered women's shelter, whichever you want.
• Call your local National Organization for Women (NOW) office for a referral.
• Call Women Against Rape (WAR) if there is one in your area.
• Call your local women's center.

If none of this leads to anything satisfactory, contact one of the regional officers of the National Coalition Against Sexual Assault (NCASA) by letter and ask for a reference to a rape crisis program near you.

NCASA

If you need a program in Connecticut, Maine, Massachusetts, New Hampshire, New Jersey, New York, Pennsylvania, Rhode Island, or Vermont, contact:

> NCASA Officer
> Albany County Rape Crisis Center
> 112 State St., No. 640
> Albany, NY 12207

If you need a program in Alabama, the District of Columbia, Kentucky, Maryland, North Carolina, South Carolina, Tennessee, Virginia, West Virginia, or Delaware, contact:

> NCASA Officer
> 5495 Murray
> Memphis, TN 38119

For Iowa, Illinois, Indiana, Michigan, Minnesota, North Dakota, South Dakota, Nebraska, Ohio, or Wisconsin, contact:

NCASA Officer
c/o Crime Victims
Illinois Attorney General's Office
12113 S. LaSalle
Chicago, IL 60628

For all other states, contact:

NCASA Officer
c/o Austin Rape Crisis Center
P.O. Box 7156
Austin, TX 78713-7156

NCPCR

To request a free directory of rape crisis programs around the country or any other information about rape, contact:

National Center for the Prevention and Control of Rape
National Institute of Mental Health
Room 6c-12, Parklawn Bldg.
5600 Fishers Lane
Rockville, MD 20857
(301) 443-1910

The following list of rape crisis programs, updated from the 1981 NCPCR directory, gives programs in each state and in Canada. The telephone numbers are all twenty-four-hour hotlines unless otherwise indicated.

You may have to wait for many rings before anyone answers when you call. Try not to give up hope—sometimes the phone is manned by an answering service inundated with calls. Sometimes you will only get a recording referring you to another number when you call, or an answering service that will want to take your name and number so that a counselor can get back to you. Counselors sometimes have to be called at home. These sorts of delays can be frustrating, but don't give up—most rape crisis lines are efficient and do want to help. And rest assured that your name, number, and problem will be kept confidential.

Because many rape crisis programs are funded by the government or by nonprofit groups and grants, they occasionally have to close down.

Between the time this list was checked and the time you try to call, some of these numbers may have become obsolete. If so, call Directory Assistance or one of the central numbers given above.

These rape crisis programs are also useful sources for finding victims' assistance programs, battered women's shelters, and counseling for men.

United States

ALABAMA

Birmingham
Rape Response Program
3600 Eighth Ave. S.
Birmingham, AL 35222
(205) 323-7273

Gadsden
C.E.D. Mental Health Center
901 Goodyear Ave.
Gadsden, AL 35903
(205) 492-7800

Montgomery
Council Against Rape/Lighthouse
830 S. Court St.
P.O. Box 4622
Montgomery, AL 36104
(205) 263-4481

Tuscaloosa
Indian Rivers Community Mental
     Health Center Crisis Line
1915 Sixth St.
P.O. Box 2190
Tuscaloosa, AL 35403
(205) 345-1600

ALASKA

Anchorage
Standing Together Against Rape
111 E. Thirteenth St.
Anchorage, AK 99510
(907) 276-7273

Fairbanks
Women In Crisis—Counseling and
     Assistance, Inc. (WICCA)
331 Fifth Ave.
Fairbanks, AK 99701
(907) 452-7273

Nome
Bering Sea Women's Group
P.O. Box 1596
Nome, AK 99762
(907) 443-5444

ARIZONA

Flagstaff
Cocomino Community Guidance
     Center, Inc.
519 N. Leroux
Flagstaff, AZ 86001
(602) 774-3351

Phoenix
Center Against Sexual Assault
    (CASA)
5555 N. Seventh Ave.
Phoenix, AZ 85013
(602) 257-8095
Scottsdale
Crisis Intervention Unit
Scottsdale Police Dept.
3739 Civic Center
Scottsdale, AZ 85251
(602) 994-2593 (Not 24 hours.)
Tucson
Tucson Rape Crisis Center, Inc.
P.O. Box 843
Tucson, AZ 85702
(602) 623-7273

ARKANSAS

Fort Smith
Rape Crisis Service
P.O. Box 2887, Station A
3111 S. Seventieth St.
Fort Smith, AR 72913
(800) 542-1031 (Toll-free within
    state.)
(501) 452-6650
Little Rock
Rape Crisis, Inc.
P.O. Box 5181, Hillcrest Station
Little Rock, AR 72205
(501) 375-5181

CALIFORNIA

Bay Area
Bay Area Women Against Rape
    (BAYWAR)
1515 Webster
Oakland, CA 94612
(415) 845-7273

Davis
Yolo County Sexual Assault Center
203 F St.
Davis, CA 95616
(916) 758-8400 (Davis hotline.)
(916) 662-1133 (Woodland
    hotline.)
(916) 371-1907 (East Yolo hotline.)
Fairfield
Upper Solano County Rape Crisis
    Service, Inc.
P.O. Box 368
Fairfield, CA 94533
(707) 422-7273
Fresno
Rape Counseling Service of
    Fresno, Inc.
3006 N. Fresno St.
Fresno, CA 93703
(209) 222-7273
Los Angeles
Los Angeles Commission on
    Assaults Against Women and
    Los Angeles Rape and
    Battering Hotline
c/o Women's Center at Council
    House
543 N. Fairfax Ave.
Los Angeles, CA 90036
(213) 392-8381
Monterey
Rape Crisis Center of the
    Monterey Peninsula
P.O. Box 862
Monterey, CA 93940
(408) 375-4357
Orange
Sexual Assault Hotline
P.O. Box 2572
Orange, CA 92669
(714) 831-9110

Palo Alto
Mid-Peninsula Rape Crisis Center
4161 Alma St.
Palo Alto, CA 94306
(415) 493-7273
Sacramento
Sacramento Rape Crisis Center
2224 J St.
Sacramento, CA 95816
(916) 447-7273
San Bernardino
San Bernardino Rape Crisis
    Intervention Services
1875 N. D St.
San Bernardino, CA 92405
(714) 882-5291
San Francisco
San Francisco Women Against
    Rape
3543 Eighteenth St.
San Francisco, CA 94110
(415) 647-7273
San Rafael
Marin Rape Crisis Center
P.O. Box 392
San Rafael, CA 94902
(415) 924-2100
Santa Cruz
Santa Cruz Women Against Rape
P.O. Box 711
Santa Cruz, CA 95061
(408) 426-7273
Santa Monica
Rape Treatment Center
Santa Monica Hospital Medical
    Center
1225 Fifteenth St.
Santa Monica, CA 90404
(213) 451-1511

Santa Rosa
Rape Crisis Center of Sonoma
    County
P.O. Box 1426
Santa Rosa, CA 95402
(707) 545-7273
Stockton
Rape Crisis Center of San Joaquin
    County
930 N. Commerce
Stockton, CA 95202
(209) 465-4997

COLORADO

Aspen
Sexual Assault Task Force
Aspen Mental Health Clinic
P.O. Box 2330
Aspen, CO 81611
(303) 925-5400
Colorado Springs
Rape Crisis Service
12 N. Meade St.
Colorado Springs, CO 80909
(303) 471-4357
Denver
Health and Hospitals Mental
    Health Program
Social Services Dept.
W. Eighth Ave. and Cherokee
Denver, CO 80204
(303) 893-7001
Pueblo
Rape Crisis Line, YWCA
801 N. Santa Fe Ave.
Pueblo, CO 81004
(303) 544-7007

CONNECTICUT

Hartford
Hartford YWCA Sexual Assault
    Crisis Service
135 Broad St.
Hartford, CT 06105
(203) 522-6666

New Haven
Rape Counseling Team
Yale-New Haven Hospital
20 York St.
New Haven, CT 06504
(203) 785-2222

DELAWARE

Wilmington
Rape Crisis Center of Wilmington
P.O. Box 1507
Wilmington, DE 19899
(302) 658-5011

DISTRICT OF COLUMBIA

Rape Crisis Center
P.O. Box 21005
Washington, DC 20009
(202) 333-7273

FLORIDA

Jacksonville
Hubbard House
222 E. Duval
Jacksonville, FL 32202
(904) 354-3114

Miami
Rape Treatment Center
1611 N.W. Twelfth Ave.
Miami, FL 33136
(305) 325-6949

Tampa
The Rape Crisis Center of
    Hillsborough, Inc.
2214 E. Henry Ave.
Tampa, FL 33610
(813) 228-7273

GEORGIA

Atlanta
Rape Crisis Center
Grady Memorial Hospital
80 Butler St., S.E.
Atlanta, GA 30335
(404) 588-4861

Augusta
Augusta Rape Crisis Line
P.O. Box 3474, Hill Station
Augusta, GA 30904
(404) 724-5200

Macon
Crisis Line of Macon and Bibb
    County
P.O. Box 56, Mercer University
Macon, GA 31207
(912) 745-9292

Savannah
Rape Crisis Center of the Coastal
    Empire, Inc.
P.O. Box 8492
Savannah, GA 31412
(912) 233-7273

HAWAII

Honolulu
Sex Abuse Treatment Center
Kapiolani Children's Hospital
1319 Punahou St.
Honolulu, HI 96826
(808) 524-7273

IDAHO

Boise
Rape Crisis Alliance
720 W. Washington St.
Boise, ID 83702
(208) 345-7273

Caldwell
Rape Crisis Emergency Line
Caldwell Memorial Hospital
1717 Arlington
Caldwell, ID 83605
(208) 454-0101

Pocatello
Rape Crisis Team, Women's
    Advocates
454 N. Garfield
Pocatello, ID 83201
(208) 232-9169

ILLINOIS

Chicago
Code R Program
Billings Hospital of the University
    of Chicago Hospitals and
    Clinics
Box 215, 950 E. Fifty-ninth St.
Chicago, IL 60637
(313) 962-6246

Women in Crisis Can Act, Inc.
    (WICCA)
1628A W. Belmont
Chicago, IL 60657
(312) 929-5150

Decatur
Dove Rape Task Force
c/o Decatur YWCA
436 N. Main St.
Decatur, IL 62523
(217) 423-2238

Evanston
Crisis Intervention and Referral
    Service
Evanston Hospital
2650 Ridge Ave.
Evanston, IL 60201
(312) 492-6500

Rockford
Rockford Rape Counseling Center,
    Inc.
P.O. Box 4027
Rockford, IL 61110
(815) 964-4044

Springfield
Rape Information and Counseling
    Service (RICS)
P.O. Box 2211
Springfield, IL 62705
(217) 753-8081

INDIANA

Evansville
Citizens Against Rape in
    Evansville (C.A.R.E.)
Deaconess Hospital
600 Mary St.
Evansville, IN 47713
(812) 424-7273

Fort Wayne
Rape Awareness
203 W. Wayne St.
Fort Wayne, IN 46802
(219) 426-7273

Gary
Calumet Women United Against
    Rape
P.O. Box 2617
Gary, IN 46403
(219) 937-0450, 980-4207,
769-3141 (Local hotlines.)

Indianapolis
Crisis Intervention Service
Gallahue Mental Health Center
Community Hospital of
    Indianapolis, Inc.
1500 N. Ritter Ave.
Indianapolis, IN 46219
(317) 353-5947
Terre Haute
Lifeline
200 S. Sixth St.
Terre Haute, IN 47807
(812) 235-8333

IOWA

Ames
Story County Sexual Assault Care
    Center
P.O. Box 1150, ISU Station
Ames, IA 50010
(515) 292-1101
Bettendorf
Rape/Sexual Assault Counseling
    Center of Scott and Rock
    Island Counties
Bettendorf Bank Bldg.
Bettendorf, IA 52722
(319) 326-9191
Cedar Rapids
Rape Crisis Services, YWCA
318 Fifth St., S.E.
Cedar Rapids, IA 52401
(319) 363-5490
Davenport
Quad Cities Rape Crisis Program
P.O. Box 190
Davenport, IA 52805
Scott County: (319) 326-9191
Rock Island County:
(309) 793-4784

Muscatine
Rape/Assault Care Services
Medical Arts Building, Suite 121
Muscatine, IA 52761
(319) 263-8080

KANSAS

Humboldt
Rape Crisis Program
Southeast Kansas Mental Health
    Center
1106 S. Ninth St.
P.O. Box 39
Humboldt, KS 66748
(316) 473-2241
Lawrence
Douglas County Rape Victim
    Support Service, Inc.
1035 Pennsylvania
Lawrence, KS 66044
(913) 841-2345
Topeka
Shawnee Community Mental
    Health Center
Emergency Services (Telephone
    contact only.)
(913) 233-1730 (To contact rape
    counselor.)
Wichita
Wichita Area Rape Center, Inc.
1801 E. Tenth St.
Wichita, KS 67214
(316) 263-3002

KENTUCKY

Lexington
Lexington Rape Crisis Center
P.O. Box 1603
Lexington, KY 40592
(606) 253-2511

Owensboro
Green River Comprehensive Care
    Center
Crisis Line, Rape Victim Services
    Project/Spouse Abuse Center
233 W. Ninth St.
Owensboro, KY 42301
(800) 482-1972 (Toll-free in
    Kentucky.)
(502) 926-7273
Somerset
Region XIV Rape Relief Services
Region XIV Community Mental
    Health Services
324 Cundiff Trade Bldg.
Somerset, KY 42501
(502) 384-5647
Louisville
R.A.P.E. Relief Center
604 S. Third St.
Louisville, KY 40202
(502) 581-7273

LOUISIANA

Alexandria
Work Against Rape, Sexual Assault
    Care Service/HELPLINE
1407 Murray St., No. 204
Alexandria, LA 71301
(318) 445-4357
Baton Rouge
Stop Rape Crisis Center
East Baton Rouge Parish District
    Attorney's Office
215 St. Louis St., No. 307
Baton Rouge, LA 70801
(504) 389-3456
New Orleans
YWCA Rape Crisis Service
601 S. Jefferson Davis Pkwy.
New Orleans, LA 70119
(504) 483-8888

Shreveport
YWCA Rape Crisis Center
710 Travis St.
Shreveport, LA 71101
(318) 222-0556

MAINE

Portland
Rape Crisis Center of Greater
    Portland
193 Middle St.
Portland, ME 04101
(207) 774-3613

MARYLAND

Annapolis
Anne Arundel County Sexual
    Offense Crisis Center and
    Hotline
62 Cathedral St.
Annapolis, MD 21401
(301) 224-1321
Baltimore
Baltimore Center for Victims of
    Sexual Assault
128 W. Franklin St.
Baltimore, MD 21201
(301) 366-7273
Bethesda
Community Crisis Center
Sexual Assault Services
4910 Auburn Ave.
Bethesda, MD 20814
(301) 656-9449
Columbia
Sexual Assault Center of Howard
    County
8045 Rte. 32
Columbia, MD 21044
(301) 997-3292

MASSACHUSETTS

Amherst
Counselors/Advocates Against
    Rape
Everywoman's Center, Wilder Hall
University of Massachusetts
Amherst, MA 01003
(413) 545-0800
Boston
Rape Crisis Intervention Program
Beth Israel Hospital
330 Brookline Ave.
Boston, MA 02215
(617) 735-3337
Cambridge
Boston Area Rape Crisis Center
Women's Center
46 Pleasant St.
Cambridge, MA 02139
(617) 492-7273
Springfield
Hotline to End Rape and Abuse
    (HERA)
25 St. James Ave.
Springfield, MA 01109
(413) 733-2561

MICHIGAN

Ann Arbor
Assault Crisis Center
4009 Washtenaw Rd.
Ann Arbor, MI 48104
(313) 994-1616
Bay City
Bay County Women's Center for
    Rape and Assault
P.O. Box 646
Bay City, MI 48707
(517) 893-4551

Detroit
Rape Counseling Center
Detroit Police Dept.
4201 St. Antoine, Room 828
Detroit, MI 48201
(313) 224-4487
East Lansing
Sexual Assault Counseling of the
    Listening Ear
547½ E. Grand River Ave.
East Lansing, MI 48823
(517) 337-1717
Flint
Domestic Violence and Sexual
    Assault Crisis Center
YWCA
310 E. Third St.
Flint, MI 48502
(313) 238-7233
Grand Rapids
1330 Bradford, N.E.
Grand Rapids, MI 49503
(616) 774-3535

MINNESOTA

Brainerd
Women's Center of Mid-
    Minnesota, Inc.
Sexual Assault Advocacy Program
P.O. Box 602,
Brainerd, MN 56401
(218) 828-1216
Duluth
Aid to Victims of Sexual Assault
2 E. Fifth St.
Duluth, MN 55805
(218) 727-8538

Fairmont
Southern Minnesota Crisis Support
    Center, Inc.
P.O. Box 214
Fairmont, MN 56031
(507) 235-3456
Minneapolis
Rape and Sexual Assault Center
122 W. Thirty-first St.
Minneapolis, MN 55408
(612) 825-4357
Rochester
Rapeline Program
515 S.W. Second St.
Rochester, MN 55902
(507) 289-0636
St. Paul
Women's Advocates
584 Grand
St. Paul, MN 55102
(612) 227-8284

MISSISSIPPI

Biloxi
Gulf Coast Women's Center
P.O. Box 333
Biloxi, MS 39533
(601) 435-1968
Jackson
Jackson Rape Crisis Center
Catholic Charities, Inc.
748 N. President St.
P.O. Box 2248
Jackson, MS 39205
(601) 355-8634 (Can refer you to
    six rape programs in the
    state.)

MISSOURI

Columbia
Abuse, Assault and Rape Crisis
    Center (AARCC)
P.O. Box 1827
Columbia, MO 65201
(314) 875-1370
Kansas City
Sexual Assault Treatment Center
St. Luke's Hospital Emergency
    Room
4400 Wornall Rd.
Kansas City, MO 64111
(816) 932-2171
St. Louis
Sex Crime Section
St. Louis Police Dept.
1200 Clark Ave.
St. Louis, MO 63103
(314) 444-5385
Springfield
Rape Crisis Assistance, Inc.
P.O. Box 1611
Springfield, MO 65805
(417) 866-1969

MONTANA

Billings
Billings Rape Task Force
1245 N. Twenty-ninth St., Room
    218
Billings, MT 59101
(406) 259-6506
Helena
Women's Support Line
Rape Awareness Program
Helena Woman's Center
146 E. Sixth Ave.
Helena, MT 59601
(406) 443-5353

Kalispell
Kalispell Rape Crisis Line
Box 1385
Kalispell, MT 59901
(406) 755-5067

Missoula
Women's Place
127 E. Main, Room 218
Missoula, MT 59801
(406) 543-7606

NEBRASKA

Lincoln
Rape/Spouse Abuse Crisis Center
1133 H St.
Lincoln, NE 68508
(402) 475-7273

Omaha
Women Against Violence
YWCA
3929 Harney St., Room 100
Omaha, NE 68131
(402) 345-7273

NEVADA

Las Vegas
Community Action Against Rape
749 Veterans Memorial Dr., Room 79
Las Vegas, NV 89101
(702) 735-7111

NEW HAMPSHIRE

Manchester
Women's Crisis Line for Rape Victims and Battered Women
YWCA
72 Concord St.
Manchester, NH 03101
(603) 668-2299

Nashua
Rape and Assault Committee for the Nashua Area, Inc.
10 Prospect St.
P.O. Box 217
Nashua, NH 03061
(603) 883-3044

NEW JERSEY

East Orange
Rape Program/Crisis Intervention Unit
East Orange General Hospital
300 Central Ave.
East Orange, NJ 07019
(201) 672-9685

Hackensack
Victim Witness Unit and Sexual Assault Crisis Center
Bergen County Prosecutor's Office
Bergen County Courthouse
Hackensack, NJ 07601
(201) 646-2057

Newark
Sexual Assault Rape Analysis Unit (S.A.R.A.)
22 Franklin St.
Newark, NJ 07102
(201) 733-7273

Paterson
Women's Haven and Family Services
P.O. Box 38
Paterson, NJ 07501
(201) 881-1450

NEW MEXICO

Albuquerque
Albuquerque Rape Crisis Center
905 Vassar, N.E.
Albuquerque, NM 87106
(505) 247-0707
Deming
Rape Crisis Center
109 E. Pine St.
Deming, NM 88030
Enterprise 333 (Toll-free number
    in state—must be dialed
    through operator.)
Santa Fe
Santa Fe Rape Crisis Center, Inc.
Box 2822
Santa Fe, NM 87501
(505) 982-4667
Taos
Community Against Rape, Inc.
Box 3170
Taos, NM 87571
(505) 758-2910

NEW YORK

Albany
Albany County Rape Crisis Center
112 State St., No. 640
Albany, NY 12207
(518) 445-7547
Buffalo
Anti-Rape Advocacy
Crisis Services, Inc.
3258 Main St.
Buffalo, NY 14214
(716) 834-3131

New York City
Victim Services Agency Hotline
2 Lafayette St., 3rd Floor
New York, NY 10007
(212) 577-7777 (On-the-spot
    phone counseling and 24-hour
    referrals to programs in all
    five boroughs.)
New York City Advisory Task
    Force on Rape
250 Church Street, 13th Floor
New York, NY 10013
(212) 553-5083 (9 A.M. to 5 P.M.,
    and then a tape recording.)
Rape Crisis Program
Dept. of Community Medicine
St. Vincent's Hospital
153 W. Eleventh St.
New York, NY 10011
(212) 790-8068/9 (9 A.M. to
    5 P.M.)
(212) 790-8000 (Call in medical
    emergencies only.)
Rape Intervention Program
St. Luke's/Roosevelt Hospital
    Center
44 Morningside Dr., No. 1
New York, NY 10025
(212) 870-1875 (9 A.M. to 5 P.M.,
    and then a tape recording.
    Hospital services are 24
    hours.)
Rochester
Rape Crisis Service of Planned
    Parenthood of Rochester and
    Monroe County
24 Windsor St.
Rochester, NY 14605
(716) 546-2595

Smithtown
Victims Information Bureau of
Suffolk, Inc.
Counseling Center
22 Lawrence Ave.
Smithtown, NY 11787
(516) 360-3606
Syracuse
Rape Crisis Center of Syracuse,
Inc.
423 W. Onondaga St.
Syracuse, NY 13202
(315) 422-7273

NORTH CAROLINA

Chapel Hill
Chapel Hill-Carrboro Rape Crisis
Center
Box 871
Chapel Hill, NC 27514
(919) 967-7273
Charlotte
Charlotte-Mecklenburg Rape Crisis
Service
P.O. Box 29055
Charlotte, NC 28212
(704) 373-0982
Durham
Helpline
c/o Durham County Mental
Health Center
P.O. Box 414
E. Main St.
Durham, NC 27701
(919) 683-8628
Greensboro
Turning Point Rape and Family
Abuse Center
1301 N. Elm St.
Greensboro, NC 27401
(919) 273-7273

Raleigh
Rape Crisis Center of Raleigh
401 E. Whitiker Mill Rd.
Raleigh, NC 27650
(919) 755-6661

NORTH DAKOTA

Fargo
Rape and Abuse Crisis Center of
Fargo-Moorhead
P.O. Box 1655
Fargo, ND 58107
(701) 293-7273
Grand Forks
Grand Forks Rape Crisis Center
319 S. Sixth St.
Grand Forks, ND 58201
(701) 746-8900

OHIO

Akron
Akron Rape Crisis Center
St. Paul's Episcopal Church
146 S. High St.
Akron, OH 44308
(216) 434-7273
Canton
Rape Crisis Center
American Red Cross
618 Second St., N.W.
Canton, OH 44703
(216) 452-1111
Cincinnati
Women Helping Women, Inc.
216 E. Ninth St.
Cincinnati, OH 45202
(513) 381-5610

Cleveland

Community Guidance and Human
    Services Mental Health
    Center
3740 Euclid
Cleveland, OH 44115
(216) 431-7774 (Office hours only,
    but 24-hour service available.)

Columbus

Women Against Rape
P.O. Box 02084
Columbus, OH 43202
(614) 221-4447

Toledo

Toledo United Against Rape
P.O. Box 4372
Toledo, OH 43609
(419) 882-6131

OKLAHOMA

Enid

YWCA Rape Crisis Center
525 S. Quincy
Enid, OK 73701
(405) 234-7644

Norman

Women's Resource Center
P.O. Box 5089
Norman, OK 73071
(405) 364-9424

Oklahoma City

YWCA Rape Crisis Line
129 N.W. Fifth St.
Oklahoma City, OK 73102
(405) 524-7273

OREGON

Corvallis

Rape Crisis Center
P.O. Box 914
216 S.W. Madison
Corvallis, OR 97330
(503) 754-0110

Eugene

Rape Crisis Network
650 W. Twelfth St.
Eugene, OR 97402
(503) 485-6700

Oregon City

Clackamas County Victim
    Assistance
1450 S. Kaen Rd.
Oregon City, OR 97045
(503) 655-8616

Portland

Rape Victim Advocate Project
Multnomah County District
    Attorney
804 Multnomah County
    Courthouse
Portland, OR 97204
(503) 248-5059

Salem

Women's Crisis Service
P.O. Box 851
Salem, OR 97308
(503) 399-7722

PENNSYLVANIA

Allentown

Rape Crisis Council of Lehigh
    Valley, Inc.
P.O. Box 1445
Allentown, PA 18105
(215) 437-6611

Erie

Erie County Rape Crisis Center
4518 Peach St.
Erie, PA 16503
(814) 868-0314

Harrisburg

Pennsylvania Coalition Against
Rape (PCAR)
2200 N. Third St.
Harrisburg, PA 17110
(800) 692-7445 (Toll-free in state.
Coordinates 35 local centers.)

Philadelphia

Women Organized Against Rape
1220 Sansom St.
Philadelphia, PA 19107
(215) 922-3434

Pittsburgh

Pittsburgh Action Against Rape
211 S. Oakland Ave.
Pittsburgh, PA 15213
(412) 765-2731

Women's Center and Shelter of
Greater Pittsburgh
P.O. Box 5147
Pittsburgh, PA 15206
(412) 661-6066

Uniontown

Rape Counseling Information
Service of Fayette County,
Inc.
62 E. Church St.
Uniontown, PA 15401
(412) 437-3737

PUERTO RICO

Caparra Heights

Centro de Ayuda a Víctimas de
Violación
Apartado CH-11321, Caparra
Heights Station
Caparra Heights, PR 00922
(809) 765-2285

Cayey

Cayey Mental Health Center
392 Jose de Diego Avenue W.
Cayey, PR 00633
(809) 738-5049/5020/2222

RHODE ISLAND

Middletown

Newport County Community
Mental Health Center, Inc.
65 Valley Rd.
Middletown, RI 02840
(401) 846-1213

Providence

Rape Crisis Center
903 Broad St.
Providence, RI 02907
(401) 941-2400

SOUTH CAROLINA

Charleston

People Against Rape
150 Meeting St.
Charleston, SC 29401
(803) 722-7273

Greenville

Rape Crisis Council of Greenville,
Inc.
700 Augusta St.
Greenville, SC 29605
(803) 232-8633

Greenwood
Rape Crisis Council of Greenwood
Beckman Center P.O. Drawer 70
Greenwood, SC 29646
(800) 223-4357 (Toll-free in state.)

SOUTH DAKOTA

Aberdeen
Aberdeen Area Rape Task Force
317 S. Kline
Aberdeen, SD 57401
(605) 226-1212
Brookings
Rape Education, Advocacy and
    Counseling Team (REACT)
Brookings Women's Center
802 Eleventh Ave.
Brookings, SD 57006
(605) 688-4518

TENNESSEE

Jackson
Women's Resources
Jackson Counseling Center
238 Summar Drive
Jackson, TN 38301
(901) 668-7273
Knoxville
Knoxville Rape Crisis Center
P.O. Box 2262
Knoxville, TN 37901
(615) 522-7273
Memphis
Rape Crisis Program
1177 Madison, Suite 401
Memphis, TN 38104
(901) 528-2161

Nashville
Rape and Sexual Abuse Center of
    Davidson County
1908 Twenty-first Ave. S.
P.O. Box 120831
Nashville, TN 37212
(615) 327-1110

TEXAS

Amarillo
Rape Crisis and Sexual Abuse
    Service
804 S. Bryan, Suite 207
Amarillo, TX 79106
(806) 373-8022
Austin
Austin Rape Crisis Center
P.O. Box 7156
Austin, TX 78713-7156
(512) 472-7273
Dallas
Dallas County Rape Crisis Center
P.O. Box 35728
Dallas, TX 75235
(214) 521-1020
El Paso
Rape Crisis Services
El Paso Mental Health/Mental
    Retardation
5308 El Paso Dr.
El Paso, TX 79905
(915) 779-1800
Fort Worth
Rape Crisis Support of Tarrant
    County
1203 Lake St., No. 208
Fort Worth, TX 76102
(817) 335-7273

Houston
People Against Rape/Abuse, Inc.
    (PARA)
P.O. Box 57535
Houston, TX 77598
(713) 488-7222
Tyler
East Texas Crisis Center
1314 S. Fleishel
Tyler, TX 75701
(214) 595-5591
Waco
Waco Rape Crisis Center
P.O. Box 464
1609 Austin Ave.
Waco, TX 76701
(817) 752-1113
Wichita Falls
First Step, Inc.
P.O. Box 773
Wichita Falls, TX 76307
(817) 767-4933

UTAH

Ogden
YWCA Women's Crisis Shelter
505 Twenty-seventh St.
Ogden, UT 84403
(801) 392-7273
Provo
Utah County Rape Crisis Line
P.O. Box 1375
Provo, UT 84601
(801) 226-8989
West Valley City
Rape Crisis Center
2140 S. 3600 W.
West Valley City, UT 84119
(801) 532-7273

VERMONT

Brattleboro
Women's Crisis Center
P.O. Box 933
Brattleboro, VT 05301
(802) 254-6954
Burlington
Women's Rape Crisis Center
P.O. Box 92
Burlington, VT 05401
(802) 863-1236
Rutland
Rutland County Rape Crisis Team
Box 121
Rutland, VT 05701
(802) 775-1000

VIRGINIA

Alexandria
Fairfax County Victim Assistance
    Network
8119 Holland Rd.
Alexandria, VA 22306
(703) 360-7273
Arlington
Arlington County Rape Victim
    Companion Service
1725 N. George Mason Dr.
Arlington, VA 22205
(703) 558-2048
Charlottesville
Charlottesville Rape Crisis Group
214 Rugby Rd.
Charlottesville, VA 22901
(804) 977-7273
Richmond
YWCA Women's Victim
    Advocacy Program
6 N. Fifth St.
Richmond, VA 23219
(804) 843-0888

WASHINGTON

Bellingham
Chrysallis Therapy Center
214 N. Commercial
Bellingham, WA 98225
(206) 647-2643
Renton
King County Rape Relief
305 S. Forty-third St.
Renton, WA 98055
(206) 226-7273
Pullman
Alternatives to Violence
P.O. Box 2615, College Station
Pullman, WA 99163
(509) 332-4357
Seattle
Seattle Rape Relief
1825 S. Jackson, No. 102
Seattle, WA 98144
(206) 632-7273
Spokane
Rape Crisis Network
1226 N. Howard St.
Spokane, WA 99201
(509) 624-7273

WEST VIRGINIA

Charleston
West Virginia Foundation for
Rape Information and
Services, Inc.
1800 E. Washington St.
Bldg. 3, Room 426
Charleston, WV 25305
(304) 348-3956 or (304) 562-3284
(Will refer you to any of the
eight rape programs in the
state.)

Huntington
Rape Crisis Counseling Team
1030 Seventh Ave.
Huntington, WV 25701
(304) 529-2382
Morgantown
Rape and Domestic Violence
Information Center
P.O. Box 4228
Morgantown, WV 26505
(304) 292-5100

WISCONSIN

Appleton
Sexual Assault Crisis Center, Fox
Cities, Inc.
P.O. Box 344
Appleton, WI 54912
(414) 733-8119
Green Bay
Green Bay Rape Crisis Center,
Ltd.
131 S. Madison St.
Green Bay, WI 54301
(414) 433-0584
Madison
Rape Crisis Center
312 E. Wilson St.
Madison, WI 53703
(608) 251-7273 (10 A.M. to 2 P.M.
or by appointment, but have
24-hour advocate service.)
Milwaukee
Women's Crisis Line
1428 N. Farwell Ave.
Milwaukee, WI 53202
(414) 964-7535

Oshkosh
Rape Crisis/Domestic Abuse
   Center
660 Oak St.
Oshkosh, WI 54901
(414) 233-7707

WYOMING

Jackson
Western Wyoming Mental Health
   Association
115 W. Snowking Ave.
P.O. Box 1868
Jackson, WY 83001
(800) 442-6383 (Toll-free in state.)
(307) 733-2046

Rock Springs
Sweetwater County Task Force on
   Sexual Assault
450 S. Main
Rock Springs, WY 82901
(307) 382-4381
Worland
Community Crisis Service, Inc.
P.O. Box 872
Worland, WY 82401
(307) 347-4991

Canada

ALBERTA

Edmonton
Rape Crisis Centre of Edmonton
416-10010-105 St.
Edmonton, AB T5J 1C4
(403) 465-1722 (Office hours only.)

BRITISH COLUMBIA

Naniamo
Mid-Island Sexual Assault Centre
105–285 Pridaux Street
Naniamo, BC V9R 2NR
(604) 753-0022
Vancouver
Vancouver Rape Relief &
   Women's Shelter
77 E. Twentieth Avenue
Vancouver, BC V5V 1L7
(604) 872-8212

Victoria
Victoria Rape/Assault Centre
1045 Linden Avenue
Victoria, BC V8V 4H3
(604) 383-5545

MANITOBA

Winnipeg
Rape Crisis and Information
   Centre (Klinic, Inc.)
545 Broadway Avenue
Winnipeg, MB R3C OW3
(204) 774-4525

NEW BRUNSWICK

Fredericton
Fredericton Rape Crisis Service
P.O. Box 174
Fredericton, NB E3B 4Y9
(506) 454-0437

NEWFOUNDLAND

St. John's
St. John's Rape Crisis and
    Information Centre
P.O. Box 6072
St. John's, Newfoundland
    A1C 5X8
(709) 726-1411

ONTARIO

Hamilton
Hamilton Rape Crisis Centre
(Address confidential)
(416) 525-4162
Ottawa
Ottawa Rape Crisis Centre
P.O. Box 35, Station B
Ottawa, ON K1P 6C3
(613) 238-6666
Marie
Algoma District Sexual Assault
    Centre
P.O. Box 785
Sault Ste. Marie, ON P68 5N3
(705) 949-5200
Toronto
Toronto Rape Crisis Centre
Box 6597, Postal Station A
Toronto, ON M5W 1X4
(416) 964-8080
Windsor
Sexual Assault Crisis Centre of
    Essex County
14 Hanna St. E.
Windsor, ON N8X 2M8
(519) 253-9667

QUEBEC

Hull
Hull Centre d'Aide et de Lutte
    Contre les Agressions
    Sexuelles
C.P. 1872, Succursale B.
Hull, PQ J8X 3Z1
(819) 771-1773
Montreal
Montreal Assistance de Femmes
    (Women's Aid)
C.P. 82, Station E.
Montreal, PQ H2T 3A5
(514) 270-8291
Mouvement Contre le Viol
    Collectif de Montreal
C.P. 391, Succursale Delormier
Montreal, PQ 82H 2N7
(514) 526-2460 (Office hours only
    or leave recorded message.)

SASKATCHEWAN

Regina
Regina Women's Community
    Centre and Sexual Assault
    Crisis Line
1810 Smith St., Room 219
Regina, SK S4P 2N4
(306) 352-0434

Victims' Assistance Programs

To find out how to get financial compensation for loss incurred because of a crime, or to get help with prosecuting and other legal matters, contact a victims' assistance program or victims' services agency in your area. The list below is of central agencies in each state that should be able to refer you to a program near you.

If the agency listed here is no longer functioning or is unable to help you, ask your local rape crisis center or police for a reference. You can also contact the National Organization for Victim Assistance (NOVA). Their address is:

> NOVA
> 1757 Park Rd. N.W.
> Washington, DC 20010
> (202) 232-8560

This list is updated from the 1983 NOVA Program Directory.

ALABAMA
District Attorney's Office
142 Washington Ave., Suite 303
Montgomery, AL 36104
(205) 263-3816

ALASKA
Assistant Attorney General
Pouch KT
Juneau, AK 99811
(907) 465-3678

ARIZONA
Victim/Witness Program
Office of the Pima County
    Attorney
900 Pima County Courts Bldg.
111 W. Congress
Tucson, AZ 85701
(602) 792-8749

ARKANSAS
Justice for Crime Victims of
    America, Inc.
P.O. Box 3906
Fort Smith, AR 72913
(501) 782-4111

CALIFORNIA
California Victim/Witness
    Assistance Program
9719 Lincoln Village Dr., Suite
    600
Sacramento, CA 95827
(916) 366-5437

COLORADO
Victim/Witness Assistance Unit
Office of the District Attorney
P.O. Box 471
Boulder, CO 80306
(303) 441-3730

CONNECTICUT
United Social and Mental Health
   Services
Victim Assistance Program
132 Mansfield Ave.
Willimantic, CT 06226
(203) 456-2261

DELAWARE
Department of Justice Victim
   Service
State Office Bldg.
820 French St.
Wilmington, DE 19801
(302) 571-2599

FLORIDA
Victim/Witness Services
Office of the State Attorney
330 E. Bay St., Room 517
Jacksonville, FL 32202
(904) 633-6634

GEORGIA
Metropolitan Atlanta Crime
   Commission
100 Edgewood Ave., N.E., Room
   128
Atlanta, GA 30303
(404) 659-6222 (24 hours)

HAWAII
Department of the Prosecuting
   Attorney
City and County of Honolulu
164 Bishop St.
Honolulu, HI 96813
(808) 523-4158/4843

IDAHO
Office of the Attorney General
State House
Boise, ID 83720
(208) 334-2400

ILLINOIS
Victim/Witness Assistance Unit
Cook County State's Attorney's
   Office
2650 S. California Ave.
Chicago, IL 60608
(312) 890-7209

INDIANA
Victim Assistance Program
Ft. Wayne Police Department
City-County Bldg.
Fort Wayne, IN 46802

IOWA
Polk County Victim Services
1915 Hickman Rd.
Des Moines, IA 50303
(515) 286-3838 (24 hours)

KANSAS
Kansas Office of the Attorney
   General
Judicial Center, 2nd Floor
Topeka, KS 66612
(913) 296-2215

KENTUCKY
Victim Information Program
Commonwealth's Attorney's Office
315 Legal Arts Bldg.
200 S. Seventh St.
Louisville, KY 40202
(502) 581-5823

LOUISIANA
Victim/Witness Assistance Bureau
Office of the District Attorney
619 S. White St.
New Orleans, LA 70119
(504) 822-2414 x553

MAINE
Billy Allison
District Attorney's Office
85 Park St.
Lewiston, ME 04240
(207) 783-7311

MARYLAND
Sexual Offense Task Force
Attention Olga Bruning
Baltimore City State's Attorney's
    Office
Room 316, Court House E
111 N. Calvert St.
Baltimore, MD 21202
(301) 396-5040

MASSACHUSETTS
Karen McLaughlin
Essex County District Attorney's
    Office
70 Washington St.
Salem, MA 01970
(617) 745-6610

MICHIGAN
Victim/Witness Services
Prosecuting Attorney's Office
227 W. Michigan Ave.
Kalamazoo, MI 49007
(606) 383-8677/8865

MINNESOTA
Minnesota Citizens' Council on
    Crime and Justice
1427 Washington Ave.
Minneapolis, MN 55454
(612) 340-5432

MISSISSIPPI
Jackson Rape Crisis Center
Catholic Charities, Inc.
748 N. President St.
P.O. Box 2248
Jackson, MS 39205
(601) 355-8634

MISSOURI
Director, Victim/Witness
    Assistance Unit
Room 330 Municipal Court Bldg.
    1320 Market St.
St. Louis, MO 63103
(314) 622-4373

MONTANA
Crime Victims Unit
Workmen's Compensation
    Division
815 Front St.
Helena, MT 59601
(406) 499-5633

NEBRASKA
Administrator, Victim/Witness
    Unit
Lincoln Police Department
233 S. Tenth St.
Lincoln, NE 68508
(402) 471-7181

NEVADA
Deputy Director of Administration
Clark County District Attorney's
    Office
300 S. Fourth St., Suite 1111
Las Vegas, NV 89101
(702) 386-4779

NEW HAMPSHIRE
Director, Victim/Witness
    Assistance Unit
Hillsborough County District
    Attorney's Office
300 Chestnut St.
Manchester, NH
    03101
(603) 669-1053

NEW JERSEY
Pam Hamilton, Victim Witness
    Coordinator
Criminal Justice Division, State of
    New Jersey
P.O. Box CN085, Justice Complex
Trenton, NJ 08625
(609) 984-7155

NEW MEXICO
President, Crime Victims
    Reparations Commission
P.O. Box 871
Albuquerque, NM 87103
(505) 842-3904

NEW YORK
Victim Services Agency
2 Lafayette St.
New York, NY 10007
(212) 577-7700

NORTH CAROLINA
Assistant to the Attorney General
    for Criminal Justice Affairs
Office of the Attorney General
P.O. Box 629
Raleigh, NC 27602
(919) 733-3377

NORTH DAKOTA
Director, Crime Victims
    Reparations
North Dakota Worker's
    Compensation Bureau
Russell Bldg.
Highway 83 N.
Bismarck, ND 58501
(707) 224-2700

OHIO
President, Ohio Victim Witness
    Association, Inc.
226 Middle Ave.
Elyria, OH 44036
(216) 329-5375

OKLAHOMA
Office of the Attorney General
State Capitol Bldg.
Oklahoma City, OK 73105
(405) 521-3921

OREGON
Director, Victims Assistance
    Program
Multnomah County District
    Attorney's Office
1021 S.W. Fourth Ave., Room 804
Portland, OR 97204
(503) 248-3222

PENNSYLVANIA
Director, Witness Assistance Unit
District Attorney's Office
2300 Centre Sq. W.
Philadelphia, PA 19102
(215) 275-6199

RHODE ISLAND
Office of the Attorney General
72 Pine St.
Providence, RI 02903
(401) 274-4400

SOUTH CAROLINA
Director, Victim/Witness
  Assistance
Room 318, Greenville County
  Courthouse
Greenville, SC 29601
(803) 298-8647

SOUTH DAKOTA
Victims' Assistance Program
Court Services Dept., 7th Judicial
  Circuit
703 Adams Rd.
Rapid City, SD 57701
(605) 394-2595

TENNESSEE
Director, Victim/Witness Unit
Criminal Justice Center
201 Poplar Ave., Suite 301
Memphis, TN 38103
(901) 577-5946

TEXAS
Director, The Victim-Witness
  Office
201 Fannin, Room 200
Houston, TX 77002
(713) 221-6655

UTAH
The Victim/Witness Counseling
  Unit
Salt Lake County Attorney's Office
460 S. 3rd East
Salt Lake City, UT 84111
(801) 535-5558

VERMONT
There are no victim assistance
  programs in Vermont. Call
  your local rape crisis program
  instead.

VIRGINIA
Victim/Witness Program
Commonwealth's Attorney's Office
City of Portsmouth
P.O. Box 1417
Portsmouth, VA 23705
(804) 393-8581

WASHINGTON
Victim/Witness Assistance Service
1033 County-City Bldg.
Tacoma, WA 98031
(206) 593-4843

WEST VIRGINIA
17th Judicial Circuit
Monongalia County Court House
Morgantown, WV 26505
(304) 291-7265

WISCONSIN
Director, Victim/Witness Services
Milwaukee County District
  Attorney's Office
412 Safety Bldg.
821 W. State St.
Milwaukee, WI 53233
(414) 278-4659

WYOMING
Western Wyoming Mental Health
  Association
115 W. Snowking Ave.
P.O. Box 1868
Jackson, WY 83001
(307) 733-2046

SELF-DEFENSE TRAINING CENTERS

To locate a self-defense class near you, call your local YWCA, women's center, rape crisis program, martial arts center, or community center. *Fighting Woman News,* a magazine available at many women's bookstores, has a directory of self-defense and martial arts classes around the country and in Canada. If you cannot find a copy, send a stamped, self-addressed envelope to the following address and ask to be referred to a class near you.

Valerie Eads, Editor and Publisher
Fighting Woman News
Box 1459, Grand Central Station
New York, NY 10163

Try also contacting these programs:

Chimera, Inc.
37 S. Wabash Ave. Suite 602
Chicago, IL 60603
(312) 332-5540
Chimera has a network of self-defense programs *for women only* in Arizona, Illinois, Indiana, Kentucky, Minnesota, Ohio, Pennsylvania, and Texas. Write or call the above, which is the central office, for a reference to a program near you.

CALIFORNIA
Los Angeles
L.A. Commission on Assaults Against Women
Women's Center at Council House
543 N. Fairfax Ave.
Los Angeles, CA 90036
(213) 938-3661
This program emphasizes both physical and verbal self-defense.

Mill Valley
The I.C.A. (Initiation, Confrontation, Altercation) Self-Protection
    Method
Joel Kirsch
P.O. Box 258
Mill Valley, CA 94941
Joel Kirsch holds one- and two-day workshops on assault prevention for corporations and community groups.

Santa Cruz
Women's Self-Defense Council
P.O. Box 8312
Santa Cruz, CA 95061
(408) 427-1687
This program emphasizes both physical and psychological self-defense for women only.

NEW YORK
The Safety & Fitness Exchange (SAFE)
541 Sixth Ave.
New York, NY 10011
(212) 242-4874/5
SAFE teaches self-defense to women, men, and children. They emphasize assault prevention, not just fighting.

Women's Martial Arts Center
16 W. Thirtieth St.
New York, NY 10001
(212) 685-4553
Street defense as well as boxing and Goju karate are taught here by women for classes of men and women. Some classes are for women only.

There are several self-defense books on the market, but reading about how to do it won't be any good unless you practice. The advantage of classes is that they make you practice and they give you the encouragement and company that only a group of people can provide.

RESOURCES FOR PART TWO

SHELTERS FOR RAPED OR BATTERED WIVES

If you cannot find a shelter near you in this list, look up "Battered Women" or "Shelters" in your telephone book. If that doesn't work, call your local rape crisis program and ask for a referral. If you still cannot find a place near you, or cannot find one that has room for you, try contacting one of these main organizations.

> National Coalition Against Domestic Violence
> 1500 Massachusetts Ave. N.W., Suite 35
> Washington, DC 20005
> (202) 347-7017

The NCADV has a list of shelters all over the country, which they keep fairly up-to-date.

> National Clearinghouse on Marital Rape (NCOMR)
> Women's History Research Center
> 2325 Oak St.
> Berkeley, CA 94708
> (415) 548-1770

The NCOMR should be able to put you in touch with a shelter near you, or tell you how to find one.

> Women Organized to Make Abuse Nonexistent (W.O.M.A.N.)
> 2940 Sixteenth St.
> San Francisco, CA 94103
> (415) 864-4722

W.O.M.A.N. can refer you to shelters and counseling services around the country, but they specialize in California. When you call, you may get a recording referring you to another number. Call that to get someone to help you. If you are in the area, they will be able to find out which shelters near you have space open at the moment, and will make the calls for you if you are unable to yourself.

> Battered Women's Network/Family Rescue
> Department of Human Services
> (Address confidential.)
> Chicago, IL
> (312) 744-5829
> (312) 375-8400

Family Rescue will be able to refer you to shelters in the Chicago area. They will call to find out which ones have room for you if you cannot do so.

> Victim Services Agency
> 2 Lafayette St.
> New York, NY 10007
> (212) 577-7777 (hotline)

VSA can refer you to shelters, counseling services, and projects that provide safe homes in the five boroughs of New York.

If one of these organizations refers you to a rape crisis program, don't be surprised—many of them double as shelters.

The following list was compiled and updated in July 1984 by the National Coalition Against Domestic Violence.

ALABAMA
Alabama Coalition Against
    Domestic Violence
Safeplace, Inc.
P.O. Box 10456
Florence, AL 35631
(205) 767-6210

ALASKA
Alaska Network On Domestic
    Violence & Sexual Assault
110 Seward St., No. 13
Juneau, AK 99801
(907) 586-3650

ARKANSAS
Arkansas Coalition Against
    Violence To Women And
    Children
P.O. Box 807
Harrison, AR 72601
(501) 741-6167

ARIZONA
Arizona State Against Domestic
    Violence
P.O. Box 27365
Tempe, AZ 85282
(602) 234-4402

CALIFORNIA
Southern California Coalition On
    Battered Women
P.O. Box 5036
Santa Monica, CA 90405
(213) 392-9874

Northern California Shelter
    Support Services
P.O. Box 1955
San Mateo, CA 94401
(415) 342-0850

Central California Coalition
    Against Domestic Violence
P.O. Box 3931
Modesto, CA 95352
(209) 575-7037

COLORADO
Colorado Domestic Violence
    Coalition
P.O. Box 18902
Denver, CO 80218
(303) 394-2810

CONNECTICUT
Connecticut Task Force On
    Abused Women
P.O. Box 14299
Hartford, CT 06114
(203) 524-5890

DISTRICT OF COLUMBIA
My Sister's Place
P.O. Box 29596
Washington, DC 20017–0796
(202) 529-5991

DELAWARE
Domestic Violence Task Force
Delaware Commission for Women
Department of Community
    Education
Carval State Bldg.
820 North French St.
Wilmington, DE 19801
(302) 571-2660

FLORIDA
Refuge Information Network Of
    Florida
P.O. Box 3762
Sarasota, FL 33578
(305) 571-2660

GEORGIA
Georgia Network Against
    Domestic Violence
1469A Pine St. N.W.
Atlanta, GA 30309
(404) 873-1766

HAWAII
Hawaii State Committee For
    Battered Women
P.O. Box 23269
Honolulu, HI 96822

IDAHO
Idaho Council On Family
    Violence
450 W. State St.
Statehouse Mail, 8th floor
Boise, ID 83720
(208) 334-2480

ILLINOIS
Illinois Coalition Against Domestic
    Violence
931 S. Fourth St.
Springfield, IL 62703
(217) 789-2830

INDIANA
Indiana Coalition Against
    Domestic Violence
919 E. Second St.
Bloomington, IN 47401
(812) 334-8378

IOWA
Iowa Coalition Against Domestic
    Violence
YWCA
309 Sycamore St.
Muscatine, IA 52761
(319) 263-7924

KANSAS
Kansas Association Of Domestic
    Violence Programs
P.O. Box 4469
Overland Park, KS 66204
(913) 432-5158

KENTUCKY
Kentucky Domestic Violence
    Association
Women's Crisis Center
321 York St.
Newport, KY 41071
(606) 581-6282

LOUISIANA
Louisiana Coalition Against
    Domestic Violence
c/o Crescent House
1231 Prythania
New Orleans, LA 70130
(504) 523-3755

MAINE
Maine Coalition For Family Crisis
    Services
P.O. Box 304
Augusta, ME 04861
(207) 623-3569

MARYLAND
Maryland Network Against
    Domestic Violence
2427 Maryland Ave.
Baltimore, MD 21218
(301) 268-4393

MASSACHUSETTS
Massachusetts Coalition Of
    Battered Women's Service
    Groups
25 West St., 5th floor
Boston, MA 02111
(617) 426-8492

MICHIGAN
Michigan Coalition Against
    Domestic Violence
10435 Lincoln
Huntington Woods, MI 48070
(313) 547-1051

MINNESOTA
Minnesota Coalition For Battered
    Women
435 Aldine St.
St. Paul, MN 55104
(612) 646-6177

MISSISSIPPI
Mississippi Coalition Against
    Domestic Violence
P.O. Box 333
Biloxi, MS 39533
(601) 436-3809

MISSOURI
Missouri Coalition Against
    Domestic Violence
27 North Newstead
St. Louis, MO 63108
(314) 531-2006

MONTANA
Montana Coalition Against
    Domestic Violence
P.O. Box 6183
Great Falls, MT 59406
(406) 228-4435

NEBRASKA
Nebraska Task Force On Domestic
    Violence & Sexual Assault
YWCA
222 South 29th St.
Omaha, NE 68131
(402) 345-6555

NEVADA
Nevada Network Against Domestic
    Violence
680 Greenbrae Drive, #270
Sparks, NV 89431
(702) 358-4214

NEW HAMPSHIRE
New Hampshire Coalition Against
    Family Violence
P.O. Box 353
Concord, NH 03301
(603) 224-8893

NEW JERSEY
New Jersey Coalition For Battered
    Women
206 W. State St.
Trenton, NJ 08608
(609) 695-1758

NEW MEXICO
The Women's Community
    Association, Inc.
P.O. Box 336
Albuquerque, NM 87103
(505) 242-3114

NEW YORK
New York State Coalition Against
    Domestic Violence
5 Neher St.
Woodstock, NY 12498
(914) 679-5231

NORTH CAROLINA
North Carolina Association Of
    Domestic Violence Programs
P.O. Box 595
Wilmington, NC 28402
(919) 343-0703

NORTH DAKOTA
North Dakota Council On Abused
    Women's Services
State Networking Office
311 Thayer, Room 127
Bismarck, ND 58501
(701) 255-6240

OHIO
Action For Battered Women In
    Ohio
P.O. Box 2421
Youngstown, OH 44509
(216) 793-3363

OKLAHOMA
Oklahoma Coalition On Domestic
    Violence & Sexual Assault
124 Colorado
Woodward, OK 73801
(405) 256-8712

OREGON
Oregon Coalition Against
    Domestic Violence & Sexual
    Assault
2336 S.E. Belmont St.
Portland, OR 97214
(503) 239-4486

PENNSYLVANIA
Pennsylvania Coalition Against
    Domestic Violence
2250 Elmerton Ave.
Harrisburg, PA 17110
(717) 652-9571 or
1-800-932-4632 (toll-free)

PUERTO RICO
Casa Julia De Burgos
P.O. Box 2433
San Juan, Puerto Rico 00936
(809) 781-2570

RHODE ISLAND
Rhode Island Council On
    Domestic Violence
P.O. Box 1829
Providence, RI 02912
(401) 272-9524

SOUTH CAROLINA
South Carolina Coalition Against
    Domestic Violence & Sexual
    Assault
P.O. Box 7291
Columbia, SC 29202
(No crisis line.)

SOUTH DAKOTA
South Dakota Coalition Against
    Domestic Violence
Resource Center for Women
317 S. Kline
Aberdeen, SD 57401
(605) 226-1212

TENNESSEE
Tennessee Coalition Against
    Domestic Violence
P.O. Box 831
Newport, TN 37821
(615) 623-3125

TEXAS
Texas Council On Family Violence
509-A West Lynn
Austin, TX 78746
(512) 482-8200

UTAH
Utah Domestic Violence Council
c/o Division of Family Services
150 West North Temple
Salt Lake City, UT 84103
(No crisis line.)

VERMONT
Herstory House
P.O. Box 313
Rutland, VT 05701
(802) 775-3232/6788

VIRGINIA
Virginians Against Domestic
    Violence
P.O. Box 5602
Richmond, VA 23220
(804) 780-3505

WASHINGTON
Washington State Shelter Network
1063 S. Capital Way No. 217
Olympia, WA 98501
(206) 753-4621

WEST VIRGINIA
West Virginia Coalition Against
    Domestic Violence
P.O. Box 2463
Elkins, WV 26241
(304) 636-3232

WISCONSIN
Wisconsin Coalition Against
    Woman Abuse
953 Jennifer St.
Madison, WI 53703
(608) 255-0539

WYOMING
Wyoming Coalition On Family
    Violence & Sexual Assault
P.O. Box 1127
Riverton, WY 82501
(No crisis line.)

COUNSELING FOR VIOLENT MEN

If you want to find help for a violent husband, boyfriend, father, or friend, ask for referrals from your local rape crisis program, from one of the regional NCASA officers listed on pages 233–34 or from one of the NCADV shelters listed on pages 261–66. Otherwise, these are some major groups that counsel men, updated from *Men on Rape* by Timothy Beneke (New York: St. Martin's Press, 1982).

CALIFORNIA
Marin County
Marin Hotline
(415) 924-1070
Men can call this number to talk
    to a male counselor.

San Francisco
M.O.V.E. (Men Overcoming
    Violence)
3004 Sixteenth St.
San Francisco, CA 94103
(415) 626-3655

Santa Monica
Los Angeles Men's Collective
2611 Fourth St. Apt. B
Santa Monica, CA 90405
(213) 396-3655

COLORADO
Denver
Amend (Abusive Men Exploring
    New Directions)
P.O. Box 61281
Denver, CO 80206
(303) 420-6759

ILLINOIS
Champaign
Men's Program Unit, University
    YMCA
1001 S. Wright St.
Champaign, IL 61820
(217) 337-1517

MASSACHUSETTS
Boston
Emerge: Men Counseling Men on
    Domestic Violence
25 Huntington Ave., Room 324
Boston, MA 02116
(617) 267-7690

MISSOURI
Kansas City
Kansas City Men's Project

Westport Allen Center

706 W. Forty-second St.

Kansas City, MO 64111

(816) 753-3844

St. Louis

RAVEN (Rape and Violence End
    Now)

P.O. Box 24159

St. Louis, MO 63190

(314) 725-6137

RAVEN provides counseling for
both violent men and men
close to victims of rape. They
primarily serve people in the
St. Louis area but will help
you find someone near you if
they can.

Most of these organizations will keep your contact with them confidential, even when you have to leave a message for them on an answering machine.

SELF-DEFENSE FOR OLDER PEOPLE AND THE DISABLED

Call your local YWCA, senior center, or community center for a reference to a self-defense class. Otherwise, contact:

The Safety & Fitness Exchange
541 Sixth Ave.
New York, NY 10011
(212) 242-4874/5

SAFE may be able to offer a program in your community, but if they cannot, they will try to refer you to an organization that can.

Jay Spiro
The Mejishi Karate Dojo
494 W. Greendale St.
Detroit, MI 48203
(313) 869-4286
Jay Spiro teaches self-defense to the elderly as well as to younger men and women. She has also taught the disabled.

Two useful publications on self-defense and assault prevention for older people and the disabled are:

Rape and Older Women: A Guide to Prevention and Protection, by Linda J. Davis and Elaine Brody. You can obtain this book *free* by writing to:
Shirley Wolock
Center for Studies of the Mental Health of the Aging
National Institute of Mental Health
5600 Fishers Ln., Room 11C03, Rockville, MD 20857

Crime Prevention Program (8th revision). You can order this book and find out how much it costs by contacting:
George Sunderland, Crime Prevention Program Coordinator
American Association of Retired Persons
1909 K St. N.W., Room 596
Washington, DC 20049
(202) 872-4700

WHERE TO GET SHRIEK ALARMS AND OTHER SAFETY DEVICES

Shriek alarms are pocket-size canisters, small and slim enough to hold in one hand, that let out an unbearably loud shriek when pressed. You can get them at some variety stores and drugstores, or order them by mail from:

The Sound Alarm
Sound Alarm Co.
1312 Washington Ave.
St. Louis, MO 63103
In his book *Crime Free,* (New York: Simon & Schuster, 1984) Michael Castleman recommends using a powerful whistle, preferably a police whistle (sports shops often carry strong whistles) or a device called Rapel, a small vial that emits a revolting skunklike stink when broken open. This can be obtained from:

Rapel Rape Deterrent
Rapel Products
P.O. Box 15227
Austin, TX 78761

TEENAGE PROGRAMS AND RAPE PREVENTION EDUCATION

All rape crisis programs will serve teenagers (and children), but the following places specialize in educating teenagers, parents, teachers, and other people who work with adolescents about sexual assault and how to prevent it. If you would like to arrange for a program to be presented at your school, Girl Scout or Boy Scout group, community center, or other such organization, contact one of these places by letter or telephone.

CALIFORNIA
Rape Prevention Education Program
University of California
Room 114, Bldg. T5
Berkeley, CA 94720
(415) 642-7310
This program will send workshops out into the community on request.

Child Abuse Program
Didi Hirsch Community Mental Health Center
4760 S. Sepulveda
Culver City, CA 90230
(213) 390-6612/6691
This program gives presentations to schools, parent groups, and child care agencies. To arrange a speaker, contact Martha Sherwood at the above numbers.

MINNESOTA
NO EASY ANSWERS
Illusion Theater
528 Hennepin Ave., No. 309
Minneapolis, MN 55403
(612) 339-4944
NO EASY ANSWERS is a theatrical presentation for adolescents that addresses such topics as emerging sexuality, incest, and aquaintance rape. The presentation takes about two hours and includes an introduction to the topic of sexual abuse and a question and answer time afterward. Curriculum manuals,

teaching aids, and training workshops are included. Illusion Theater will perform *anywhere in the country* on request and for varying costs.

NEW YORK

The Door Center of Alternatives
618 Avenue of the Americas
New York, N.Y. 10011
(212) 691-6161 (Monday to Friday, 2 P.M.–10 P.M.)

The Door provides counseling for victims of incest and rape, ages twelve to twenty-one. It also has services for runaways. If you call on any weekday but Friday, ask for the Health Program if you need help for a sexual assault. On Fridays, ask for S.O.S.

The Safety & Fitness Exchange
541 Sixth Ave.
New York, N.Y. 10011
(212) 242-4874/5

SAFE offers self-defense and awareness training for children, parents, schools, and corporations. They also have a special pamphlet for young people on how to prevent sexual assault, which can be mailed to you on request.

OHIO

Child Assault Prevention
Women Against Rape
P.O. Box 02084
Columbus, OH 43202
(614) 291-9751

CAP has programs for children and teenagers, parents and teachers. They teach women and children how to protect themselves and they teach other people how to teach them. They will speak in schools and community groups.

WASHINGTON

Coalition for Child Advocacy
SOAP Box Players
Whatcom County Opportunity Council
P.O. Box 159
Bellingham, WA 98227
(206) 734-5121

The SOAP Box Players present a film called *The Touching Problem* that dramatizes the facts about sexual abuse, sexual abusers, and the emotional repercussions on the child and family. They also present workshops on sexual abuse. The programs are offered *around the country* for varying prices. The film and workshop can be ordered separately by contacting the above address or number.

GAY AND LESBIAN SERVICES

If there isn't a local center for gays or lesbians listed in your telephone book, try contacting the following:

National Gay Task Force (NGTF)
Hotline outside of New York State (toll-free): (800) 221-7044
Hotline for New York State, Alaska, and Hawaii: (212) 807-6016

New York City Gay/Lesbian Anti-Violence Project
132 W. 24th St.
New York, NY 10011
(212) 772-0404 (confidential hotline)

These numbers should be able either to provide telephone counseling immediately or refer you to an appropriate organization near you.

Notes

Introduction

1. Ellen Ferris, "Long-term Consequences of Adult Rape," *Response* 6, no. 1 (January/February 1983): 5. *(Response* is a publication of the Center for Women Policy Studies.)
2. Ellen Frank and Barbara Duffy Stewart, "Treatment of Depressed Rape Victims: An Approach to Stress-Induced Symptomology," in *Treatment of Depression: Old Controversies and New Approaches*, ed. P. J. Clayton and J. E. Barrett (New York: Raven Press, 1983), p. 329.
3. Ibid., p. 316.
4. Ibid.
5. Ibid.
6. Interview with Deborah West, Ph.D., a member of Ellen Frank's ongoing study, "The Rape Victim: Her Response and Treatment" at the Western Psychiatric Institute, Pittsburgh, Pa.
7. Dudley Clendinen, "Barroom Rapists Are Given Sentences of Up to 12 Years," New York *Times*, March 27, 1984.
8. Susan Brownmiller, *Against Our Will: Men, Women and Rape* (New York: Simon & Schuster, 1975), p. 270.
9. Ibid., pp. 368–74.
10. Frank and Stewart, op. cit., p. 329.
11. Ann Burgess and Lynda Holmstrom, *Rape: Crisis and Recovery* (Bowie, Md.: Brady, 1979), p. 222.
12. A. Nicholas Groth and Ann Wolbert Burgess, "Male Rape: Offenders and Victims," *American Journal of Psychiatry* 137, no. 7 (July 1980): 807.
13. Menachim Amir, *Patterns in Forcible Rape* (Chicago: University of Chicago Press, 1971), p. 341.
14. A. Nicholas Groth and H. J. Birnbaum, *Men Who Rape: The Psychology of the Offender* (New York: Plenum Press, 1979).
15. Groth and Burgess, op. cit., p. 808.
16. Interview with Gene G. Abel, M.D., director of the Sexual Behavior Clinic of the New York State Psychiatric Institute in Manhattan and professor of clinical psychiatry at the Columbia University College of Physicians and Surgeons.

17. Brownmiller, op. cit., pp. 187–94. Also Groth and Burgess, op. cit., p. 808.
18. Burgess and Holmstrom, op. cit., pp. 443–44.
19. Michael S. Serrill, "Castration or Incarceration?" *Time*, December 12, 1983, p. 70.
20. Diana E. H. Russell, *Rape in Marriage* (New York: Macmillan Co., Collier Books, 1982), pp. 64–65.
21. U.S. Department of Justice, Federal Bureau of Investigation, *Uniform Crime Reports for the United States, 1980* (Washington, D.C.: GPO, 1981), p. 15.
22. Ibid.
23. M. Joan McDermott, *Rape Victimization in 26 American Cities*, a U.S. Department of Justice report from the Criminal Justice Research Center, (Washington, D.C.: GPO, 1979), p. 13.
24. Amir, op. cit., p. 117.
25. Groth and Birnbaum, op. cit., p. 98.
26. Ibid., p. 109.
27. McDermott, op. cit., p. 48.
28. "Reports to Police Questioned in New Bedford Rape Trials," New York *Times*, February 28, 1984.
29. Victims reported at St. Vincent's Hospital, New York.
30. McDermott, op. cit., p. xi.
31. FBI *Uniform Crime Reports, 1980*, p. 6.
32. Robert L. Geiser, *The Hidden Victim: The Sexual Abuse of Children* (Boston: Beacon Press, 1979), pp. 9, 10.
33. U.S. Department of Health and Human Services, Office of Human Development Services, Administration for Children, Youth, and Families, Children's Bureau, National Center on Child Abuse and Neglect, *Child Sexual Abuse: Incest, Assault, and Sexual Exploitation* (Washington, D.C.: GPO, 1981), p. 3.
34. Frank and Stewart, op. cit., p. 329.
35. Quoted in Perry Lang, "The Secret Anguish of Men Who Are Raped," San Francisco *Chronicle*, November 4, 1981.

Chapter 1

1. Frank and Stewart, "Treatment of Depressed Rape Victims," p. 309.
2. "Rape—Prevention and Resistance," an unpublished report by the Queen's Bench Foundation in San Francisco, 1976, p. 21.
3. McDermott, *Rape Victimization in 26 American Cities*, p. 20.
4. "Rape—Prevention and Resistance," p. 21.
5. McDermott, op. cit., p. 36.
6. "Rape—Prevention and Resistance," p. 22.

7. Reactions documented by Burgess and Holmstrom in *Rape: Crisis and Recovery;* Frank and Stewart, "Treatment of Depressed Rape Victims"; Dean G. Kilpatrick, Lois J. Veronen, and Patricia A. Resick, "The Aftermath of Rape: Recent Empirical Findings," *American Journal of Orthopsychiatry* 49, no. 4 (October 1979): 658–69; Lois J. Veronen and Dean G. Kilpatrick, "Self-reported Fears of Rape Victims: A Preliminary Investigation," *Behavior Modification* 4, no. 3 (July 1980): 383–96; Veronen and Kilpatrick, "Rape: A Precursor of Change" in *Proceedings of the 7th Life-Span Developmental Psychology Conference: Non-normative Life Events,* ed. E. J. Callahan and K. A. McCluskey (New York: Plenum, forthcoming.) Information also from interviews with Frank, Veronen, and others.

8. Ferris, "Long-term Consequences of Adult Rape," p. 5.

9. Ibid., p. 6.

10. Frank and Stewart, op. cit., p. 310.

11. Case quoted by Flora Colao, founder of the St. Vincent's Hospital Community Medicine Crisis Program and coauthor, with Tamar Hosansky, of *Your Children Should Know* (Indianapolis: Bobbs-Merrill, 1983), in an interview.

12. Brownmiller, *Against Our Will,* p. 363.

13. Burgess and Holmstrom, *Rape: Crisis and Recovery,* p. 338.

14. Ann Wolbert Burgess and Lynda Lytle Holmstrom, "Rape Trauma Syndrome," *American Journal of Psychiatry* 131 no. 9 (September 1974): 981–86.

15. Ibid.

16. Andra Medea and Kathleen Thompson, *Against Rape* (New York: Farrar, Straus & Giroux, 1974), p. 105. Also, Timothy Beneke, *Men on Rape* (New York: St. Martin's Press, 1982), p. 133.

17. Burgess and Holmstrom, *Rape: Crisis and Recovery,* p. 415.

18. Ibid., p. 423–24.

19. Ibid., p. 433.

20. Frank and Stewart, op. cit., p. 309. Also, FBI *Uniform Crime Reports, 1980,* p. 6—one forcible rape every six minutes.

21. Interview with Marie Brathwaite, Women's Treatment Coordinator, Addiction Research and Treatment Corporation, Brooklyn, N.Y.

22. Burgess and Holmstrom, *Rape: Crisis and Recovery,* p. 257.

23. Noreen Connell and Cassandra Wilson, eds., *Rape: The First Sourcebook for Women* (New York: New American Library, 1974), p. 44.

24. Burgess and Holmstrom, *Rape: Crisis and Recovery,* p. 415.

25. Ferris, op. cit., p. 6.

26. Ibid., pp. 5–6. Also, Burgess and Holmstrom, *Rape: Crisis and Recovery,* p. 415.

27. "Rape: A Personal Account," *Health & Social Work* 1, no. 3, (August 1976): 83–95.
28. Interview with Judith Becker, Ph.D., associate professor at the Columbia College of Physicians and Surgeons, Department of Psychiatry, and research scientist at the New York State Psychiatric Institute and the Victim Research Clinic at Columbia University. Also, J. V. Becker et al., "Incidence and Types of Sexual Dysfunction in Rape and Incest Victims," *Journal of Sex and Marital Therapy*, 8 (1982): 65–74.
29. Interview with Becker.
30. Becker et al., loc. cit.
31. Interview with Becker.

Chapter 2

1. Frank and Stewart, "Treatment of Depressed Rape Victims," p. 316.
2. C. Nadelson et al., "A Follow-up Study of Rape Victims," *American Journal of Psychiatry* 139, no. 10, (1982): 1266–70.
3. A. Nicholas Groth and Ann Wolbert Burgess, "Rape: A Sexual Deviation," *American Journal of Orthopsychiatry*, 47, no. 3 (July 1977): 403.
4. William R. Miller, Ann Marie Williams, and Mark H. Bernstein, "The Effects of Rape on Marital and Sexual Adjustment," *American Journal of Family Therapy* 10, no. 1 (1982): 52.
5. Frank and Stewart, op. cit., pp. 316, 322.
6. Groth and Burgess, "Rape: A Sexual Deviation," p. 403.
7. Burgess and Holmstrom, *Rape: Crisis and Recovery*, pp. 82–87.
8. Ibid., p. 87.
9. Interview with Assistant District Attorney Linda Fairstein, chief of the Sex Crimes Bureau, Manhattan District Attorney's Office, New York.
10. An estimate based on Brownmiller, *Against Our Will*, p. 175; McDermott, *Rape Victimization in 26 American Cities*, p. 43; FBI *Uniform Crime Reports, 1980*, p. 15.
11. Connell and Wilson, eds., *Rape: The First Sourcebook for Women*, p. 44.
12. Interview with Fairstein.
13. Burgess and Holmstrom, *Rape: Crisis and Recovery*, p. 351.
14. Ibid., p. 113. Also, Kay Weiss, *What the Rape Victim (or Anyone) Should Know about the "Morning-After Pill,"* a booklet from Advocates for Medical Information, 2120 Bissone, Houston, Texas 77005.
15. Burgess and Holmstrom, *Rape: Crisis and Recovery*, p. 114.
16. Groth and Burgess, "Rape: A Sexual Deviation," p. 403.
17. Boston Women's Health Book Collective, *Our Bodies, Ourselves* (New York: Simon & Schuster, 1979), pp. 207–11.
18. Burgess and Holmstrom, *Rape: Crisis and Recovery*, pp. 238–40.

19. Ibid., p. 114.

20. There are several evidence collection kits on the market that are becoming widely available to hospitals.

21. Ann W. Burgess and Lynda L. Holmstrom, "Adaptive Strategies and Recovery from Rape, *American Journal of Psychiatry* 136 (1979): 1278–82.

22. "Rape: A Personal Account," loc. cit.

23. Therapeutic suggestions from interviews with Ellen Frank, Ph.D., a psychologist at Western Psychiatric Institute and Clinic in Pittsburgh, Pa.; Lois J. Veronen, Ph.D., a clinical psychologist at the Medical University of South Carolina in Charleston and a member of People Against Rape; Anne Sparks and Doris Ullendorff, co-coordinators of the Rape Crisis Program at St. Vincent's Hospital, New York. Also, Burgess and Holmstrom, *Rape: Crisis and Recovery*, pt. 6; Frank and Stewart, op. cit., p. 317.

24. Burgess and Holmstrom, *Rape: Crisis and Recovery*, pp. 417, 430. Also, Jane E. Brody, "Self-Blame Held to Be Important in Victims' Recovery," New York *Times*, January 17, 1984.

25. Interview with Judith Becker.

26. Connell and Wilson, eds., *Rape: The First Sourcebook for Women*, p. 44.

27. Interview with William R. Miller, Ph.D. Also, William R. Miller et al., loc. cit.

28. Brownmiller, op. cit., pp. 315–25. Also, Florence Rush, *The Best-Kept Secret* (New York: McGraw-Hill, 1980), chap. 7, "A Freudian Cover-up."

29. Samuel M. Turner and Ellen Frank, "Behavior Therapy in the Treatment of Rape Victims," *Future Perspectives in Behavior Therapy*, ed. L. Michelson, M. Hersen, and S. M. Turner (New York: Plenum, 1981), p. 275.

30. Daniel Goleman, "Sexual Fantasies: What Are Their Hidden Meanings?" New York *Times*, February 28, 1984.

31. Ibid.

32. Colao and Hosansky, *Your Children Should Know*, p. 137.

33. "Rape: A Personal Account," loc. cit.

34. Interview with Miller.

35. Interview with Becker.

36. Self-defense information from the Safety & Fitness Exchange (SAFE), 451 Sixth Ave., New York, NY 10011; Women's Martial Arts Center, Inc., 16 W. Thirtieth St., New York, NY 10001; and Helen Benedict, "Rape: What You Should Know About Resistance—Now," *Glamour*, April 1983, pp. 140–44.

Chapter 3

1. Frank and Stewart, "Treatment of Depressed Rape Victims," p. 316.
2. Helen Benedict, "The Hidden Rape Victim," *Glamour*, March 1982, pp. 304–8.
3. Brownmiller, *Against Our Will*, pp. 366, 444–45.
4. Montana case from interview with Claire.
5. Burgess and Holmstrom, *Rape: Crisis and Recovery*, pp. 329–30.
6. Ibid., pp. 238–40.
7. Case quoted by Flora Colao in interview.
8. Questions suggested by Burgess and Holmstrom in *Rape: Crisis and Recovery*, pts. 5 and 6.
9. Interview with Deborah West (see note 6 for the Introduction).
10. Linda Tschirhart Sanford, *The Silent Children* (New York: McGraw-Hill, 1980), p. 3. Also, John H. Gagnon, "Female Child Victims of Sex Offenses," *Social Problems* 13 (Fall 1965): 176–92.
11. U.S. Department of Health and Human Services, *Child Sexual Abuse: Incest, Assault, and Sexual Exploitation*, p. 2.
12. Lawrence I. Rodkin, E. Joan Hunt, and Suzi Dunstan Cowan, "A Men's Support Group for Significant Others of Rape Victims," *Journal of Marital and Family Therapy*, January 1982, p. 95.
13. Interview with Becker (see note 28 for chap. 1).
14. Interview with Miller (see note 27 for chap. 2).
15. Breakup rate of 40 percent quoted by Becker in interview; breakup rate of 85–87 percent quoted by Frank in interview; breakup rate of 80–90 percent quoted by Theresa Crenshaw, Ph.D., a psychotherapist for marital and sexual problems in San Diego, California, in Helen Benedict, "Rape: How men react to an attack on loved one," "The Sunday Magazine" of the Richmond *Independent & Gazette*, June 8, 1980.
16. Benedict, "Rape: How men react to an attack on loved one."
17. Told by Carolyn Craven in a press conference in Berkeley, California, 1978.

Chapter 4

1. *Surviving Sexual Assault*, ed. Rochel Grossman with Joan Sutherland for the Los Angeles Commission on Assaults Against Women (New York: Congdon & Weed, 1983), p. 18.
2. ". . . The conviction rate in New York County for felony sex offenses after trial has been between 70% and 90% each year for the past five years." "Criminal Prosecution of a Felony Sex Offense: A Guide for Coun-

selors & Advocates," an unpublished paper prepared by the Criminal Justice Committee, New York City Advisory Task Force on Rape, p. 8.

3. Timothy Beneke, *Men on Rape*, pp. 118–19.

4. Information on "Procedures" from "Criminal Prosecution of a Felony Sex Offense"; *Surviving Sexual Assault*; and interview with Linda Fairstein, assistant district attorney, New York (see note 9 for chap. 2).

5. John Adams, *Legal Papers of John Adams*, ed. L. Kinvin Wroth and Hiller B. Zobel (Cambridge: Harvard University Press, 1965), 3:242.

6. Lynda Lytle Holmstrom and Ann Wolbert Burgess, "Rape: The Husband's and Boyfriend's Initial Reactions," *The Family Coordinator*, July 1979, pp. 322, 328.

7. "Reports to Police Questioned in New Bedford Rape Trials," New York *Times*, February 28, 1984.

8. Connie Borkenhagen, "You Asked for It," *Student Lawyer*, September 1975, p. 47. Reprinted with permission of *Student Lawyer*, American Bar Association, © 1975.

9. Rodkin, Hunt, and Cowan, "A Men's Support Group for Significant Others of Rape Victims," p. 95.

10. Holmstrom and Burgess, "Rape: The Husband's and Boyfriend's Initial Reactions," p. 329.

Chapter 5

1. Diana E. H. Russell, *Rape in Marriage*, p. 329.

2. Ibid., p. 81.

3. Ibid., p. 82.

4. Ibid., p. 112—husbands used weapons in 17 percent of the cases; McDermott, *Rape Victimization in 26 American Cities*, p. 20—weapons used in two thirds of stranger rapes.

5. Court records obtained from National Clearinghouse on Marital Rape, 2325 Oak St., Berkeley, CA 94708.

6. Ibid., *Pennsylvania Socio-Legal Chart of Marital Rape Cases*, © Women's History Research Center.

7. Russell, op. cit., p. 112.

8. Ibid., p. 180.

9. Ibid., p. 197.

10. List of states from National Clearinghouse on Marital Rape, updated to April 1984.

11. Ibid., p. 17.

12. Ibid., pp. 375–81.

13. U.S. Department of Justice, Bureau of Justice Statistics, *Report to the*

Nation on Crime and Justice, (Washington, D.C.: The Department, 1983), p. 2.

14. Russell, op. cit., p. 57.
15. Louie Andrews, "Family Violence in Florida's Panhandle," *Ms.*, March 1984, p. 23.
16. Interview with Laura X, director of the National Clearinghouse on Marital Rape.
17. Some theories are from Russell, op. cit., pp. 132–55; and Groth and Birnbaum, *Men Who Rape*, pp. 178–79. Some are my speculations.
18. Ibid.
19. "You've Got To Beat Me To Keep Me" by Grainger, *Louis Armstrong in New York*, Archive of Jazz, vol. 26, BYG Records.
20. "Why Battered Wives Don't Leave Home," letter to the editor, New York *Times*, December 29, 1983.
21. Ibid.
22. Ibid.
23. Russell, op. cit., p. 314.
24. Ibid., p. 315.
25. Ibid.
26. Ibid., p. 316.
27. Ibid., pp. 220, 250.
28. Andrews, loc. cit.
29. Nancy Baker, "Why Women Stay with Men Who Beat Them," *Glamour*, August 1983, p. 367.
30. Russell, op. cit., p. 317.
31. Ibid., p. 313.
32. Ann Jones, *Women Who Kill* (New York: Holt, Rinehart & Winston, 1980), pp. 304–5.
33. Interviews with rape crisis counselors who have worked with police to sensitize them to rape.
34. Jane O'Reilly, "Wife Beating: The Silent Crime," *Time*, September 5, 1983, p. 26.
35. Interview with Laura X.
36. Russell, op. cit., pp. 78–79.

Chapter 6

1. Case and other material from interview with David MacEnulty, a former counselor with St. Vincent's Hospital's Rape Crisis Program.
2. Interview with A. Nicholas Groth; and Perry Lang, "The Secret Anguish of Men Who Are Raped," San Francisco *Chronicle*, November 4, 1981. Rise in male rape victims reported also by Bellevue Hospital in New York

and rape crisis centers in San Jose, San Francisco, Palo Alto, and Berkeley, all in California.

3. Frank and Stewart, "Treatment of Depressed Rape Victims," p. 329.
4. Ibid.
5. Helen Benedict, "Men Get Raped, Too," *The Soho News*, March 16, 1982.
6. Groth and Birnbaum, *Men Who Rape*, p. 139.
7. A. Nicholas Groth, and Ann Wolbert Burgess, "Male Rape: Offenders and Victims," *American Journal of Psychiatry* 137, no. 7 (July 1980): 807.
8. Lang, loc. cit.
9. Daniel Lockwood, *Prison Sexual Violence* (New York: Elsevier/North Holland, 1980).
10. Interview with Groth.
11. Groth and Birnbaum, op. cit., p. 148.
12. Groth and Burgess, "Male Rape: Offenders and Victims," p. 808.
13. Groth and Birnbaum, op. cit., p. 132.
14. Lockwood, op. cit., p. 93.
15. "Rape in Another Gender," *Emergency Medicine*, July 15, 1980, p. 107. Also, Arthur Kaufman, et al., "Male Rape Victims: Noninstitutionalized Assault," *American Journal of Psychiatry*, 137, no. 2, (February 1980): 221.
16. Gordon W. Josephson, "The Male Rape Victim: Evaluation and Treatment," *Journal of the American College of Emergency Physicians* 8, no. 1, (January 1979): 14.
17. "Rape in Another Gender," p. 107.
18. Lockwood, op. cit., p. 97.
19. Ibid.
20. Groth and Burgess, "Male Rape: Offenders and Victims," p. 809.
21. Information on automatic ejaculation from interview with Groth and with Dr. John O'Connor, a psychiatrist and founder of the Sexual Therapy Program at the Columbia Presbyterian Medical Center, New York.
22. Lois Timnick, "When Women Rape Men," *Psychology Today*, September 1983, p. 74.
23. Ibid.; and Groth and Birnbaum, op. cit., pp. 185–88.
24. Groth and Birnbaum, op. cit., p. 189.
25. Timnick, loc. cit.
26. Groth and Birnbaum, loc. cit.
27. Timnick, loc. cit.
28. Ibid., p. 75.
29. Leigh Bienen, "Rape IV," *Women's Rights Law Reporter* (Rutgers Law School), supplement to Vol. 6, no. 3 (Summer 1980): 2–61.

Chapter 7

1. Linda J. Davis and Elaine M. Brody, *Rape and Older Women: A Guide to Prevention and Protection*, written for the National Institute of Mental Health; U.S. Department of Health and Human Services, (Washington, D.C.: GPO, 1979).

2. Ibid., pp. 31–32; and McDermott, *Rape Victimization in 26 American Cities*, p. 5.

3. McDermott, op. cit., pp. 5, 6, 8, 17.

4. Davis and Brody, op. cit., p. 33.

5. Groth and Birnbaum, *Men Who Rape*, p. 172.

6. Ibid., p. 164.

7. Davis and Brody, op. cit., p. 12.

8. Mike Pearl and Bernard Bard, "Aged widow's rape tale taped: she may not live until the trial," New York *Post*, July 18, 1980.

9. Interview with Tamar Hosansky and Pam McDonnell, cofounders of the Safety and Fitness Exchange (SAFE) in New York and instructors there.

10. Self-defense techniques from SAFE (see note 36 for chap. 2) and Davis and Brody, op. cit., pp. 63–67.

11. Davis and Brody, op. cit., p. 33.

12. Ibid., p. 16.

13. Jane E. Brody, "Self-blame Held to Be Important in Victims' Recovery," New York *Times*, January 17, 1984.

14. Interview with McDonnell.

15. Ibid.; and Davis and Brody, op. cit., pp. 63–67.

Chapter 8

1. McDermott, *Rape Victimization in 26 American Cities*, p. 5.

2. Robert L. Geiser, *The Hidden Victim: The Sexual Abuse of Children* (Boston: Beacon Press, 1979) pp. 9–10. One out of five rape victims is under twelve.

3. John H. Gagnon, "Female Child Victims of Sex Offenses," *Social Problems* 13 (Fall 1965): 176–92. Gagnon cites findings that 24 percent of 4,441 female, white, middle-class, college-educated women were the victim of sexual attacks "while prepubescent" and that 20–25 percent reported a sexual incident before the age of thirteen—findings of Kinsey.

4. U.S. Department of Health and Human Services, *Child Sexual Abuse: Incest, Assault, and Sexual Exploitation*, p. 3.

5. Glenn Collins, "Sexual Abuse of Children Is Widespread," New York *Times*, May 13, 1983.

6. Groth and Birnbaum, op. cit., p. 181.
7. McDermott, op. cit., p. 12.
8. Ibid., p. 13.
9. Groth and Birnbaum, op. cit., p. 148.
10. School account from Colao and Hosansky, *Your Children Should Know,* p. xi.
11. Ibid., pp. 113–14.
12. From "Emotional First-Aid for Teens," a letter from a victim, © St. Vincent's Rape Crisis Center, New York.
13. Baker, "Why Women Stay with Men Who Beat Them," p. 365.
14. "Emotional First-Aid For Teens."
15. Interview with Tamar Hosansky, author of *Your Children Should Know* and cofounder of SAFE.
16. Collins, loc. cit. and Sandra Butler, *Conspiracy of Silence: The Trauma of Incest* (San Francisco: Volcano Press, 1978), p. 16—"Other studies conclude that 80 percent of all children are victimized by an adult they know and trust."
17. Collins, loc. cit.
18. Ibid.
19. Helen Benedict, "Prostitution: Its roots often lie in child abuse," "The Sunday Magazine" of the Richmond *Independent & Gazette,* November 23, 1980. Report on research by the Delancey Street Foundation in San Francisco that found that over 60 percent of two hundred prostitutes were sexually abused as children.
20. Butler, op. cit., p. 16.
21. Sanford, *The Silent Children,* p. 151.
22. "Emotional First-Aid For Parents," letter for parents of child victims given out by St. Vincent's Hospital, New York. © St. Vincent's.

Chapter 9

1. Much of the information on lesbian reactions to rape comes from Tamar Hosansky of SAFE (see note 36 for chap. 2).
2. R. H. Gundlach, "Sexual Molestation and Rape Reported by Homosexual and Heterosexual Women," *Journal of Homosexuality* 2, no. 4 (Summer 1977): 367–84.
3. Interview with Becker (see note 28 for chap. 1).
4. Letter from a victim distributed to other victims, © St. Vincent's Hospital Rape Crisis Program, New York.
5. Much of the information on gay men's reactions to rape comes from Lance Bradley, C.S.W., psychotherapist.

6. Case from David MacEnulty, a former counselor at St. Vincent's Hospital's Rape Crisis Program, New York.
7. Case from David Feuerstein, rape counselor at St. Vincent's Hospital.
8. Groth and Birnbaum, *Men Who Rape*, p. 148.
9. Information from Lance Bradley.
10. Daniel Goleman, "Sexual Fantasies: What Are Their Hidden Meanings?" New York *Times*, February 28, 1984.
11. Interview with A. Nicholas Groth.
12. U.S. Department of Health and Human Services, *Child Sexual Abuse: Incest, Assault, and Sexual Exploitation*, p. 2.
13. *The Rights of Gay People*, An American Civil Liberties Union Handbook (New York: Bantam Books, 1983), pp. 131–66.

Index

aspects, members); relations of victims with and self-perception after assaults, 41–42; teenage rape and, 205–10, 213–14. *See also* Relatives; specific aspects, developments, members, problems, victims

Fantasies: rape, 68–69, 71, 103, 225; revenge, 36–37, 99

Fathers, 92, 93, 202–4; and help for teenagers, 205–10; and incest, 202–4; of rape victims, 209. *See also* Families; Parents

Father's Days (Brady), 204

Fear (terror), 1, 25, 29, 31, 33, 35–36, 37–40, 68, 87, 88, 95, 97–99, 102, 120; of being alone after being raped, 24, 29, 31, 34, 35–36, 58, 63, 88, 89–90, 173, 176; homosexual rape and, 217, 218, 219, 227; incest and, 203; male rape and, 157–58; nervous or compulsive habits and, 28–29; older victims and, 173, 176, 180, 184; and phobias, 28, 35, 102, 182, 210; self-defense courses for, 61, 75–77 *(see also* Self-defense); of sex following assaults, 29–30, 38–40, 72–74, 159–60, 196; teenage rape and, 188–90, 200, 203, 205, 208. *See also* Anxiety; Depression; Shock; Trauma; specific aspects, developments

Feminists (feminist movement), xiii–xiv, 6, 96. *See also* specific developments, groups, individuals

Fertility, pregnancy following rape and, 53

Fighting Woman News, 259

Financial compensation. *See* Compensation, financial

Flashbacks, rape experience and, 26, 38–39, 73, 157, 167

Flirting, teenage rape and, 62, 197

Fluctuating emotions (mood swings), 25, 88

For Yourself: The Fulfillment of Female Sexuality (Barbach), 131n.

Freudian therapy, 67–68

Friends (acquaintances), 42–45, 47, 57–58, 64–66, 70, 71–72, 109–11, 125–26; abused wives and, 149–51; help for teenagers by, 212–13; homosexuals and, 220–22, 228–29; older victims and, 176, 178; problems faced by and

help from, 109–11, 125–26, 149–51, 176, 178, 212–13, 228–29; teenage rape and, 195–96, 197–98, 199, 200, 212–13

Fyfe, James J., 145

Gang rape (group sex assaults), 6, 8, 10, 27, 53, 97, 119, 156–57, 187, 217

Gay men, 222–30; child rape myth and, 187; male rape and myths and, 154–55, 159–60, 165, 166, 167; rape of, 222–30 *(see also* Homosexuals); services and agencies for, 271 *(see also* specific agencies, kinds)

"General Hospital" (TV soap opera), 6

Gonorrhea, 54, 171. *See also* Veneral (sexual) diseases

Grandparents, and incest, 202–4

Griffin, Susan, xiii

Groth, A. Nicholas, 7, 153–54, 155, 159, 170, 186, 272, 275

Group rape. *See* Gang rape

Group therapy, 69–70, 75

Guilt feelings, 32, 45, 64, 75, 83, 102, 103, 111, 183; homosexual rape and, 215–16, 218–19, 222–24. *See also* Blame; Shame

Headaches, as a reaction to rape, 24, 26

Hindu women, 30

Hitchhiking, 61–62

Holmstrom, Lynda L., 6, 8, 27, 28, 32, 50–51, 53, 85–86, 126, 272

Homosexuals, rape of, 215–30; gay men, 222–30, 271 *(see also* Gay men); help from others, 219–22, 228–29, 271; helping yourself, 218–19, 225–28; lesbians, 72, 215–22, 226, 271 *(see also* Lesbians); reporting and prosecuting, 229–30; services, 271 *(see also* specific agencies, kinds)

Hosansky, Tamar, 69, 94, 127, 217

Hospitals (doctors, nurses), 46, 52–57, 69, 84, 86–87; counseling (rape crisis programs) and, 46, 47, 50, 53, 55, 56, 69, 174; and examinations following assaults, 54–56, 174, 200; homosexual rape and, 225; and kits for collecting rape evidence, 55–56; male rape and, 163–64; marital rape and, 145–46; mixed experiences in, 55–57; older victims and, 171–72, 174–75; teenage